MW00710648

London Gothic:
Place, Space and the Gothic Imagination

Also available from Continuum

London Narratives, Lawrence Phillips
Recalling London, Alex Murray

London Gothic:
Place, Space and the Gothic Imagination

Edited by
Lawrence Phillips and Anne Witchard

Continuum Literary Studies

continuum

Continuum International Publishing Group

The Tower Building   80 Maiden Lane
11 York Road   Suite 704
London, SE1 7NX   New York, NY 10038

www.continuumbooks.com

British Library Cataloguing-in-Publication Data
A catalogue record for this book is available from the British Library.

ISBN: 978-1-4411-0682-7 (hardcover)

Library of Congress Cataloging-in-Publication Data
A catalog record for this book is available from the Library of Congress.

Typeset by Newgen Imaging Systems Pvt Ltd, Chennai, India
Printed and bound in Great Britain by the MPG Books Group

Contents

Part Three: Sites, Performance and Film

List of Illustrations

Chapter 3

Chapter 10

Notes on Contributors

Jenny Bavidge is Lecturer in English at the University of Greenwich. She has published on various aspects of children's literature and children's geographies, alongside work on urban theory and contemporary London writing.

Fred Botting is Professor of English at the University of Lancaster. He is the author of *Gothic* (Routledge, 1996), *Sex, Machines and Navels* (Manchester University Press, 1999), and with Scott Wilson, *The Tarantinian Ethics* (Sage, 2001), and *Bataille* (Palgrave, 2001), as well as the co-editor of *Gothic: Critical Concepts in Literary and Cultural Studies*, 4 vols (Routledge, 2004).

Amanda Mordavsky Caleb is a lecturer at the University of Tennessee. She is the editor of *(Re)creating Science in Nineteenth-Century Britain* (Cambridge: Scholars Publishing, 2007), and is currently working on a monograph which considers the intersection of decadence and science at the *fin de siècle*. Her primary research interests lie in the interdisciplinary study of science and literature.

Nick Freeman is a Senior Lecturer in English in the Department of English and Drama, Loughborough University. He has published widely on Victorian and twentieth-century literature and cultural history, with recent articles on Edward Thomas, Somerset Maugham, E. Nesbit, and the 'Raffles' stories of E. W. Hornung. He is also the author of *Conceiving the City: London, Literature, and Art 1870–1914* (Oxford University Press, 2007).

Roger Luckhurst is Professor in Modern and Comparative Literature at Birkbeck College, University of London and is the author of books on science fiction and the history of science. His current project is an investigation of the British Museum mummy curse.

J. S. Mackley teaches at the University of Northampton. His research and publication interests include the medieval perception and reception of apocryphal legends, British mythology and folklore, and Medieval astronomy and cosmography. He is the author of *The Legend of Brendan: A Comparative Study of the Latin And Anglo-Norman Versions* (Leiden, Brill: 2008), has written articles on the medieval legend of Judas Iscariot and is currently editing and translating a fourteenth-century treatise on cosmography.

Emma McEvoy is Lecturer in English Literature at the University of Westminster, London. She co-edited the *Routledge Companion to the Gothic* with Catherine Spooner and contributed essays on 'Gothic and the Romantics' and 'Contemporary Gothic Theatre' to the volume. She has also published work on J. Meade Falkner, G. K. Chesterton, Mary Shelley, Ann Radcliffe, Nick Cave, the Picturesque and Gothic Music in Film. She provided the introduction and notes for the Oxford University Press World's Classics edition of Matthew Lewis's *The Monk* (1995). *Beginning Gothic*, co-written with Catherine Spooner, is forthcoming.

Alex Murray is Lecturer in English at the University of Exeter. He is the author of *Recalling London* (Continuum, 2007) and editor, with Nick Heron and Justin Clemens, of *The Work of Giorgio Agamben* (Edinburgh, 2008).

Lawrence Phillips is Reader in English at the University of Northampton. His recent books include *London Narratives: Post War Fiction and the City* (Continuum, 2006) and as editor, *A Mighty Mass of Brick and Smoke: Edwardian and Victorian Representations of London* (Rodopi, 2007), and *The Swarming Streets: Twentieth-Century Representations of London* (Rodopi, 2004). He is the founding editor of the journal *Literary London: Interdisciplinary Studies in the Representation of London* (ISSN 1744-0807).

Catherine Spooner is Senior Lecturer in English Literature at Lancaster University, UK. She is the author of *Fashioning Gothic Bodies* (2004), *Contemporary Gothic* (2006) and the co-editor, with Emma McEvoy, of the *Routledge Companion to Gothic* (2007). She is currently working on a series of essays on twenty-first century Gothic, Gothic geographies, and literature and fashion.

Anne Witchard is Lecturer in the department of English, Linguistics and Cultural Studies at the University of Westminster, London. She is the author of *Thomas Burke's Dark Chinoiserie: Limehouse Nights and the Queer Spell of Chinatown* (Ashgate, 2009). *Lao She, London and China's Literary Revolution* is forthcoming (Hong Kong University Press).

Julian Wolfreys is Professor of Modern Literature and Culture at Loughborough University, and the author or editor of around 40 books, his most recent being *Thomas Hardy* (Palgrave) and *Literature, in Theory: Tropes, Subjectivities, Responses and Responsibilities* (Continuum). He is currently compiling *The Derrida Concordance*.

Chapter 1

Introduction

Anne Witchard and Lawrence Phillips

London Gothic as a specific category can be seen as important for understanding ourselves today as it has been for thinking about the cultural productions of the late nineteenth century. While certain texts such as *Strange Case of Dr Jekyll and Mr Hyde* (1886), *The Picture of Dorian Gray* (1891)) and *Dracula* (1897) have become canonic, Gothic representations of London are to be found across a diverse array of texts, not only those that correspond with the emergence of the genre in fiction and the industrial era's expansion of the capital, but as J. S. Mackley's chapter explores, from the legends of its earliest origins. Although the Gothic is considered to represent an eighteenth-century reconstruction of a barbaric past, the Guildhall statues of Gog and Magog, mythical giants 'who guard this ancient city' (Dickens 1907, 275) testify to Gothic narrative as fundamental to socio-cultural self perception.

London Gothic is currently a topic of major interest to film-makers. Since the Hughes brothers' adaptation *From Hell* (2001), cinema's neo-Victorian reassertions of 'darkest London' iconography with evil and corruption have continued in a slew of recent blockbusters, *Dorian Gray* (2009), *A Christmas Carol* (2009) and *Sherlock Holmes* (2009), their self-parodic hyper-realism, providing to a greater or lesser extent a postmodern interrogation of nineteenth-century industrial capitalism. The Gothic London of contemporary film, in its commodified pastiche of the generic traditions of Victorian popular culture, the penny dreadful, the melodrama and the sensation novel, foregrounds fin-de-siècle London's stratification of class, race and gender. In Tim Burton's *Sweeney Todd: The Demon Barber of Fleet Street* (2007), London stands for the cannibalism of post-industrial consumer culture, a city that literally devours its populace. In 'Living in the Slashing Grounds: Jack the Ripper, Monopoly Rent and the New Heritage'(Warwick and Willis 2007), David Cunningham has described the ways in which the heritage industry's Gothicized mythology of place continues to have disturbing consequences for East London's economic, social and cultural existence.

In the nineteenth century the Gothic was utilized as a perceptual mode of evoking the metropolis not just as a site of terror but, via its occult topographies, as a site of potential resistance. It is some ten years since Robert Mighall's insistence on a socio-political rather than psychoanalytically attention to the Gothic (1999). He identified the urban Gothic of George Reynolds' mid-nineteenth century series, *The Mysteries of London* (1844–1848) as a demonstration of modern concerns about the growth of an information culture and its correlative production of secrets as commodities, their exchange value being related to power. The city itself becomes implicated in the motives, desires and conflicts of the characters. As Roger Luckhurst has pointed out elsewhere, London Gothic found the conditions to prosper again in the era after the abolition of the GLC in 1986 ('The Contemporary London Gothic and the Limits of the "Spectral Turn"' (2002)). With the Thatcherite 'return' to Victorian values, the white-collar crimes of advanced capitalism that determined the plots of mid-Victorian London Gothic, chiefly fraud, forgery and blackmail, emerged with renewed relevance in fiction by Christopher Fowler, China Miéville, and others. Gothic tropes of paranoia, alienation, contagion and erotic fascination continue to inform our literary relation to the city and a response to what some see as its inexplicability. A self-aware, or reflexive, Gothic historiography of London might be seen as an attempt to resolve this 'inexplicability'. Iain Sinclair's work, and its simplification in Peter Ackroyd's, participates in an intense longing for the Gothic and its various possibilities. Yet Sinclair's quest for an alternative 'occult heritage', having undergone the move from counter-cultural to mainstream commodification, has ultimately rendered the Gothic, 'official heritage'. The ghosts of de Quincey's Oxford Street now provide the blueprint for Marylebone's rebranded gastropubs with their gin cellars and opium lounges. The question remains, does East End gentrification, Jack the Ripper walking tours, or the 'tourist gothic' of Madame Tussaud's and the London Dungeon, negate any subversive or transgressive possibilities? Where do we now locate London's progress or civilization and where its Gothic antithesis?

The chapters in this volume focus in various ways on Gothic representations of London, and approach the subject from diverse theoretical premises. The volume is divided into three sections. Victorians to Moderns begins with Julian Wolfreys' exploration of Charles Dickens' magazine and journal articles in which subjectivity or the narrating self is, he argues, constructed through its encounter with London locations, courts and alleys, suburban wastelands and gloomy squares that are identifiably Gothic. Dickensian urban subjectivity gives voice to a strikingly modern consciousness that reveals how closely the empirical and phenomenological interanimate one another. Dickens's London Gothic is considered here as a tropological field, a Gothic of the senses of reception and interpretation rather than empirical location, composed through techniques of distortion, disorientation, anxiety and astonishment that illuminate the historically determined concerns and observations of the perceiver. In excess of the factual empiricism of later anthropological and political writers such as Mayhew or Engels, Wolfreys suggests that Dickens risks a phenomenological discourse that wakes up from the nightmare of the inescapably mimetic and realist which merely reinscribes the political and social horrors it seeks to denounce.

Attention to nineteenth-century London Gothic writing has tended to focus on the dockside opium dens and labyrinthine slums familiar from the fin-de-siècle fictions of Wilde, Stevenson, Stoker and Machen. Anne Witchard's chapter considers the ways in which London's suburban expansion at the very beginning of the nineteenth century evoked responses that employ Gothic tropes and motifs across a range of writing, including essays and journalism, urban sketches and pseudo-autobiography. London's new suburbs would be developed as distinctly Gothic locations in the mid-Victorian novel by Dickens and Wilkie Collins. Collins' struggle to depict 'modern life' evinces a conservative anxiety that the demarcations of social class were proving as permeable as those of London's ever devolving boundaries. The Gothic articulates the failure of symbolic order and the nineteenth-century suburb would invite Gothic treatment as a space where boundaries are undermined and meaning collapses. This 'othering' of London's sprawl is symptomatic of the vulnerability induced by the changes within bourgeois culture and the rise of the suburb as it altered the meaning of the city and what it meant to be a Londoner.

Ultimately our attention to the terrain of a Gothicized London serves to emphasize the significance of the built environment for the ways in which it functions as a metaphor for socio-psychological crisis. Arthur Machen's *The Hill of Dreams* (1907) reflects the spatial and temporal anxieties associated with London and its outer suburbs. Machen's novel juxtaposes the ancient rural past with the urban present, the pagan with the prosaic, and urban with suburban. Amanda Caleb reads Machen's engagement with space, time, and cognitive dissociation in *The Hill of Dreams*, as it charts the protagonist's psychic breakdown. His failure to rationalize the cityscape, exacerbated by increasing drug use and paranoia, results in an inability to maintain his own sense of being. This internal conflict addresses the notions of Decadent identity and the emergence of the modern self.

In a consideration of the virtues and vices of our persistent Gothicized apprehension of London's cultural geography, Roger Luckhurst turns back to the certainty of the map to investigate the uncanny concentration of spooky sites in central London's Bloomsbury. Between about 1870 and 1945, the area was famed for its cluster of Spiritualist mediums, institutions and meeting halls, the full materialization of the spirit of Katie King, the astral travel of Mrs Guppy the medium, the anthropological researches of the famous Oxford ethnologist Edward Tylor among the Spiritualists, and the researchers of the Society for Psychical Research. Urban Gothic fictions have similarly used the area for its settings, from Arthur Machen to Charles Williams. Luckhurst uses the mapping techniques developed by Franco Morretti in *The Atlas of the European Novel* (1998) to suggest why London's obsession with the supernatural found such a significant cluster amidst the dusty demi-monde of disreputable Bloomsbury. Rather than rely on the Peter Ackroyd's transhistorical instancing of such collective phenomena as examples of London's *genius loci,* the psychogeograph-ical notions of the Situationists, or Derridean hauntology, Luckhurst tracks the shifting economic and class status, the spatial distribution of Bloomsbury's specific topography that has made it the quarter for hermetic, marginal or otherwise occult knowledges.

The stability of a notion such as 'Gothic London' is brought into focus by Alex Murray's contribution to the second section, Contemporary Prose Narrative, as he pursues a category that has its origins in a tourist construction of the city, but also the attractions of the notion as it imports suggestions of alterity and a politics of dispersed and deferred identity associated with the Gothic London alignments of Sinclair and Ackroyd. In turn Murray maps the terms of a debate that threads through this collection by contrasting the respec-tive critical positions of Julian Wolfreys and Roger Luckhurst for which he wishes to argue for a 'cultural cartography' that preserves the culturally contin-gent construction of space and place while not succumbing to the temptation to entrench an essentialist conception of the city and its cultural representa-tion, leaving both 'London' Gothic if not a 'London' literature problematic to say the least. This he finds in Stewart Home's experimental novel *Down and Out in Shoreditch and Hoxton* (2004) which questions both to the point of collapse.

A not dissimilar effect can be found in Hilary Mantel's *Beyond Black* (2005) and the London novels of Derek Raymond, the subjects of Catharine Spooner's and Nick Freeman's chapters. In both cases the 'centre' is probed from the periphery, both in terms of locales, from the orbit of the M25 and the rootless-ness of outer suburbs in search of a connection via spiritualism in the case of Mantel's novel, to the narrative construction of popular crime procedurals deliberately undermined by Derek Raymond's sergeant, similarly invoking the dead through 'a compassionate immersion in the minutiae of ruined lives'. In each instance the essentializing pressure that Murray suggests is at risk through a category such as 'London Gothic', is carefully refuted by confound-ing the expectations of the popular genres from which Mantel and Raymond write. In both it is the interior rather than literal landscape that generates a Gothic construction of place which signals a rather surprising warmth that is not quite community but is arguably a 'lived' experience nonetheless.

The gardens and green spaces of London's built environment are not often considered in terms of the Gothic. Jenny Bavidge investigates their horrors as she describes how nature's return lends itself to narratives of irruption and destabilization as the Gothic noses its way out through cracks in the pavements, grows from seeds in suburban gardens or accumulates through the steady drip of rainwater. Nature when it re-emerges in the city comes back 'wrong' in the form of extreme weather, killer plants, pests and disease.

The Gothic mythmaking of London constructed via Performance and Film, our third section, is tackled by J. S. Mackley and Emma McEvoy each from quite different perspectives. Mackley traces the history of the Gog and Magog legend that has become closely associated with the city and materially expressed in the statues that still guard the City from the Guildhall. Their persistent symbolism and surprising history in the city defy the best attempts of fiction to exceed the melting pot of London's, and indeed Britain's, mythological origins. If Mackley traces the history of such mythmaking, McEvoy traces the contemporary in process by exploring the narratives, created spaces and consumption of London Gothic tourism. It doesn't take much of a leap of the historical imagination to see the faux-historical narratives of ghost tours, the Clink Museum and Madame Tussaud's as the engines of London's ongoing myth-making machine. It is of course profoundly performative and a Gothic history stands in for and challenges essentialist assumptions about history and experience.

These questions also inform the two final chapters in this volume which both deal with film. Indeed, Gothic film horror proves a fertile genre/medium to pursue further questions of myth and history. Phillips examines two films that revive the supernatural inflected serial killer 'myth' that has been popular since the very real murders of 1888 were so effectively mythologized by the sensationalist press of the time and maintained by an international Gothicized popular culture industry every since (and continues to provide material for various 'Ripper Walks' as part of the Gothic tourist industry explored by McEvoy). Both Films, *Death Line* from 1972 and *Creep* from 2005, explore very real issues of class and material inequality by evoking the Gothic frame of the Ripper murders conjoined with London's great symbol of technological modernity, the London Underground, which itself has been reconstructed as the disturbing underbelly of the city's wealth acquiring the patina of age. This is of course another of those paradoxical binaries which symbolize the city and pepper the Gothic histories of Sinclair and Ackroyd; both modern and ancient; technological innovation and atavistic throwback. Botting also exposes the symbolic rendition of the city, capital and the Gothicization of modernity in the film *28 Days Later* (2002) and its sequel *28 Weeks Later* (2007). Drawing upon a broader palette that enables an exploration of contemporary global capital and resurgent experimentation with empire in a city and nation overridden by zombies (of the genre-breaking, fast moving zoombies of his title) and preternaturally deserted, the near empty city occupied by UN sponsored American troops. Echoing the distorted 'everyday life at the point of a gun' of occupied Baghdad, the RAGE virus suggests the 'dog eat dog' world of international finance that is literally consuming itself.

As Robert Mighall argues, the 'Gothic' is by definition about history and geography. Rarely do such categories seem so self evidently destabilized as one finds in London Gothic.

Part One

Victorians to Moderns

Chapter 2

Toward a Phenomenology of Urban Gothic: The Example of Dickens

Julian Wolfreys

'Self-consciousness', observes Hegel in the *Phenomenology of Spirit*, 'is only *something*, it only has *reality*, insofar as it estranges itself' (Hegel 363–64). In this chapter, I argue that the Dickensian subject is always estranged by London. Indeed, consciousness arrives as a self-consciousness of one's place and time through the estrangement that the encounter with London causes. The Dickensian subject is produced, moreover, even as he, or occasionally she, produces himself or herself through a self-conscious subjectivity engendered by the experience of London that is often recognizably Gothic; that is to say, in order to 'invent' the modern urban self in the face of the material conditions of the city, Dickens has frequent recourse to the language, the tropes, of Gothic fiction.

In particular, while I will consider certain characters, my principal concern is with the implied subject perceived *as* or *through* the narrator or narrator-effect, and imagined as the place onto which the city is projected and from which a text is written or, seemingly, spoken. It is not that one might think the Dickensian narrator as having a body, albeit that such a figure appears to embody material experience through representation. It might be said, instead, that this shadowy character is maintained through an incarnation, a coming that takes place between, in the 'inter-space [*l'entre-deux*]' (Nancy 64–65); a consciousness coming into being 'between-two' and constituted through place and consciousness, *as* the truth of historicized attestation, for the reader. The Dickensian urban subject, or, more properly, Dickensian urban subjectivity, is both a phenomenon of the city and a screen onto which the materiality of the early nineteenth-century metropolis is projected. The subject as 'form' – a form given shape through narration in response and as witness to the city – *consists in this, that a now becomes constituted by means of an impression*' (emphasis added), and furthermore, that impression is constituted through 'a trail of retentions and a horizon of protentions . . . [as this] abiding form supports the consciousness of constant change' (Husserl 1991 118). The successive *now* of any narrating, narrated representation of the city is, therefore, always the impression left by the material historicity of place, which must subsequently be given form through available language. But it is formulated, in the singular example of Dickensian writing through the retention of the Gothic trope, as fictive memory appropriate to the representation of the city.

While there is much more to be said about Hegel's theorization of the subject, with which I began, for now, in order to proceed, let me suggest apropos subjectivity in Dickens that the subject always begins as an estranged subject, subject to its own knowledge as participant *and* observer, through the encounter with and experience of the event of the city, of what takes place and comes to pass. There is no subjectivity for Dickens without the earliest experiences and representations of London. Dickens gives voice to a strikingly modern consciousness, a consciousness estranged in the condition of its nascent modernity. London shapes – or deforms – subjectivity. And this subject is both modern *and* Gothic: modern because of the phenomenological register and reinscription of subjectivity as mediating identity and medium for the other; and Gothic because subjectivity, in being displaced, doubled, deferred from any pure presence, finds itself, is taken by surprise by its other self, as *always already* perceived, and perceives itself as being a haunted structure within which the flight and flux of becoming is rendered momentarily available. That hauntedness of being is only available to expression through the language of Gothic narrative, and to the tropological reinscription in encrypted fashion of some of its most enduring images and figures.

Moreover (as already implied), this anachronistically modern subjectivity assumes most often in Dickens's journalism an anonymous, but partial and positioned, rather than an objective, universal worldview. Consider momentarily the commentary on Seven Dials, first published in *Bell's Life in London*, 27 September 1837. 'Where', inquires our narrator, 'is there such another maze of streets, courts, lanes and alleys . . . as in this complicated part of London?' (Dickens 1994 71–72). Here is a place, unlike any other – except that, in Dickens, every singular site is just like every other singular site in its difference – comprising 'obscure passages' and an 'irregular square'. A 'stranger', it is imagined, who has 'plunged' into this square, will perceive himself as lost, disorientated, as the streets and courts 'dart in all directions until they are lost in the unwholesome vapour which hangs over the house tops, and renders the dirty perspective uncertain and confined' (Dickens 1994 72). Something fascinating and complex is in motion here, as a result of plunging into 'these streets' with their 'peculiar character' (Dickens 1994 73). The narrator and the stranger are, in effect, one and the same; or, to invert this, each is the displaced, estranged and doubled figure of the other: the one invisible, paused, observing in detail that which would keep one's 'curiosity and attention awake for no inconsiderable time' (Dickens 1994 72), the other unable to orientate himself. Already doubled, the narrator's selfhood has no greater vantage point than that of the stranger, his other, and so is demoted from transcendental primacy. In this, the reader apprehends narratorial subjectivity as 'the condition of the experience of the other' (Henry 110). And as the stranger is lost, so too are the streets, becoming invisible at a certain distance, from flagstones to rooftops. Elements in the scene appear momentarily, pausing before that plunge, that disappearance and anonymity. All we witness, our narrating subject assures us, 'would fill any mind but a regular Londoner's with astonishment' (Dickens 1994 72). That mind, the stranger's, we already know and will continue to find out, is confronted by confusion, complication, excess, indecipherability, and 'bewilderment'. No further familiarity with the streets or their character will 'decrease the bewilderment in which the unexperienced wayfarer . . . finds himself involved' (Dickens 1994 72). And every street bears, in character if not in appearance, a 'close resemblance [to] . . . its neighbour' (Dickens 1994 73). There is here a serial iterability, a duplication in which self gives way to perception, and the stranger is reduced to the being of a thing, uncannily alive *and* dead, through a perceptual experience that is scarcely delimitable.

Not yet obviously Gothic in its figural work, the passage nonetheless invents a mode of representation that, in the modernity of its subjective partiality and loss, bespeaks in an original manner that constellation of sensations and apprehension attributed to the Gothic subject. Confusion, loss, doubling and iterable fragmentation, disorientation, anxiety and one's suddenly perceiving oneself as being caught up in something beyond one's knowledge, all elements of Gothic sensibility if not narration, are figured here *just as* the identity of one London district *and*, simultaneously, the event of perception for narrator and stranger alike. Such experience is implied as that which the contours of that district are capable of projecting onto, thereby determining the subject. This district only serves to heighten, furthermore, the subject's anonymity in the experience in which, if we recall the phrase, 'he finds himself involved'. Subjectivity is illuminated only through being estranged and becoming conscious of itself, as estranged and as an other, always on the threshold of abjection. If, as Maurice Natanson claims in his exploration of 'Phenomenology, Anonymity, and Alienation', '[e]ssentially, the way in which I know the Other is through the largely tacit construction of a miniature ideal type' (Natanson 535), then in 'Seven Dials', the only way I know the Other is to see him iterated and divided between the stranger and the analogous apperception of the narrating subject, and to perceive myself in both of those. Concomitantly, the transcendental privilege my Ego affords me is diminished, if not lost, also. There is a close resemblance between a character and his neighbour, to transfer the Dickensian representation from architecture to persona. That being so, my loss of self, that estrangement of relation comes in seeing how, like those figures of the other, visible and invisible, I am unable to extricate myself from this labyrinthine and threatening location, in which *I find myself involved.*

I use this phrase of Dickens's again, for it is, I think, appropriate to the perceptual experience of reading. The written passages of 'Seven Dials' act on the reading subject in a manner analogous to the effect of the architectural and topographical passages encountered by the stranger and the narrator. I refer to the 'narrator' advisedly for this phantom figure who is both there and not there is, on the one hand, capable of presenting in detail all there is, while, on the other hand, admitting to the limits of representational power, and confessing furthermore that the city is ultimately unknowable, impenetrable in its mysteries, and therefore undecidable. The assumed universality of narrative realism, in its attention to detail, collapses back into the partiality and interpretive provisionality of phenomenological perception. Recall the observation that all but the minds of 'regular Londoners' would be filled with astonishment. Who is this regular Londoner? Where can one be found? None are in Seven Dials certainly, not even the narrator, who projects and reproduces the astonishment of the estranged subject. The passage thus closes in its play around an evacuated centre, as the expression of a perceptual experience of a modernity, which has become another *now*, and which, therefore, is also *my* experience. This recursion is not however a failure, but a reduction, which, in freeing the elements of composition from their being enchained in mimetic service, makes their fragmentary and iterable signs appear to *my* consciousness as the signs of historicity, thereby exceeding the merely historical and the merely factual. Thus freed, communication of perceptual experience becomes, in Husserl's term 'virtual . . . sensibly experienceable. . . . Accordingly, then, the writing-down effects a transformation of the original mode of being of the meaning structure' (Husserl 1989 164).

The processes so far described may appear closer to London's transformation, if not a Londoner's perception, of the sublime, rather than the Gothic. In questioning, however implicitly what it meant to be a subject of the city, and to be, moreover the subject of a city unlike any other in the 1830s, thereby subjected to an irregular, monstrous and deformed but mutable modernity what might have been felt as awe and wonder could all too easily have been experienced as terror and abjection. If, as Peter de Bolla argues, 'every age has its own concept of selfhood, and every succeeding "age" may or may not choose to interpret this concept in its own fashion, and very often in its own self-image' (de Bolla 5), the 'age' of London's subject – which epoch is still ours and which we have yet to leave – imposes a daunting task on its readers in the formation of a consciousness capable of bearing witness to the city, which singular event, though never repeatable in its experience, is nonetheless open to transmission and translation. The frequent use of present tense in Dickens's journalism, makes the transport between discrete moments or locations possible, through the illusion of a 'first-timeliness', Husserlian *Erstmaligkeit*, 'as pertaining to a transcendental history' which opens, in Derrida's reading of Husserl, a 'profoundly reconceived, newly understood, "historical ground"' (Kates 139) that is produced in the mediation and the material of language itself. Dickens's narrator-effect is, thus the medium, not only between distinct modes of being, the estranged being of the stranger and my estranged mode as reader, but also between modern consciousness and Gothic as an other sensibly experienceable virtual reality producing not dissimilar experiences.

In this mediumistic transformation of the reader, the Dickensian representation of the perceptual experience of the city partakes of the less obvious,
and more playful aspects of Gothic discourse. If the Gothic consists in part of
elements of carnivalesque, as Robert Miles asserts, along with 'contending discourses', having 'as their foci issues of . . . origin, the sublime, . . . vision, reverie',
this 'congeries' (as Miles calls it, in a term which echoes Dickens' manner of
figuring urban representations (Miles 6)) comprising London is thus all the
more disquieting. Carnivalesque tropes, particularly those informing Gothic,
are arguably the very discourses by which Dickens builds his urban location.
A performative writing, Dickensian urban narration does not merely show, it
acts out, even as it induces, or seeks to induce the experience for the perception of the reader. And this, in small measure, addresses if not answers that
question concerning Dickens's readership concerning the distinction between
'Londoners' and 'non-Londoners' (a division, I am sure, which, according
to the laws of the city, will not hold). London as knowable, orderable totality
is ungraspable. However, in more immediately material and historical terms, it
has to be argued that London, only ever its districts, boroughs, and neighbourhoods, transforms so rapidly and unceasingly throughout the nineteenth century that, in the process of assimilation, those who move to the city, expanding
its population, do not have the leisure to become *flâneurs*. Work proscribes
knowledge. These are regular Londoners, they become regular Londoners, but
in moving between home and work know nothing other than their route and
their locality (rather as if they were still, and remained strangers). At the same
time, given that there are Londoners who are more established and also wealth-
ier, this is not to presume that they know any more of 'their' city than their own
partial worlds. Because of the perceived and real 'dangers' of certain districts,
perceptions and realities belonging as much to the city of the eighteenth century, 'London' is apprehended as multiple and heterogeneous, with areas that
are 'off-limits', 'dark', 'threatening', and even monstrous. As Dickens remarks
of the suburbs of the early part of the century, before being connected 'with the
main body of the city and its environs . . . many of them [were] a place of resort
for the worst and most desperate characters' (Dickens 1994 364). Thus the
margins of London become read as a domestic Gothic environment.

It is not that Dickens's urban writing is necessarily or overtly Gothic, at least
in its earliest published examples. What can be argued, instead, is that Dickens's
writing has recourse to a Gothic 'turn' in order to explain the inexplicable, to
give expression to that for which there is no language. Gothic considered as a
tropological field rather than as a genre informs the determination of representation in the face of what would otherwise remain unpassable, inexpressible.
What changes is that with demographic and economic transformation, the
rapid expansion of suburbs further out from the centre creates a margin greater
than the centre in which live 'regular Londoners' who know from first-hand
experience almost as little as readers of Dickens of this other London. In that

Dickens frequently writes of a London where, like the writing of Gothic, the writing of the city, expressed through a language that maps a problematized consciousness, reveals a 'deeper wound' or 'fracture, an imbalance, a "gap" in the social self which would not go away' (Punter 26), thus the act of writing London comes to be shaped by what can be called an encrypted, tropic Gothic, rather than one composed of surface grand guignol effects, and mundane narratives of monstrosity. The representation of Walworth from one of Dickens's earliest tales, 'The Black Veil', a story written particularly for the first collected edition of *Sketches by Boz* in 1836, is instructive in this regard:

> The back part of Walworth, at its greatest distance from town, is a straggling miserable place enough, even in these days; but, five-and-thirty years ago, the greater portion of it was little better than a dreary waste, inhabited by a few scattered people of questionable character, whose poverty prevented their living in any better neighbourhood, or whose pursuits or mode of life rendered its solitude desirable. Very many of the houses which have since sprung up on all sides, . . . were of the rudest and most miserable description.
>
> The appearance of the place . . . was not calculated to raise the spirits . . . or to dispel any feeling of anxiety or depression. . . . [the] way lay across a marshy common, through irregular lanes, with here and there a ruinous and dismantled cottage fast falling to pieces with decay and neglect. A stunted tree, or pool of stagnant water, roused into a sluggish action by the heavy rain of the preceding night, skirted the path occasionally; and, now and then, a miserable patch of garden ground, with a few old boards knocked together for a summer house, and old palings imperfectly mended with stakes pilfered from the neighbouring hedges bore testimony, at once to the poverty of the inhabitants, and the little scruple they entertained in appropriating the property of other people to their own use. . . . scarcely anything was stirring around; and so much of the prospect as could be faintly traced through the cold damp mist which hung heavily over it, presented a lonely and dreary appearance perfectly in keeping with the objects we have described. (Dickens 1994 363–64)

The representation of a south London suburb moves between objective or documentary representation and subjective interpretation that develops its mode of apprehension through access to the effect of place on perception. Clearly not a material Gothic setting, yet the register here is such that, with the 'appearance' of dismal gloominess that lowers the spirits even as it is imbued with the power implicitly to induce anxiety, a Gothic of the senses takes effect. Particular objects or phenomena – the ruined cottage, the stunted tree, the suggestion of danger and isolation, the mist and residue of rain – in their abject or ruinous condition maintain or intensify the effect on the one who bears witness, even as they appear, collectively as a suburban, domestic transformation of the conventions of Gothic landscape. Dickens is careful to trace the connection between the empirical and the subjective, between the material and its appearance for the viewing – and reading – subject. Though confronted with a 'real' landscape, the urban subject is placed under the sign of the Gothic in his perception and this perception is transmitted to, and so reduplicated in, the reader, as empirical location is subsumed within phantasmic reception. Dickens thus produces a countersignature to the picturesque, through the 'givenness of the impression, whose essence is the pure fact of being impressed as such, is stripped of its role in givenness, in favour of an originary consciousness' (Henry 25) perfectly in keeping, as Dickens has it, 'with the objects we have described'. Such Gothic effects thus place the reading subject in the midst of a complex problem of perception and orientation.

Here, one is forced to respond, not to documentary verisimilitude, but rather to what Robert Miles calls 'Gothic's discursive practices' rendering problematic 'what it is possible to say with clarity and the slippery nature of language itself; between the territory of social experience narrative allows [the writer] to map out, and the uncharted character of' phenomenological apprehension that is not, itself, 'immediately intelligible' to Dickens as such (Miles 143). Hence the struggle, the 'apposition' of dialogic, as Miles calls it, between journalistic observation and the discursive matrix of Gothic, 'to make their articulations discernible' (Miles 144). And, as another commentator on Gothic, Robert Mighall, remarks in his commentary on W. M. Reynolds' *The Mysteries of London*, 'a closely-knit collection of courts and alleys is one thing – an observable topographical phenomenon that can be charted . . . [However,] to label even the most architectural complex "labyrinthine"' (Mighall 33), not only imports 'effects from the earlier [Gothic] literary tradition' (Mighall 31), it also 'reveals less about its actual condition than [it does] the concerns of the perceiver and these are . . . historically determined' (Mighall 33).

This is what Dickens enables – the historically determined concerns and perceptions of the perceiver. What we in turn receive are the signs of an immanent phenomenological structure and mode of perception. An 'irreducible historicity is recognized' therefore, in that this mode of perception arrives through the dialogic struggle 'only *after* the fact of the event' (Derrida 49); which event is double: on the one hand constituted through the writing subject's encounter with the city; on the other hand, produced through the demand to transform the materiality of history and experience into the materiality of the letter, whereby the irreducible historicity might be transmitted. London thus gives Dickens, and therefore those of us who read the city after Dickens, the singular emergence of a discourse not yet articulated in the 1830s, and 'whose unity is still *to come* on the basis of what is announced' (Derrida 53). If London erupts in Dickens as monstrous, sublime, ineffable, undecidable, it enables not a retreat from the political into a restatement of aporetic suspension, but rather a necessary abstention and so a break 'from . . . historicist empiricism' (Derrida 59) to institute a movement towards a truth, which 'is really that of a concrete and specific history – the foundations of which are a temporal and creative subjectivity's acts based on the sensible world and the life world as cultural world' (Derrida 60). Between London and its witnessing subject interconnections are originated, interconnections of 'what is, in the fullest sense of the word, *history itself*' (Derrida 65), 'the possibility of which is *language*' (Derrida 66).

But this London, these Londons, are everywhere. They make possible the expression, through the agency of Dickensian subjectivity in its interconnection of documentary journalism and Gothic, 'the possibility of history as the possibility of language' enabling 'a phenomenology of historicity' (Derrida 69). Nowhere permanently, they erupt and interrupt with an insistent if irregular rhythm in the author's journalism, like so many more obviously Gothic horrors. Dickens risks everything on the Gothic trope in a gesture that anticipates not only Husserl but also Joyce, in the expression of a will to 'awake' from the nightmare of history, so as to 'master that nightmare in a total and present resumption' (Derrida 103). Dickens's urban Gothic, in excess of the merely factual and historicist empiricism to which later anthropological and political writers such as Mayhew or Engels succumb, risks a phenomenological discourse that wakes up from the nightmare of the inescapably mimetic and realist, which merely reinscribes the political and social horrors it seeks to denounce.

Beyond or, perhaps more accurately, *before* representation and the narrative that binds content though, there are those structural aspects, constituent parts or facets that, in their complex formal relation serve to constitute in turn that which makes London Gothic peculiarly and singularly what it is: a Gothic, on the one hand, of complex, repeated formal structures, traces and interanimating architectural and topographical parts; and a Gothic, on the other hand, of affect, emotion, sensate apprehension and apperception – a topology therefore tending towards provisional ontological reinscription and the reading or interrogation through that topological and tropological formation of the translation or communication of the conscious experience of place and event, wherein the event of encounter with what is objectively real is irreversibly interiorized as the phantasmic perception of the materiality of place as phenomena. Experience becomes, in this relation, revelation, and so illumination, for the experiencing and reading subject, of an inner force or truth, if you will, of that which is London's identity.

This broad sketch requires qualification if we are to move forward. It is therefore necessary to explicate the relationship between a phenomenology of perception and those aspects of an ontology of the Gothic more explicitly where materiality of place and the concatenation of objects that constitute place overlap with the perception of what place might harbour, or which, immanent within its structures, might without direct revelation nevertheless cause to erupt within the subject as the anticipation of what is to come. 'Communication', writes Maurice Merleau-Ponty, 'is an appearance' (Merleau-Ponty 7), and this is seen, in the example of Seven Dials. This is not to say that communication is, or can be, always, if ever direct, straightforward, or successful. Dickens apprehends this question of causing or making something to appear, and so communicate, and the fraught conditions under which it might occur. But to insist again on this point, Dickens comes to this realization through the initial and lifelong encounter, experience and re-acquaintance with the places that make up both the material condition and the identity of London. In order to cause the city to appear, not *as such* but *as it is*, Dickens risks everything on the ruin of communication filtered through the discourse of the Gothic, with its evasiveness, its fragmentation and its tantalizing, yet addictive narrative frustrations.

Dickens' writing of the city moves therefore through manifestations of the urban for a subject constituted by and placed within those manifestations, which present themselves sequentially and serially. An object, or fragment of an object, is presented, only to be supplemented by another, as each 'builds' in the imagination through a concatenation not objectively explicit. This is given us to read at the opening of an article titled 'Wapping Workhouse', published in *All the Year Round* early in 1860. In directing himself towards the 'East-end of London', and on leaving Covent Garden, the narrator, having 'got past the India House', is caused to reflect in desultory fashion on 'Tippoo-Sahib and Charles Lamb'. These phantasms are supplanted in turn by the little wooden mid-shipman, Aldgate Pump, the Saracen's Head, his already 'swarthy countenance' disfigured by an 'ignominious rash of posting bills' (Dickens 1997 366). These phenomena are juxtaposed with an 'ancient neighbour', another Inn, the name of which is not to be remembered distinctly as a result of its having long disappeared, and its becoming conflated with another coaching inn, The Bull, which was to be torn down six years after this article was published.

While items, names, images and objects accumulate, already in meaningful ways, the journey moves forward but the narrating subject displaces himself from the present both spatially and temporally. Names and figures – India House, Tippoo-Sahib, and the Saracen's Head – hint at an 'orientation' which is also a disorientation, the journey to the East of London invoking another, Orientalist East, and with that, other temporal and historical frames. Topographical motion brings about a slippage in the mind, into Gothic codes of 'the barbaric or Oriental' (Miles 44), as if the physical act of perambulation, in its causing the chance encounter with various signs of alterity, releases an unconscious desire, as language itself succumbs to an inadvertent revelation of the perception or anticipation of excess. A doubling temporality is opened from within the present for the subject, who later confesses himself, in another Orientalist turn, in a 'Turkish frame of mind' (Dickens 1997 367), for he walks on quite blind to place and historical moment, lost in the pasts of coaching inns and a phantasmic, quite possibly Gothicized East, before emerging in both 'the age of railways' and Whitechapel Church (Dickens 1997 366). The signs of the city lose the subject in a phenomenological miasma between Leadenhall Market and Hawksmoor's St Anne's, a distance just over 1.5 miles. In the presentation of objects, a street scene, the details of atmosphere, the listing of proper names by encounter and association, or, as elsewhere details of a building

or room, the object or group of objects being represented, manifesting themselves through the communication of traces in an often febrile adumbration,
disappear behind the phantasm woven out of the collective web of signs.
Concomitantly, the urban subject finds himself lost, once more. As the narrator
had found himself in a disorientating experience in Seven Dials almost three
decades before, so here, it is confessed that 'I gave myself up as having lost
my way, and abandoning myself to the narrow streets in a Turkish frame of
mind' (Dickens 1997 367). As if to enforce the Gothic transformation of place
and subject, the narrator then recounts how a young man is encountered,
whose 'puffed sallow face, and . . . figure all dirty and shiny and slimy . . . may
have been . . . the drowned man' of local advertizing hoardings (Dickens 1997
367). This 'figure' defined three times as an 'apparition' and having a ghastly
grin and a watery gurgle for a laugh (Dickens 1997 367) erases the narrator's
own sense of individualism, causing the latter to feel himself to be anonymous,
a 'General Cove, or member of the miscellaneous public' (Dickens 1997 368).

The subject is given up, and gives himself up to the city. Being addressed by
it, he becomes a psychic palimpsest of its structures, flows and manifestations.
Objects and places are revealed as being veiled by the traces of themselves,
traces which bespeak the tenor, the tone if you will, of other identities, mean-
ings and times, and which in turn direct the subject away from the present
materiality, through the lightning flash impressions that they leave perceptually.
Moreover, the object in Dickens, that material form belonging to the technique
of urban representation, is 'never grasped as distinct from what reveals it'.
In short, observes Renaud Barbaras (on whose phenomenology of perception
I am drawing), 'the manifestation presents the object [whichever experience
of London, whichever location, event or scene to which Dickens addresses
himself, and by which he is addressed] as what itself remains unpresentable'
(Barbaras 14) – hence the fabricated Gothic East with its wild boar, dismem-
bered Muslims, and aqueous ghouls.

The concern I am stressing here though is that Dickensian urban mapping
and representation proceeds by telegraphic shorthand and phatic adumbration, in order simultaneously to outline the experience of perception and to
present that which is unavailable to full presentation. That very act of sketching
nevertheless presents the object 'rigorously as what requires formulation',
which is to say the subject's apperception of the truth of the urban, as the object
transforms itself into perceived subject and as the subject who perceives must
necessarily receive, decipher and so perceive both 'the manifestation and what
appears, [as these are] affected by a double constitutive ambiguity' (Barbaras 14).
Perception, always the perception of some subject, thus reveals itself as the
'identity' of that other subject, the city for the human subject who, in producing
this identity, obliterates the objective reality. And 'as for the object', Barbaras
continues, 'it is [therefore] simultaneously present in the sense that it is attained
in person and indefinitely absent in the sense that no series of adumbrations

can exhaust the tenor of being'. The Dickensian manifestations of London generated in fragmentary surges – themselves communicated through the fragment, the ruin, the otherwise unorderable collocation of traces, elements and aspects both structural and phantasmic – project, rather than represent, 'the identity of a coming to presence and a retreat into the unpresentable' (Barbaras 14). The subject sees the city. The subject *is* the city. Conscious experience becomes the place where, and the screen on which, the apparent unity of the urban is found and projected contingently, before giving way to the haunting implication, always at work, of 'an eidetic abyss between experience and reality' (Barbaras 14). Half glimpsed as it were, the city in full retreats, its various manifestations never becoming a totality but perceived as an ungraspable totality, which can only be apprehended in the present if it is linked with an historical or fictive past – hence, that drive we identify through the adjective *Dickensian*, that restless rapid pulse at the heart of urban representation in the text of Dickens. And if 'the Gothic novel remains unhistorical precisely because it lacks this link' between the 'historical reality' of the past and 'the present' (Iser 84), then Dickens situates the interconnection explicitly between historical reality and subjective historicity, through the tropes of Gothic discourse.

   What I wish to suggest about Dickens' response to London and thus, by extension, about the ways in which representation in writing is translated by the subject's experience of the metropolis, is that the phenomenon that is London from the early nineteenth century onwards causes or gives to be known a radically different mode of apprehension and representation, in which it is no longer possible to represent the material world 'as if there were only a single manner of existing and therefore a single adequate modality of access to existing' (Barbaras 16). London brings about the revelation of the ruin of representation – its reduction to 'nothing other than the vital movement of the coexistence and the interweaving of original formations and sedimentations of meaning' (Husserl 1989 174) – in terms of the limits of a purely presentist mimetic adequation, and so forces on the subject a new identity, with an historically and materially grounded urban specificity, from which must be generated an inventive 'idiocultural' writing. Such inscription, while grounded in empirical or historical fact, whether solicited 'in the present through experience or . . . as a fact in the past, necessarily has its *inner structure of meaning*' (emphasis added) and thus is founded on an 'immense structural a priori', the disclosure of which gives to the act of writing its 'historical becoming' (Husserl 1989 174). Such a writing is 'inventive' in the sense that the writing subject is forced by the object to find the trace of alterity within what is already there, rather than create some wholly new mode, in order to communicate perception and experience from its partial and subjective location as this takes place. And it is 'idiocultural', to borrow and adapt this term of Derek Attridge's, inasmuch as Dickensian urban invention, through its adumbrated and telegraphic phatic fluxes, attests in a performative manner, thereby doing in words the very thing it describes, to the 'individual's grasp on the world [of the modern city, as this] is mediated by a changing array of [historically given] interlocking, overlapping and often contradictory cultural systems' that mark the urban scene as a 'complex', and which therefore is 'necessary unstable and subject to constant change' (Attridge 21).

Thus, Dickens' writing of London 'comes into being as a challenge to cultural norms [of representation] and retain[s] that challenge . . . because it is never fully accommodated' (Attridge 46). Yet, although it cannot be fully accommodated, there is, nevertheless, that strange, disquieting feeling of the 'experience of intimacy . . . a sense that the work speaks to my inmost, most secret being', its haunting and uncanny singularity striking me 'afresh' (Attridge 78). At the same time, the demand made on me is clearly akin to the demand made on Dickens by the city. The demand that London imposes on Dickens is also a demand that 'this specific collocation of words, allusions, and cultural references makes on me, in the event of my reading, *here and now*' (Attridge 67; emphasis added). I read the Dickensian subject encountering the city: I *am* that subject – or at the very least, phantasmically, it is *as if* I were that subject. This experience and perception are thus the manifestation of a singularity, and the 'experience of singularity involves an apprehension of *otherness*, registered in the event of apprehension' (Attridge 67). So it is that we find ourselves back, once again, with that abyss between experience and perception. In this, we therefore are simultaneously at a remove and yet impossibly close to Dickens' own encounter with the abyss, that very opening which writing could never suture, and which intuition may serve in part to explain the motivation behind the Dickensian invention of a specifically modern, idiocultural urban Gothic. Or, let us just suggest, for Dickens, the urban *was* Gothic and what was Gothic was precisely the apprehension of a terror in the face of an abyss which could never be bridged or closed, and which, in turn, drove Dickens on to write repeatedly of the city as a topography and architecture that could never be mapped or given totalized, finite representation. Reading Dickens on the city, the experience becomes one involving something akin to Dickens' encounters with London: an inventive and singular – singular every time I pick up another text – appreciation and *analogical apperception;* as Attridge has it, this is a 'living through, of the invention that makes the work not just different but the creative re-imagination of cultural materials' and material culture (Attridge 67).

If I experience that sense of a 'living through' – in the sense of duration and its endurance – as vicarious, phantasmic event, it is in Dickens' creative re-imagining of various dimensions of the Gothic in culturally and historically specific terms iterable in the urban contexts. Additionally, my phenomenal, haunting experience is marked by both the replication and iteration of Dickensian subjectivity's fall, into the world and anonymity. The anonymous narrator-effect delivers us to, and marks the limits of, a threshold between subject and world and the Gothic translated is all the more immanently troubling, if less solidly represented, because identity is lost in the urban. The anonymous comes to pass, glimpsed in this act and articulation of the city in its bearing witness to place and what takes place; for: 'the anonymous is a constitutive feature of the social' (Natanson 534). As the anonymous subject disappears into the urban (think if you will of Master Humphrey's 'disappearance'), so I too experience this estranged, ironic displacement. Therefore, the anxiety in the face of London's haunting traces is more nearly felt, more intimately available, if not to perception, then to apperception. In indirect apprehension the city is experienced or suffered as a possibly occult threatening, inhuman, yet vital force, which can swallow us, suffocate us, lose us forever, and prevent our escape. The flows of London consolidate around the nameless subject all too easily, becoming reified as both material locations *and* Gothic structures of the imagination.

Works Cited

Attridge, D. (2004), *The Singularity of Literature*, London: Routledge

Barbaras, R. (2006), *Desire and Distance: Introduction to a Phenomenology of Perception*, trans. Paul B. Milan, Stanford: Stanford University Press

de Bolla, P. (1989), *The Discourse of the Sublime: History, Aesthetics and the Subject*, Oxford: Blackwell

Derrida, J. (1989), *Edmund Husserl's Origin of Geometry: An Introduction*, trans. with Preface and Afterword by John P. Leavey, Jr. Lincoln: University of Nebraska Press

Dickens, C. (1986), *Nicholas Nickleby*, Harmondsworth: Penguin

Dickens, C. (1994), *Sketches By Boz and Other Early Papers 1833–1839*, London: J. M. Dent

Dickens, C. (1997), *Selected Journalism 1850–1870*, London: Penguin

Freeman, N. (2007), *Conceiving the City: London, Literature, and Art 1870–1914*, Oxford: Oxford University Press

Hegel, G. W. F. (1977), *Phenomenology of Spirit*, trans. A. V. Miller. Foreword by J. N. Findlay, Oxford: Oxford University Press

Henry, M. (2008), *Material Phenomenology*, trans. Scott Davidson, New York: Fordham University Press

Husserl, E. (1989), *The Origin of Geometry*, trans. David Carr. In Jacques Derrida *Edmund Husserl's Origin of Geometry: An Introduction*, trans. with a Preface and Afterword by John P. Leavey, Jr. Lincoln: University of Nebraska Press

Husserl, E. (1991), *On the Phenomenology of the Consciousness of Internal Time (1893–1917)*, trans. John Barnett Brough, Dordrecht: Kluwer Academic

Iser, W. (1974), *The Implied Reader: Patterns of Communication in Prose Fiction from Bunyan to Beckett*, trans. anon., Baltimore: The Johns Hopkins University Press

Kates, J. F. (2008), *Derrida: Philosophy, Literary Criticism, History, and the Work of Deconstruction*, New York: Fordham University Press

Merleau-Ponty, M. (1973), *The Prose of the World*, (ed.) Claude Lefort, trans. John O'Neil, Evanston: Northwestern University Press

Mighall, R. (1999), *A Geography of Victorian Gothic Fiction: Mapping History's Nightmares*, Oxford: Oxford University Press

Miles, R. (1993), *Gothic Writing 1750–1820: A Genealogy*, London: Routledge

Nancy, J-L (2008), *Corpus*, trans. Richard A. Rand, New York: Fordham University Press

Natanson, M. (Spring 1979), 'Phenomenology, Anonymity, and Alienation', *New Literary History*, 10(3) , 533–46

Chapter 3

'A Fatal Freshness': Mid-Victorian Suburbophobia

Anne Witchard

The Storms of London: A Preamble

In the evening of a late September day in the Indian summer of 1802, Thomas De Quincey, aged seventeen, left behind the golden splendour of Snowdonia's twilit peaks for the uproar of the 'dreadful', 'beckoning' metropolis: 'I made my farewell adieus to summer. All through the day, Wales and her grand mountain ranges... had divided my thoughts with London. But now rose London – sole, dark, infinite – brooding over the whole capacities of my heart' (De Quincey 2000 192). De Quincey's association of Snowdonia's 'grand mountain ranges' with the 'infinite' metropolis registers a more intense trepidation than is usual in a young man setting off to seek his way in the world: 'I stood upon the brink of a precipice; and the local circumstances around me deepened and intensified these reflections, impressed upon them solemnity and terror, sometimes even horror' (De Quincey 2000 192). De Quincey's recall of this moment owes much of course to Edmund Burke's theory of the sublime. In De Quincey though, as Deeanne Westbrook observes, 'the sacred is transformed into something like the Uncanny as that term is now understood. The expansive, the exalted, the sublime, and the transcendent . . . turn dark and terrifying' under his scrutiny (Westbrook 159).[1]

By midnight, De Quincey had reached Shrewsbury on the Welsh border. Here he waits for the two a.m. Holyhead-to-London mailcoach in a sumptuous hotel room, a 'ball-room of noble proportions' (De Quincey 2000 193). A wild storm is blowing up and the lofty dimensions of the room and its seasonal disuse (the chandeliers are shrouded in wrappings) set in chain further associations that inform De Quincey's anticipation of the city in terms of a Gothic sublime:

the rooms – their unusual altitude, and the echoing hollowness . . . together with crowding and evanescent images of the flying feet that so often had spread gladness through these halls on the wings of youth and hope at seasons when every room rang with music – all this, rising in tumultuous vision, whilst the dead hours of night were stealing along . . . [and] against the windows more and more the storm outside was raving, and to all appearances endlessly growing, threw me into the deadliest condition of nervous emotion under contradictory forces, high over which predominated horror recoiling from that unfathomed abyss in London into which I was now so wilfully precipitating myself. (De Quincey 2000 193)

The subsequent 'calamaties of [De Quincey's] noviciate in London' chief of which is his fruitless search for the disappeared street girl, Ann, confirm what may well be a retrospective configuration of how he felt at seventeen, but given his peculiar cast of mind was perhaps ever likely to be a self-fulfilling prophesy (De Quincey 1821 353).[2] For De Quincey, London's wilderness of streets is 'amplified to an extent of unutterable and self-repeating infinity' (Burke 1928 169). He nightly paces 'the never-ending terraces' of Oxford Street in his search for Ann, the mushrooming thoroughfares of Bloomsbury and Fitzrovia confounding him in their 'imprisoning web' (De Quincey 2000 214).[3] His 'consolation' though, is 'on moonlight nights . . . to gaze from Oxford-street up every avenue in succession which pierces through the heart of Marylebone to the fields and the woods', beyond which he can envision the north, Grasmere (home of his idolized Wordsworth) and its associated 'comfort' (De Quincey 2000 214).

De Quincey's neurosis that manifests a terror of London principally in terms of its labyrinthine streets is quite singular at this point. Before long it would have a wide resonance. While the development of Regents Park in 1812 would preserve grassy stretches that might still be glimpsed from Oxford Street today, the green fields, babbling brooks, hedge-row walks and wooded glades of Marylebone were beginning to be encroached upon (Larwood 311). Charles Molloy Westmacott in *The English Spy* (1826), describes a 'country' stroll taken just north of the new park by Bernard Blackmantle and his pal Crony: 'At the foot of Primrose Hill we are amazed by coming upon a large complication of streets . . . The rustic and primeval meadows of Kilburn are also filling with raw buildings and incipient roads; to say nothing of the charming neighbourhood of St. John's Wood farm, and other spots nearer town' (Westmacott 72). Crony declares himself 'doomed to deplore' modern times and 'the destructive advances' of what generally goes by the name of improvement: 'the rage for building fills every pleasant outlet with bricks, mortar, rubbish and eternal scaffold-poles, which, whether you walk east, west, north, or south, seem to be running after you . . . It is certainly astonishing: one would think the builders used magic or steam at least' (Westmacott 72).[4] William Cobbett, in 1822, had set out from his smallholding in the village of Kensington on a journey south that took him past the 'clusters of new houses at Stockwell and the stucco villas which lined one side of the long slope up Brixton Hill' (Sheppard 83). Cobbett famously likened London to 'an infernal Wen' and he was horrified by the 'miles of stock-jobbers' houses' which were 'with accelerated force . . . added to the Wen' (Cobbett 60). How, he bewails, 'is this Wen to be *dispersed?* I know not whether it is to be done by knife or by caustic; but dispersed it must be!' (Cobbett 60).

We can see then that from the beginning of the nineteenth century, responses to London's suburban development employ a variety of Gothic tropes and motifs across a range of writing that encompasses essays and journalism, urban sketches, memoirs and autobiography. The 'sprawling phase' of suburban growth, while it 'gratified landowners, developers [and] builders' and lured occupants with prospects of 'status and happiness', pleased 'practically no one else' (Thompson 2). For De Quincey, London was a gargantuan phenomenon, unfathomable but nevertheless a discrete structure. Cobbett responds with clinical revulsion to the city's organic rapacity while the alarming rapidity and proliferation of suburban development is conceived by Westmacott as a misalliance of technology and enchantment which George Cruikshank's illustration, *London Going Out of Town - Or - the March of Bricks and Mortar!* (1829) visualizes as a robotic army of bricks and chimney pots mindlessly advancing towards Hampstead Heath from what we now know as Camden Town. Like the buckets and brooms in Goethe's poem, 'The Sorcerer's Apprentice' (1797), the brick kilns have escaped from their masters and are careering wildly out of control.

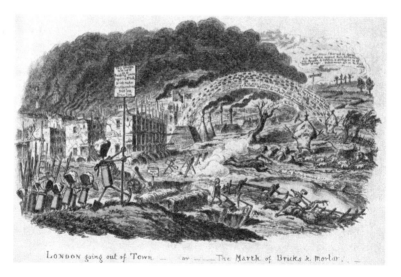

FIGURE 3.1 *London going out of town - or - the march of bricks and mortar! (1829)* by George Cruikshank

In 1829 Sir Thomas Wilson introduced a bill for the enclosure and development of Hampstead Heath.

The placard reads: 'This Ground To Be Lett on a Building Lease Enquire of Mr Goth, Brick Maker, Bricklayers Arms, Brick Lane, Brixton'.

Attention paid to Gothic figurations of nineteenth-century London tend to focus on the *fin-de-siècle* fictions of Oscar Wilde, Robert Louis Stevenson and Bram Stoker, as 'the moment when a distinctively urban Gothic was crystallized' (Luckhurst 530). In the late-Victorian and Edwardian imaginaries London becomes the symbolic where boundaries threatened to dissolve; Count Dracula is sighted in Piccadilly, Dr Jekyll undergoes his metamorphosis in a respectable West End square. What I want to do in this chapter is to show how the development and spread of London's suburbs early in the nineteenth century might be seen to underpin this Gothic writing about the city. Responses to the outward push of (what is now central) London's perimeter, where dissolved boundaries are both metaphoric and literal, inaugurate the premise of an urban Gothic in an efferent division of the civilized from the barbarous.

Alexandra Warwick locates the general shift from a post-Romantic lull to the beginnings of a literary Gothic revival in the 1840s, with the translation of the Gothic from rural to urban settings, and to the bourgeois domestic scenarios of the Sensation genre (Spooner and McEvoy 33–34). While a Gothicized apprehension of inner London's maze of dismal courts and alleys emerges in G. W. M. Reynolds' *Mysteries of London* (1844–1856), London's new suburban outgrowths were being developed as distinctly Gothic locations firstly by Charles Dickens and particularly by Wilkie Collins. By the end of the century London suburbia was regularly resorted to by writers of the Gothic short story.

Outer Limits

Metropolitan tentacles had been reaching out to the 'the quiet rural villages that were London's nervous neighbours' since the middle of the eighteenth century (Hill 113). The Georgian exodus of successful merchants and tradesmen from the City's stinks to the rarefied reaches of Hackney and Islington was facilitated in varying degrees by the canals and the horse-drawn omnibus, and would be accelerated by the railways and the electric tram. Beyond Marylebone, a rural spot in De Quincey's youth, north London's inner suburbs arose from the fields with breathtaking speed. St John's Wood, Maida Vale, Camden Town, Hampstead, Kilburn and Holloway, swathes of 'Stucconia' proliferated.[5] Often these were shoddy and badly drained developments that would quickly deteriorate, 'interstitial suburban slums, caught and held, as Charles Booth observed, in successive railway loops' (Reeder 19) or marooned in urban wastelands of 'rough grazing and piggeries' (Porter 215).[6] The surrounding 'country' was the 'squalid edge-of town type represented by muddy lanes, pitch-black streets and blasted fields' (White 89), as Dickens described in *Our Mutual Friend* (1865), where 'tiles and bricks were burnt, bones were boiled, carpets were beat, rubbish was shot, dogs were fought, and dust was heaped by contractors' (*Our Mutual Friend* 42). There is 'nothing more wretched' observed the architect, James Elmes, 'than the first process of planting and making roads' (Elmes 97).

It is an entropic process that entails the city producing a wasteland of itself. Elmes described the stretch thrown up between Oxford Street and the former village of Marylebone in the 1750s as a 'dreary monotonous waste of dank pasturage'. By the 1860s a 'suburban Sahara' had engulfed the 'fields and trees' of rural Holloway, where the hellish light of the brick kiln-fires now made 'lurid smears on the fog' (*Our Mutual Friend* 42).[7]

The 'planting' of railway stations in the fields around the city encouraged developers to buy up smallholdings, but the small builder, as Jerry White so Gothickly puts it, was 'as evanescent as London fog and just as pernicious' (White 81). In the speculative free-for-all that prevailed, many developments remained half-lighted quagmires with 'stinking drains leeching into the subsoil for the whole of the period until building was finished' which might take twenty or even forty years (White 81). Dickens described this process as it was happening in Camden Town in *Dombey and Son* (1848). The 'Railroad was in progress . . . But as yet, the neighbourhood was shy to own the Railroad. One or two bold speculators had projected streets; and one had built a little, but had stopped among the mud and ashes to consider farther of it' (*Dombey and Son* 79). Here, 'at the very door of the Railway' are still 'frowzy fields, and cow-houses, and dunghills, and dustheaps (*Dombey and Son* 80). Dickens employs London's transient outposts as settings for those whose lives are in social flux and uses metaphors of pantomime sorcery to evoke the fearful rapidity of London's socio-geographical transformations. The disgraced John Carker and his loyal sister Harriet live in a 'poor, small house' in a peripheral district 'where the busy great north road of bygone days' thanks to the railway 'is silent and almost deserted, except by wayfarers who toil along on foot' (*Dombey and Son* 514). The place 'is neither of the town nor country. The former, like the giant in his travelling boots, has made a stride and passed it, and has set his brick-and-mortar heel a long way in advance; but the intermediate space between the giant's feet, as yet, is only blighted country' (*Dombey and Son* 515). The 'frowzy and uneven patch of ground which lay before their house . . . had once (long ago) been a pleasant meadow, and was now a very waste, with a disorderly crop of the beginnings of mean houses, rising out of the rubbish, as if they had been unskilfully sown there' (*Dombey and Son* 517). It is here, passing in front of her house in a howling rain storm, that Harriet Carker first encounters Edith Dombey's double, the 'fallen' Alice Marwood, making her vengeful return to the metropolis after penal exile in the colonies. Even as the city casts itself and its inhabitants outwards, it continues to exert a diabolic magnetism:[8]

> Day after day, such travellers crept past, but always, as [Harriet] thought, in one direction – always towards the town. Swallowed up in one phase or other of its immensity, towards which they seemed impelled by a desperate fascination . . . Food for the hospitals, the churchyards, the prisons, the river, fever, madness, vice and death, – they passed on to the monster, roaring in the distance, and were lost. (*Dombey and Son* 523)

It is in this same spot, on 'the lonely high-road' (*Woman in White* 14) that leads from Hampstead 'to St Johns Wood and the Regent's Park' (15), that Walter Hartright encounters fiction's most famous Gothic double, the ghostly Anne Catherick in Wilkie Collins' *The Woman in White* (1868), 'her hand pointing to the dark cloud over London' (14). Collins would develop Dickens' treatment of north London's suburbs as dismal wastelands into what Tamara Wagner describes as 'rapidly denigrated epitomes of a new sense of bourgeois respectability' (Wagner 200). In an earlier novel, *Basil: A Story of Modern Life* (1852) a visceral disgust for the new suburban class is the source of the title's self-proclaimed modernity. Collins aligns the petty bourgeois self-confinement of London's brick-box new crescents spiralling north of Regents Park with the terrors central to eighteenth-century Gothic: 'those ghastly heart-tragedies . . . which are acted and re-acted scene by scene, and year by year, in the secret theatre of home' (*Basil* 75).

A metropolitan abject

In tracing the 'phases' of London's 'immensity' as Dickens put it, historians date the genesis of London's suburbia as 'unlovely, sprawling artefact' to the post-Waterloo house-building boom of the years following the end of the Napoleonic wars, and as taking place in three clear stages of devolving class distinction that correlate to the expansion of London's public transport systems. The first phase, from around 1800 to the end of the 1830s was broadly bourgeois in tone, making its biggest push in the north and west, its principal mode of communication the omnibus. The next four decades were more mixed in their class appeal, pushing in every direction, alongside the railway system. By the end of the century the appeal of the suburb had spread definitively to the lower-middle and artisan classes. Of the literary responses that correspond to these phases what is consistent to each is the articulation of anxieties over social boundaries and the disruption of the city's topography as it was seen to relate to class structures.

From its earliest usage in the fourteenth century until the mid-eighteenth century, a 'suburbe' or 'settlement on the urban fringe' meant, in the definition of the *Oxford English Dictionary*, a 'place of inferior, debased and especially licentious habits of life' (Fishman 6).[9] Before 1800, the fields on which Bloomsbury would shortly be built, 'lay waste and useless', described as 'the resort of degraded wretches, whose amusements consisted chiefly in fighting pitched battles, and other disorderly sports, especially on the Sabbath day' (Dobie 176). City limits are traditionally 'off limits', symbolic of disruptive tendencies. Drawing on Mary Douglas's study of human pollution rituals and liminality, *Purity and Danger* (1966), Julia Kristeva's *Powers of Horror: An Essay on Abjection* (1982) explains the responses of queasiness and revulsion elicited by the dissolution of boundary markers in terms of psychoanalysis: 'Any phenomenon that "disturbs identity, system, order" and that "does not respect borders, positions, rules" . . . reminds one of traumatic infantile efforts to construct oneself as an ego, or discrete subject, from out of an undifferentiated pre-Oedipal state' (Kristeva 4). Self differentiation is 'to identify the I from the not-I and then repudiate it as other, what is loathsome must be displaced and projected elsewhere' (Kristeva 3). Liminality is a key aspect of the abject according to Douglas, abjection happens in the light of the parts of ourselves that we exclude, the abject meaning 'to cast off' or 'cast away' to edges, peripheries, hinterlands or occluded spaces. London's urban fringes had always been places of shanty towns, transient labouring colonies and noxious manufacture. For example at Battle Bridge, later Kings Cross, 'great rubbish heaps – "mountains of cinders and filth", "hillocks of horse dung" and piles of stinking "waste grains and hop-husks" had accumulated over generations' before Dickens made them pivotal to *Our Mutual Friend* (White 488).

Kristeva's account of the loathing felt towards 'filth, waste, or dung . . . sewage, and muck' as secretions that threaten bodily containment, and their relevance to Gothic horror are well rehearsed. We use rituals, specifically those of defilement, in order to define our boundaries, to keep them clearly marked. According to Douglas: 'Any structure of ideas is vulnerable at its margin' and societies imagine their boundaries or outlines, as containing power 'to reward conformity and repulse attack' (Douglas 50, 41). Margins are perilous places insofar as 'if they are pulled this way or that the shape of fundamental experience is altered (Douglas 50). Nineteenth-century suburban development would invite Gothic treatment as spaces where boundaries are undermined and meaning collapses. (Douglas 50). In *Metropolitan Improvements* (1827), his paean to state sponsored architecture and the delights of the new Regent's Park, James Elmes expresses this discomfort with regard to the activities of the 'jerry-builders' beyond its perimeters: 'It would be curious to ask those gentleman in what part of the neighbouring counties they intend London should end. The precincts of London have more the appearance of a newly-discovered colony than the suburbs of an ancient city' (Elmes 85). In Collins' *Basil*, an act of adultery and an attempted murder are committed in 'a very lonely place – a colony of half-finished streets, and half-inhabited houses, which had grown up in the neighbourhood of a great railway station'(*Basil* 158).[10] This 'othering' of London's sprawl is symptomatic of the vulnerability induced by the changes within bourgeois culture and the rise of the suburb as it altered the meaning of the city and what it meant to be a Londoner.

A Fatal Freshness

Except for some childhood years spent in the village of Hampstead (1826–1828), Wilkie Collins was to live until his death in various houses in the part of Marylebone so familiar to De Quincey, defined by Regents Park to the north,

Oxford Street to the south, the new suburban streets of Bayswater to the west, and Tottenham Court Road to the east. In fact he rarely resided more than a few streets away from Regents Park, a place which comes so often to stand for the kind of civilized metropolitan values 'under attack' from 'a more modern kind of urban savagery present in the new suburbs' (Law and Maunder 65). One contemporary reviewer of *Basil* succinctly summed up the threat: its eponymous upper-class hero 'sees a pretty girl in an omnibus; and he – goes to his doom *Bentley's Miscellany* (576–86). Readers today, as Lara Whelan notes, in her investigation of the Victorian 'suburban ideal', may be surprised at the idea of any kind of terror being present in the new suburb.[11] This is because of our familiarity with its chief vehicle of propaganda, the nineteenth-century domestic novel. The suburban ideal was founded in what would become the cornerstone of Victorian ideology and the principle of separate spheres, the radical disassociation of home and work environments: 'The growth of suburbia was to build into the physical environment that division between the feminine / natural / emotional world of family and the masculine / rational / urban world of work' (Fishman 62). Evangelical ideology was crucial to this separation. A valorization of domestic life founded in Evangelical notions of innate female virtue, together with a more traditional notion of female susceptibility to vice, required that wives and daughters be segregated from the profane metropolis. One of the seminal features of the Sensation novel was that the suburban ideal is called into question or explicitly undermined, now implicating gender as well as class.

Because of his seemingly bohemian lifestyle and an unusual sympathy demonstrated in his writing with the restrictions imposed upon women's lives, critics tend to read Collins as a thoroughgoing radical. Yet Collins had an ambivalent relationship to Victorian patriarchy. While he was vigorously opposed to Evangelical earnestness, high Tory politics, and the Grundyish 'respectability' of his times, he was always to shy away from any commitment to revolutionary, social or political change. He created strong female characters who challenge bourgeois social and sexual boundaries, but he never 'supported any movement to allow women full legal equality or access to the public sphere' (Law and Maunder 4). These unresolved tensions are played out in his fictional deployment of London's new suburbs, beginning with *Basil*, the prototype of the Sensation novel. In each of Collins' novels the relationship between character and environment entails a negotiation of the challenges posed by metropolitan modernity, particularly to codes of social status. The novels depict London as a city of immediate social contrast where, 'the mansion and the hovel' are 'neighbours in situation', but what is truly sinister for Collins is not what is in the adjacent slum but in the remote suburb, the sites and eerie silences of the half-built 'colonies' and alien wastelands of north London's developing edges (*I Say No* 60). The architecture of the Gothic, the decaying ancestral mansions hemmed in by impenetrable forests find a parallel in 'the abortive, half-formed villa-dom that was ringing London in his lifetime. In novel after novel, the scaffolding of the half-built replaces the ruined castle or the tumbledown tenement to become the haunt of modern evil' (Peters 119).

Basil is principally concerned with what it is to be a gentleman. Collins' struggle to depict 'modern life' and the pursuit of a 'poetry of everyday truth' (Preface) evinces a conservative anxiety that the demarcations of social class were proving as permeable as those of London's ever devolving boundaries. Anti-suburban snobbery sprang from the aristocratic fear of new money and 'the mushroom aristocracy of trade' as Richard Phillips in *A Morning's Walk from London to Kew* (1817) describes the class that fuelled the first phase of suburbia (Phillips 101). They are a 'dull and monotonous' people, 'whose rank, in its first generation, affords no palpable ground of introduction . . . whose importance, [is] founded on the chances of yesterday, . . . whose consequence grows neither out of manners, intellectual endowments, superior taste, nor polished connections' (Phillips 100). It is 'not to be wondered at' he continues, that most of their 'showy mansions' are 'points of repulsion rather than of attraction' (Phillips 101). Nevertheless the author allows that many of these families are 'hospitable, charitable, sociable and anxious to be agreeable' and were they 'properly directed' in 'such establishments as book-clubs', might prove worthy of some 'more liberal intercourse' (Phillips 101). Dickens would read something more sinister in the type he mocks as the Veneerings, 'bran-new people in a bran-new house in a bran-new quarter of London' (*Our Mutual Friend* 17). The political establishment as member for Pocket Breaches of the vote-buying Mr Veneering, 'a too, too smiling man, with a *fatal* freshness on him' (*Our Mutual Friend* 19), suggests the advancement of a class that is beyond being 'directed'. Mr Veneering has become 'all of a sudden . . . a representative man' (*Our Mutual Friend* 243). This social threat is made manifest in *Basil,* in which the denizens of Hollyoake Square are 'fiend-souls' in 'fiend-shapes' (*Basil* 174).

In *Basil*, evils flourish in these susceptible spaces where social divisions are fluctuating and unsettled. Having glimpsed the beautiful linen-draper's daughter, Margaret Sherwin, on an impulsively boarded omnibus, Basil is compelled to stay on until the last stop. This leads ultimately to a scenario of domesticity, the very newness of which indicates an inherent corruption. Basil follows Margaret and her maid to:

> a suburb of new houses, intermingled with wretched patches of waste land, half built over. Unfinished streets, unfinished crescents, unfinished squares, unfinished shops, unfinished gardens, surrounded us. At last they stopped at a new square, and rang the bell at one of the newest of the new houses. (*Basil* 32)

Basil, younger scion of an ancient family is inveigled by the Sherwins into a marriage that is to remain secret and unconsummated pending his inheritance. The relationship ends in betrayal, insanity and death. A moral and cultural malaise, assumed to be attendant on the rapid material prosperity that raised tradesmen to the ranks of the middle class, is signified by a shiny newness that can never appropriate the patina of the *bourgeoise propre*.

> Everything was oppressively new. The brilliantly-varnished door cracked with a report like a pistol when it was opened; the paper on the walls, with its gaudy pattern of birds, trellis-work, and flowers, in gold, red, and green on a white ground, looked hardly dry yet; the showy window-curtains of white and sky-blue, and the still showier carpet of red and yellow, seemed as if they had come out of the shop yesterday; the round rosewood table was in a painfully high state of polish; the morocco-bound picture books that lay on it, looked as if they had never been moved or opened since they had been bought; not one leaf even of the music on the piano was dogs-eared or worn. Never was a richly furnished room more thoroughly comfortless than this – the eye ached at looking round it. (*Basil* 61)

The class revulsion that Basil demonstrates here was famously depicted in William Holman Hunt's, *The Awakening Conscience* (1851–1853). John Ruskin was moved to write a letter to *The Times* in order to explain to a bemused (because suburban?) public the significance of the painting's 'ghastly and unendurable distinctness':

> There is not a single object in all that room, common, modern, vulgar (in the vulgar sense, as it may be), but it becomes tragical, if rightly read. That furniture, so carefully painted, even to the last vein of the rosewood – is there nothing to be learned from that terrible lustre of it, from its fatal newness; nothing there that has the old thoughts of home upon it, or that is ever to become a part of home? Those embossed books, vain and useless – they are also new-marked with no happy wearing of beloved leaves.[12]

'To let, a genteel house, up this road.'

For the sake of verisimilitude in rendering the moral turpitude of suburban life Hunt rented Woodbine Villa, a house in St John's Wood. The former strolling ground of Blackmantle and Crony was favoured for the installing of mistresses because of the privacy of its low-density 'villas' compared to London's more typical terraced housing. Count Fosco 'takes a furnished house in St John's Wood' in which he imprisons Anne Catherick in *The Woman in White*, and St John's Wood is the location of North Villa, 1, Hollyoake Square where the Sherwins live. What strikes the modern reader is that despite its proximity to 'the Regent's Park, the northern portion of which' to Basil's relief 'was close at hand' (*Basil* 32) it is described as a desolate place, edged by 'sooty London fields' (*Basil* 49). In 1853, estate agent Albert Cox's *Landlord and Tenant's Guide* states the current impossibility of mapping St John's Wood: 'that district north-west of London which lies between the Regent's Park and Maida Hill, and is so much enlarging in the northern direction, that the definition of its locality will shortly be more accurate when stated as lying between Haverstock Hill and Kilburn'.[13]

The ruthless rapidity of the city's self-immolation at the hands of profiteers is described in polemic detail in Collins' next novel *Hide and Seek* (1854). Baregrove Square

> in the year 1837 was the farthest square from the city, and the nearest to the country, of any then existing in the north-western suburb of London . . . But, by . . . the year 1851 . . . other streets, crescents, rows, and villa-residences had forced themselves pitilessly between the old suburb and the country, and had suspended for ever the once neighbourly relations between the pavement of Baregrove Square and the pathways of the pleasant fields. (*Hide and Seek* 26)

Not even the metaphor of fallen empire, that ready conveyor of doom to Victorians, can express the irreversible loss wrought by London's expansion:

> Alexander's armies were great makers of conquests; and Napoleon's armies were great makers of conquests; but the modern Guerilla regiments of the hod, the trowel, and the brick-kiln, are the greatest conquerors of all; for they hold the longest the soil that they have once possessed. How mighty the devastation which follows in the wake of these tremendous aggressors, as they march through the kingdom of nature, triumphantly bricklaying beauty wherever they go! What dismantled castle, with the enemy's flag flying over its crumbling walls, ever looked so utterly forlorn as a poor field-fortress of nature, imprisoned on all sides by the walled camp of the enemy, and degraded by a hostile banner of pole and board, with the conqueror's device inscribed on it – "THIS GROUND TO BE LETT ON BUILDING LEASES"? (*Hide and Seek* 26).

While Collins mourns the loss of green fields and trees to the 'greenly-festering stucco of a finished Paradise Row, or the naked scaffolding poles of a half-completed Prospect Place' (*Hide and Seek* 27) what is registered most intensely is the loss of self-containment of a city structured by the divisions of a pre-industrial class system in which a leisured, literate elite reside in the city centre with the lower class and outcaste groups scattered centrifugally towards the city's perimeters. Collins notes how the dwellings and modes of life of London's new suburban middle class mimic the 'three distinct subdivisions' of the wider English class system. The pomposity of those with large incomes and the meanness of those with meagre incomes are heinous but less offensive than 'those who occupy the neutral ground of the moderate incomes; turning it into the dullest, the dreariest, the most oppressively conventional division of the whole suburb' (*Hide and Seek* 30). Collins' alignment of the suburb with the stultifying convention and cultural mediocrity of this new class indicts them and their genteel aspirations as the source of horror. Ruskin, for whom its architecture 'constitutes the identity of a nation' (Ruskin 2004 25) had spelled this out in *The Lamp of Memory* (1849). It is 'not merely with sorrow for a desecrated landscape' that he bemoans 'those pitiful concretations of lime and clay which spring up in mildewed forwardness out of the kneaded fields about our capital'– but for the fact that those 'dwellings are the signs of a great and spreading spirit of popular discontent; that they mark the time when every man's aim is to be in some more elevated sphere than his natural one' (Ruskin 2004 19).

As institutional power shifted irreversibly from a landed class to the industrial capital, and as the suburban spread moved into its second and third phases, Collins' treatment of the suburbs began to detail, amongst the rubble of modernity, the vestigial traces of this social order. In *Armadale* (1866) a new suburb 'situated below the high ground of Hampstead' is the location of the Sanitarium, a commercially run lunatic asylum with its own state of the art fumigation-cum-lethal gas chamber. Fairweather Vale is a 'wilderness of open ground with half-finished villas dotted about, and a hideous litter of boards, wheelbarrows and building materials of all sorts scattered in every direction' (*Armadale* 711). The Sanitarium, a dismal house, 'plastered with drab-coloured stucco' is approached 'by a new road running between trees, which might once have been the park-avenue of a country house'. In *The Law and the Lady* (1875) Miserrimus Dexter assumes a disreputable eighteenth-century dandy aesthetic in his stand against 'the brutish contempt for beauty in the age in which I live' (*Law and the Lady* 216). Byronically handsome but deprived of his lower limbs, Dexter is a relic of a bygone age and of a man. One of Dexter's 'madnesses' we learn is his house (*Law and the Lady* 189). It lies on the outskirts of the 'great northern suburb of London' where there are 'dreary patches of waste ground which seemed to be neither town nor country' and half-completed foundations of new houses in their first stage of existence' (*Law and the Lady* 189). Collins' suburban Gothic landscape is familiar, yet this time, amongst the 'gaunt scaffolding poles' that 'rose like the branchless trees of the brick desert' and 'the oyster shells and broken crockery, that strewed the ground' is a 'long low and ancient house' (*Law and the Lady* 189). We are told that

> It was originally the manor-house of the district. Dexter purchased it many years since in one of his freaks of fancy. He has no old family associations with the place; the walls are all but tumbling about his ears; the money offered would really be of use to him. But no! He refused the proposal of the enterprizing speculators by letter in these words: 'My house is a standing monument of the picturesque and beautiful, amid the mean, dishonest, and grovelling constructions of a mean, dishonest, and grovelling age. I keep my house, gentlemen, as a useful lesson to you. Look at it while you are building around me, and blush, if you can, for your work.' Was there ever such an absurd letter written yet? (*Law and the Lady* 189–90)'

While he would have applauded Dexter's sentiments, John Ruskin deplored the deformed and 'truncated' characters of Collins' fiction as 'the very sign manual of the plague' of modernity (Ruskin 1899 22). In *Fiction Fair and Foul* (1880–1881), Ruskin posits a direct correlation between the 'peculiar forces of devastation' wrought by the city's suburban excrescence and 'the material of modern fiction' which he deems to be 'of languidly monstrous character developed in an atmosphere of low vitality' (Ruskin 1899 224). As the scholastic or artistic issue of 'infinite nastiness', modern fiction was intrinsically debased: 'Our real wealth and progress in creative power' he writes 'are indicated only by the Babylonian wildernesses of brickfield, white with slime, by a continual festering cancer of waste ground among skeletons of buildings, rotten before they are inhabited' (Ruskin 1905 210). Contemporary novels are peopled by characters he describes as 'the sweepings out of a Pentonville omnibus' and are written to feed 'the demands of the rows of similar brick houses, which branch in devouring cancer', the occupants of which, being 'thoroughly trained Londoners', are 'numb to all fictional entertainment' but that which varies 'to his fancy the modes' and defines 'for his dullness the horrors, of Death' (Ruskin 1899 145–46). Despite having described this literary correspondence in some detail and with particular reference to Dickens' *Bleak House,* such are 'the peculiar forces of devastation induced by modern city life' Ruskin declares, that 'no existing terms of language' are enough for him to be able to adequately describe its 'forms of filth and modes of ruin' (Ruskin 1899 4). He goes on though, to use the same language of Gothic abjection, of defilement and repulsion that Dickens, in his lists of detritus and waste, detailed the spaces of suburban growth in North London, when he writes about the transformation by 'the wild crossings and concurrencies of three railroads' of his childhood haunts in south London's formerly rural Herne Hill:

> the gashed ground: the lane itself, now entirely grassless, is a deep-rutted, heavy-hillocked cart-road, diverging gatelessly into various brickfields or pieces of waste; and bordered on each side by heaps of – Hades only knows what! – mixed dust of every unclean thing that can crumble in drought, and mildew of every unclean thing that can rot or rust in damp: ashes and rags, beer-bottles and old shoes, battered pans, smashed crockery, shreds of nameless clothes, door-sweepings, floor-sweepings, kitchen garbage, back-garden sewage, old iron, rotten timber jagged with out-torn nails, cigar-ends, pipe-bowls, cinders, bones, and ordure, indescribable; and, variously kneaded into, sticking to, or fluttering foully here and there over all these, remnants, broadcast, of every manner of newspaper, advertisement or big-lettered bill, festering and flaunting out their last publicity in the pits of stinking dust and mortal slime. (Ruskin 1899 5)

The hellish foulness, the slime and dust of Herne Hill indicates for Ruskin what is fallen: 'Where there is dirt there is system. Dirt is the by-product of a systematic ordering and classification of matter, in so far as ordering involves rejecting inappropriate elements' (Douglas 35–36). The Gothic articulates the failure of symbolic order thus our attention to the Gothicizing of London's suburbs serves to emphasize or underscore the ways in which the built environment, as Warwick points out, functions so frequently as a metaphor for dynastic, physical or psychic crisis. Ruskin, for whom the forces of industrial capitalism and technological progress were responsible for the moral and social collapse of England, replicates in his rhetoric the fictional mode he abhors.

At the same time as Ruskin was predicting 'infinite nastiness, prevailing as a fixed condition of the universe, over the face of nature', the Gothic settings employed by Wilkie Collins crept inexorably outwards. In *Heart and Science: A Story of the Present Time* (1883), the vivisectionist, Dr Benjulia has his laboratory near the remote village of Hendon: 'Between Hendon and Willesden, there are pastoral solitudes within an hour's drive of Oxford Street – wooded lanes and wild flowers, farms and cornfields, still unprofaned by the devastating brickwork of the builder of modern times' (*Heart and Science* 129). Here 'in a desolate field' – in some lost suburban neighbourhood that nobody can discover. Benjulia has built a 'hideous . . . yellow brick house' wherein he conducts his horrific experiments. London's momentum is such that as outer become inner suburbs, it encompasses undiscoverable neighbourhoods. Making use of cheaper transport, artisans and clerks filled the terraces of the newest redbrick and stucco outposts that saw London's outlying villages such as Walthamstow 'cocknified and choked up by the jerry-builder' as William Morris wrote of his birthplace (Tames 6).

Writers of the 1880s and 1890s used the suburbs to explore the social upheavals of the *fin-de-siècle*. New Woman writer, George Egerton, sets 'Wedlock' (1893) a story of infanticide, amongst 'new jerry-built houses in genteel suburbs' where, along with the builders' refuse, relics of fine old houses – 'a granite urn, portions of a deftly carven shield, a mailed hand and a knight's casque' lie smashed and trampled in the remains of 'a grand old garden' ('Wedlock' 115). Such remains are often portals to prelapsarian fantasy for writers such as Arthur Machen, E. M. Forster and G. K. Chesterton who wrote stories of ghosts, revenants, occult histories and pagan enchantments, evoked by the very dullness, drabness and uniformity of the suburban.

In 1921 the London writer, Thomas Burke, incredulous at having to admit himself lost in his native city discovers he is in Sherrick Green, just 'ten minutes to Willesden' (*Outer Circle* 11). In *The Outer Circle* he celebrates these scorned dormitories: 'We know the histories of your worm eaten Gothic piles but the potentialities of the history of that red brick villa in that clay-soil suburb are too vast' (*Outer Circle* 14). A new egalitarian spirit in literary depictions of London's suburbia had emerged, now that the clerks were getting to write their own stories.[14] Burke follows Arnold Bennett whose *A Man From the North* (1898) hailed this development: 'people have got into a way of sneering at the suburbs' (*Man From the North* 46) comments Mr Aked: the 'eighty or so houses in each suburban street' are indeed eighty theatres as Collins would have it but of 'splendid' rather than 'ghastly heart-tragedies' and not just of hate, greed and tyranny, but of love, endeavour and especially character (*Man From the North* 44). Burke later pinched the plot of a ghost story by Edith Nesbit, 'The Mystery of the Semi-Detached' (1893), rewriting it as 'Desirable Villa' (1931) in which a strangling witnessed in a new villa turns out to be a prophetic haunting, a crime that actually takes place some months later. We can tell that Burke had read his Dickens, Collins, and Ruskin too. The protagonist finds himself in 'the northern rim of that cup which holds London . . . On what speck of the map he was he didn't know, but he was in a land that some dark corner of his soul told him was very much like hell. It was neither town nor country nor suburb but something that blasphemed all three . . . The grass of the fields was sore with eruptions of brick and pole' ('Desirable Villa' 171). But here Burke interrupts the narrative and debunks this conjunction of new suburb and horror, stating: 'The sight of this business of making houses affects most of us as an hour in a slaughter house would affect a lover of pork' ('Desirable Villa' 171). He explains that 'At all points of the outer circle you may come upon these spots of horror. They are not of the stuff or the spirit of horror – merely a necessary part of "developing" a residential estate' ('Desirable Villa' 171). It is a revealing interruption. By the interwar period, the Victorian premise of his suburban ghost story had become both a commonplace and an anachronism.

Notes

[1] De Quincey, Westbrook reminds us, was able to recall from his fifth year the '"shuddering horror" of "the truth that [he] was in a world of evil and strife" (Westbrook 159). See also, Lindop, Grevel (ed.) (2000), *The Works of Thomas De Quincey*, volumes 19: 7 and 15: 138.

[2] For an excellent discussion of the operations of such 'memory released from time' in De Quincey's vision, see Shilstone, Frederick W. (1983), 'Autobiography as "Involute": De Quincey on the Therapies of Memory', *South Atlantic Review*, 48(1), 20–34, 22.

[3] De Quincey writes in his *Autobiography from 1785–1803* of London's tremendous force dragging people in as if to the centre of some imprisoning web, see Masson, David (ed.) (1890), *The Collected Writings of Thomas De Quincey*, 1, 178.

[4] Westmacott is citing James Elmes' (1827) *Metropolitan Improvements*, London: Jones and Co., 85.

[5] Stucconia is a coinage in Dickens' *Our Mutual Friend*, home to the nouveau riche Veneerings. Stucco and veneer are both artificial surfaces used to give the illusion of luxury to buildings and furniture of cheap construction.

[6] Booth analyses the relationship between spatial and social segregation, describing how the poor were located in pockets of streets lying between railway and canal districts and cut off from the mainstream of urban life. See Booth, Charles (1892–1897), *Life and Labour of the People in London*, (14 volumes), London: Macmillan.

[7] The cityscapes of *Our Mutual Friend* which T. S. Eliot was reading when he wrote the poem, foreshadow *The Waste Land* (1922) and its themes of urban degeneration and decay.

[8] H. G. Wells would refer to this as 'the whirlpool' effect, after the theme of social mobility in Gissing's novel *The Whirlpool* (1897), see Wells (1924), 'The Probable Diffusion of Great Cities' (1900) in *Anticipations and Other Papers*, volume. 4 of *The Works of H. G. Wells*, New York: Scribner's, 39.

[9] Fishman notes that in Shakespeare's London, because brothels were moved to the outskirts, a whore was called 'a suburb sinner' and to call a man a 'surburbanite' was defamatory.

[10] In the novel's first version the place to which Basil follows his wife and her seducer is a brothel, or house of assignation. In the published version it is 'an hotel – a neglected, deserted, dreary-looking building', see Peters, Catherine (1991), *The King of Inventors: A Life of Wilkie Collins*, Princeton: Princeton University Press, 115.

[11] Whelan, L. (2003), 'Unburying Bits of Rubbish: Deconstruction of the Victorian Suburban Ideal', *Literary London: Interdisciplinary Studies in the Representation of London*, 1 (2) http://www.literarylondon.org/london-journal/september2003/whelan.html, accessed 25 January 2010.

[12] Letter to the Editor, *The London Times*, 25 May 1854.

[13] http://www.wilkie-collins.info/home_sjwood.htm.

[14] See Rose, Jonathan (1994), 'Intellectuals Among the Masses: Or, What Was Leonard Bast Really Like?' *Biblion*, 2, 3–18.

Works Cited

Bennett, A. (1994), *A Man From the North* (1898), Gloucestershire: Alan Sutton Publishing

Booth, C. (1892–1897), *Life and Labour of the People in London,* (14 volumes), London: Macmillan

Burke, T. (1921), *The Outer Circle: Rambles in Remote London*, London: George Allen and Unwin

Burke, T. (1928), *The Ecstasies of Thomas De Quincey*, London: George Harrap

Burke, T. (1931), *The Pleasantries of Old Quong*, London: Constable

Cobbett, W. (1930), *Rural Rides Volume 1*, (3 volumes), G. D. H. and Margaret Cole (eds), London: Peter Davies

Collins, W. (1884), *"I Say No" Or The Love-Letter Answered*, New York: Harper Bros

Collins, W. (1990), *Basil: A Story of Modern Life* (1852), Oxford: Oxford University Press

Collins, W. (1994), *The Woman in White* (1868), London: Penguin Books

Collins, W. (1998), *The Law and the Lady* (1875), London: Penguin Books

Collins, W. (1999), *Hide and Seek* (1854), Oxford: Oxford University Press

Collins, W. (2008), *Armadale* (1866), Oxford: Oxford University Press

De Quincey, T. (1821), *The London Magazine Volume IV*, London: Taylor and Hessey

De Quincey, T. (2000), *Confessions of an English Opium-Eater* (1821–1856), in Grevel Lindop (ed.) *The Works of Thomas De Quincey Volume 2*, (21 volumes), London: Pickering and Chatto

Dickens, C. (1997), *Our Mutual Friend* (1865), London: Penguin Books

Dickens, C. (2002), *Dombey and Son* (1848), London: Penguin Books

Dobie, R. (1829), *The History of the United Parishes of St. Giles in the Fields and St. George Bloomsbury*, London: F. Marshall

Douglas, M. (1966), *Purity and Danger: An Analysis of the Concepts of Pollution and Taboo*, London: Routledge and Kegan Paul

Egerton, G. (2006), *Keynotes and Discords* (ed.) Sally Ledger, London: Continuum

Elmes, J. (1827), *Metropolitan Improvements*, London: Jones and Co

Fishman, R. (1987), *Bourgeois Utopias: The Rise and Fall of Suburbia*, New York: Basic Books

Hill, D. (1970), *Georgian London*, London: Macdonald

Kristeva, J. (1982), *Powers of Horror: An Essay on Abjection*, New York: Columbia University Press

Larwood, J. (1867), *The History of Signboards from Earliest Times to the Present* Day, London: John Camden Hotton

Law, G., and Andrew Maunder (2008), *Wilkie Collins: A Literary Life*, London: Palgrave Macmillan

Luckhurst, R. (2002), 'The Contemporary London Gothic and the Limits of the Spectral Turn', *Textual Practice*, 16(3), 527–46

Masson, D. (ed.) (1890), *The Collected Writings of Thomas De Quincey Volume 1*, (14 volumes), London: Adam and Charles Black

Peters, C. (1991), *The King of Inventors: A Life of Wilkie Collins*, Princeton: Princeton University Press

Reeder, D. A. (1980), *Suburbanity and the Victorian City*, Leicester: Leicester University Press

Ruskin J. (1899), *On The Old Road Volume 3*, London: George Allen

Ruskin, J. (1905), *Works*, volume 19, London: Cook Dumas Wedderburn

Ruskin, J. (2004), *John Ruskin Selected Writings*, (ed.) Dinah Birch, Oxford: Oxford University Press

Sheppard, F. (1971), *London 1808–1870: The Infernal Wen*, London: Secker and Warburg

Shilstone, F. W. (1983), 'Autobiography as "Involute": De Quincey on the Therapies of Memory', *South Atlantic Review*, 48(1), 20–34

Tames, R. (2003), *William Morris: An Illustrated Life of William Morris, 1834–1896*, Princes Risborough: Shire

Thompson, F. M. L. (ed.) (1982), *The Rise Of Suburbia*, Leicester: Leicester University Press

Unsigned Review 'Esmond and Basil', *Bentley's Miscellany*, (Dec 1852), 32, 576–86

Wagner, T. S. (2006), 'Sensationalising Victorian Suburbia: Wilkie Collins's *Basil*', in Kimberley Harrison and Richard Fantina (eds), *Victorian Sensations: Essays on a Scandalous Genre*, Columbus: The Ohio State University Press, 200–10

Warwick, A. (2007), 'Victorian Gothic', in Catherine Spooner and Emma McEvoy (eds), *The Routledge Companion to Gothic*, London and New York: Routledge

Westbrook, D. (2003), 'Deciphering Oracle: De Quincey's Textual Epistemology', *The Wordsworth Circle*, 34, 158–71

Westmacott, C. M. (1826), *The English Spy*, London: Sherwood Gilbert and Piper

Whelan, L. (2003), 'Unburying Bits of Rubbish: Deconstruction of the Victorian Suburban Ideal', *Literary London: Interdisciplinary Studies in the Representation of*

London, 1(2), http://www.literarylondon.org/london journal/september2003/ whelan.html, accessed 25 January 2010

White, J. (2007), *London in the Nineteenth Century: 'A Human Awful Wonder of God'*, London: Jonathan Cape

Chapter 4

'A City of Nightmares': Suburban Anxiety in Arthur Machen's London Gothic

Amanda Mordavsky Caleb

You may think you know life, and London, and what goes on day and night in this dreadful city; for all I can say you may have heard the talk of the vilest, but I tell you can have no conception of what I know, no, not in your most fantastic, hideous dreams can you have imaged forth the faintest shadow of what I have heard – and seen.

The Great God Pan 34

W. T. Stead (1885) referred to London as a 'Modern Babylon'; James Thomson (1909) lamented that it was 'the city of dreadful night'; Oscar Wilde (1891) portrayed it as the 'grey monstrous London of ours'; and for Arthur Machen (1895) it was 'a city of nightmares'. These depictions of London evoke the Gothic encounter with the late nineteenth-century metropolis that by now encompassed its environs. While London's suburbs did not present the anxieties defined by the crime and squalor of the inner slum, their relentless spread evoked less tangible fears. In *Black's Guide to London and its Environs*, A.R. Hope Moncrieff emphasizes the lack of spatial definition that was the suburb's most worrying aspect: 'A patient philosopher might be invited to exercise his brains on the question: Where do the suburbs of London begin then remains the still harder one: Where do they end?'(Moncrieff 138). Ged Pope has echoed this notion of indeterminacy by suggesting the suburbs were 'too close and yet agonizingly distant, contiguous and alien, intertwined with the urban core and sharing some of its features, but also displaced, even off the map' (Pope). Yet the maps themselves were proving unreliable records of London's topography. After 1888, the post office's renaming and renumbering of many streets, provoked outcry: 'it is easier today to discover the house of a man who died two hundred years ago, before the streets were numbered at all, than to identify the houses of men who have died within a few years' (Hutton vii).

Arthur Machen's *The Hill of Dreams* (1907) reflects these spatial and temporal anxieties associated with the London suburbs. In his engagement with space, time, and cognitive dissociation, Machen's novel juxtaposes past with present, pagan with prosaic and urban with suburban in an exploration of the protagonist's psychic breakdown. In *Things Near and Far* (1923), his first attempt at an autobiography, Machen recalled how his explorations led him to realize the vastness of London, and 'to appreciate the fact that if you set out, without a map, from your house at 36 Great Russell Street and walk for an hour eastward or northward you are in fact in an unknown region, a new world' (*Near and Far* 79). Here Machen experiences the contrast between middle-class streets and those of the working poor, a divide that is socio-temporal as well as spatial. He Gothicizes this distance by comparing the neighbourhood in which he finds himself (it is Islington) to 'the ultimate parts of Libya, and the lands of the Mountains of the Moon' (*Near and Far* 79). Oriental-ized and other-worldly, Islington's chief consolations are in its nevertheless 'material historicity of place' (see Wolfreys' chapter in this volume). In describing the tottering houses, Machen notes on the front of one house a sign for a Buhl Maker, a retention of a discernable past which he finds exciting, contrast-ing the decay of 'this forsaken, climbing street [with] that right eighteenth-century art of brass and tortoiseshell, fashioning curious cabinets and escritoires!' (*Near and Far* 80). Machen contrasts his own perception with that of a friend who finds venturing away from the West End disconcerting. Machen explains that his friend

> grew silent as the streets grew greyer and the squares dimmer and the remote-ness of the whole region from any conceivable London that he knew filtered through his soul. His London was Piccadilly, the Haymarket, St. James's, and the many polite neighbourhoods where there are flats and calls are paid and tea is taken and literary and theatrical and artistic circles meet and gather. But this London that was a grey wilderness, these streets that went to the beyond and beyond, these squares which nobody that my friend could ever have known could ever inhabit: it was all too much for him. (*Near and Far* 87–88)

Machen's choice of London as the setting for many of his stories and novels is, in part, also an attempt at autobiography, in understanding his own journey from rural Wales to inner London and eventually to the suburbs. These stories that move from country to city to suburb are also reflective of the history of the suburb and of the Gothic. As Roger Luckhurst has argued; Machen's move-ment from the Welsh countryside to London in *The Great God Pan* demonstrates 'the geographical drift of the Gothic from its first inception' (Luckhurst xxix). This is particularly evident in *The Hill of Dreams*, in which the mysticism and supernatural elements of the Welsh countryside travel with Lucian Taylor to haunt him in the London suburbs.

Machen felt uneasy about the city, claiming '"alone in London" has become a phrase, it is a title associated, I think, with some flaring melodrama; but the reality is a deadly thing' (*Near and Far* 19). The deadliness of being isolated in a metropolis, or its surrounding suburbs, is at the heart of *The Hill of Dreams*. In *Things Near and Far*, Machen describes the genesis of the novel, claiming the novel to be 'a "Robinson Crusoe" of the mind': 'It was to represent', Machen explains, 'loneliness not of body on a desert island, but loneliness of soul and mind and spirit in the midst of myriads and myriads of men' (*Near and Far* 163). This urban loneliness is represented in *The Hill of Dreams* by the character of Lucian Taylor, a castaway in his own mind, trying to navigate the real world in relation to his imaginative understanding of it. This leads to a disjointed view of London and its suburbs, one that consumes him, leading to his eventual death.

Lucian's imagining of his environment, his mental construction of the suburb in which he resides, engages with the artificiality and perversity of Decadence. Lucian comes to London 'to escape, to set himself free in the wilderness of London, and to be secure amidst the murmur of modern streets' (*Hill of Dreams* 46). His description of what he imagines London to be anticipates the anonymity that London would provide him. When he first arrives this is exactly what he finds, 'the city of the unending murmuring streets' where he is 'a part of the stirring shadow, of the amber-lighted gloom' (*Hill of Dreams* 168). Lucian immediately aligns himself with the city, claiming an affinity to its gloom, embracing the seedier side of London's western suburb, between Shepherd's Bush and Acton Vale. The location reflects an expanded London, one that has accommodated an overflow from the inner suburbs, and was seen as lacking in any value, whether economic or aesthetic. T. W. H. Crosland writes of the

> God-forsaken suburbs. . . . devoid of graciousness to a degree which appals. Deserts of sand, or alkali, or scrub were paradise by comparison. For it is a country . . . where the principal objects of cultivation are the stunted cabbage and the bedraggled geranium; where everybody's portion is soot and grime and slush; where the only streams are sewers, and the gardens are all black. (Crossland 15–16)

This, though, is the ideal backdrop for Lucian's psychological journey, undertaken: 'in the waste places of London. . . . On every side monotonous grey streets, each house the replica of its neighbour, to the east an unexplored wilderness, north and west and south the brickfields and market-gardens, everywhere the ruins of the country' (*Hill of Dreams* 179). The narrator explains that

> as he went farther afield a sense of immensity slowly grew upon him: it was as if, from the little island of his room, that one friendly place, he pushed out into the grey unknown, into a city that for him was uninhabited as the desert. (*Hill of Dreams* 203)

Lucian describes an indeterminable space that is defined only by neither being part of a town or the country. Instead it is the decay of the country, the representation of modernity's impact on nature, and as such the ideal location for a Decadent novel. Lucian embraces the suburbs, the space between the extremes of city and country, finding himself 'curiously strengthened by the change from the hills to the streets. There could be no doubt', he muses, 'that living a lonely life, interested only in himself and his own thoughts, he had become in a measure inhuman' (*Hill of Dreams* 118). The isolation Lucian feels is a reflection of Machen's own experiences when he first arrived in London, a period which served as inspiration for much of the novel. He explains:

> I knew what it was to live on a little in a little room, what it meant to pass day after day, week after week, month after month through the *inextricabilis error* of the London streets, to tread a grey labyrinth whose paths had no issue, no escape, no end. (*Hill of Dreams* 163–64)

The feeling becomes so overwhelming for Lucian that he claims soon to have 'lost the sense of humanity [and] was wretched because he was an alien and a stranger amongst citizens' (*Hill of Dreams* 225). Yet the crowds of the suburbs are inexplicably tied into Lucian's attempts at writing his novel, which both thrives and suffers in relation to suburban humanity. When these crowds disappear during the particularly harsh winter, Lucian finds himself 'reduced to impotence', unable to write or develop his thoughts (*Hill of Dreams* 206). In order to avoid the madness of writer's block – and the beginnings of his own mental breakdown – Lucian 'knew his only hope was to walk till he was physically exhausted, so that he might come home almost fainting with fatigue, but ready to fall asleep the moment he got into bed' (*Hill of Dreams* 212). He initially tries to avoid crowds, opting instead 'for remote and desolate places', yet he longs 'for some sound and murmur of life' (*Hill of Dreams* 209). Lucian's engagement with the suburbs is one that reflects the paradoxical view of the suburb that positions it as remote and yet crowded, desolate and full of life.

His alienation growing, Lucian reflects that in the surrounding streets 'stood a symbol of his life, chill and dreary and grey and vexed with a horrible wind . . . a maze of unprofitable dreariness and desolation' (*Hill of Dreams* 192). His affiliation with the suburb lies also in its isolation outside of the main traffic of the city, which is reflective of his own Decadent removal from bourgeois society. He imagines himself at night as 'being on a tower, remote and apart and high above all the troubles of the earth . . . it was as if he alone stirred and looked out amidst a host sleeping at his feet' (*Hill of Dreams* 198–99). Lucian's view of himself above the multitudes of sleeping suburbanites demonstrates his artistic estrangement from the common man and from the capitalist workplace. He imagines himself as a daily commuter from the suburbs to London, 'going dutifully every morning to the City on the bus, and returning in the evening for high tea', an image which strengthens his resolve regarding his own work and life outside the city centre (*Hill of Dreams* 198). His symbolic relation to the suburbs and their streets is extended through his description of the abject modernity of the suburbs. He describes:

> the row of common shops, full of common things, the blatant public-houses, the Independent chapel, a horrible stucco parody of a Greek temple with a façade of hideous columns that was a nightmare, villas like smug Pharisees, shops again, a church in cheap Gothic. (*Hill of Dreams* 192)

As Alex Warwick has noted, Lucian sees the suburb as 'a jumbled collection of faint imitations of the great work of the past, interspersed with the rubbish commodity culture' (Warwick 135). If he sees the suburbs as symbolic of himself and his life, then he too represents a 'jumbled collection' of past and present, high and low art. This internal conflict addresses the notions of Decadent identity and the emergence of the modern self: while Lucian outwardly rejects the artificiality of the suburbs, inwardly he identifies with them.

Machen extends this paradoxical representation of the suburbs through a vision of the suburbs as both historical and contemporary, at once mundane and exotic. Lucian's initial draw to London is for literary inspiration and to escape his debauched hallucinations of an ancient Roman fort in Wales. Yet before long Lucian realizes that although he had 'changed the fauns' singing for the murmur of the streets, the black pools for the shadows and amber light of London . . . the truth was that he had merely exchanged one drug for another' (*Hill of Dreams* 210). His rejection of the woods and hills in favour of a more social life in London ultimately leads to the same isolation and subsequent hallucinations, whereby he finds himself wondering 'whether there were some drop of the fairy blood in his body that made him foreign and a stranger in the world' (*Hill of Dreams* 210). Lucian's view of himself as a hybrid being, both mortal and mystical, becomes reflective of the paradox of the suburbs with which he associates himself.

The temporal locality of the suburbs in *The Hill of Dreams* is simultaneously historical and contemporary. Lucian compares the London suburbs to Herculaneum because of its 'shadowy villas' that remind him of the buried city (*Hill of Dreams* 214).The comparison of the suburbs to a victim of Mount Vesuvius suggests a buried past of the suburbs, as well as 'an analogy of repression', which preserves past, present, and future through its lava encasement and future excavation (Freud 40). The suburbs' buried past lies in the urban sprawl that similarly covered the countryside in the black ash of London's industry. This comparison between Herculaneum and the London suburbs also anticipates the future ruin of London, 'a city doomed from ages' (*Hill of Dreams* 228). Lucian draws further connections between greater London and a mythical land as he ventures into a remoter suburb during a particularly foggy day. He believes that 'he had strayed into a city that had suffered some inconceivable doom, that he alone wandered where myriads had once dwelt. It was a town great as Babylon, terrible as Rome, marvellous as Lost Atlantis' (*Hill of*

Dreams 223). Machen collapses time by overlaying the ancient past (Babylon) with the existing present (London). Lucian to place himself in a definite temporal position (the present) results in his inability to maintain his own sense of being (*Hill of Dreams* 223).

Lucian's connection to the suburbs described as 'an infinitely desolate plain, abandoned from ages' and his alienation from society and reality culminates in his vision of greater London as being a part of a pagan ceremony: 'All London was one grey temple of an awful rite, ring within ring of wizard stones circled about some central place, every circle was an initiation, every initiation eternal loss' (*Hill of Dreams* 223). The description here suggests central London as being at the heart of these rings, each representing the outward movement into the suburbs. This is reflective of Sydney Low's image of the future of urban planning:

> the inevitable tendency . . . is leaving the costly sites in the inner circles of the towns to be used as places of business and public resort of all kinds, while the mass of the middle and working-class population, the bone and sinew of the country, are . . . housed in ever larger and wider concentric rings of suburbs. (Low 558)

While one might interpret Machen and Low's descriptions as suggesting London is in control of its outer rings, this is also suggestive of the rings of the outer suburbs controlling and containing London. The danger here is that the power dynamic no longer clearly defines the other, signifying that if the suburbs gain power, the city becomes the other. This shift in viewing the suburbs causes Lucian to become disassociated from them after an initial identification. In other words, as the temporal boundaries dissolve away, Lucian's ability to find definition also fades. He views himself now as trapped by these suburbs, reflecting that 'it was awful to think that all his goings were surrounded, that in the darkness he was watched and surveyed, that every step but led him deeper and deeper into the labyrinth' (*Hill of Dreams* 224). This paranoia of being watched, along with his fear of being lost in the labyrinth of the suburbs, is a by-product of his drug use which causes an altered view of self and surrounding, and a literary representation of suburban anxiety connected by Lucian to the hallucinatory experience of London described by Thomas De Quincey, as both 'had chosen the subtle in exchange for the more tangible pains' (*Hill of Dreams* 223). The reference is to De Quincey's *Confessions of an English Opium Eater* – a novel that Lucian first buys in Wales and takes with him to London. De Quincey's account also reveals an inability to rationalize the cityscape exacerbated by increasing drug use and paranoia. He encounters a London that overwhelms him imagining himself standing 'upon the brink of a precipice; and the local circumstances around me deepened and intensified these reflections, impressed upon them solemnity and terror, sometimes even horror' (*Opium Eater* 195). This daytime Gothic dream leads him to a nightmare in which London is an 'unfathomed abyss . . . expanding her visionary gates to receive me, like some dreadful mouth of Acheron' (*Opium Eater* 196). Time in the city collapses again, this time accompanied by an image of consumption, that London will take the narrator to an otherworld, from which he cannot return. Lucian echoes this sentiment in his wanderings through the suburbs, indicating that when he 'turned back towards London . . . the mist folded him in its thick darkness', consuming him (*Hill of Dreams* 232). The suburban streets become an obsession for Lucian, one that he both embraces and dreads. He imagines the suburb to be Babylon, and its underbelly a place in which 'every instinct of religion, of civilization even, was swept away' (*Hill of Dreams* 238). He has expected to find 'the English working class, "the best-behaved and the best-tempered crowd in the world"', yet what he finds is 'wonderful orgies' (*Hill of Dreams* 235, 236). Yet another collapse of suburban definition occurs here. Sydney Low argued that the suburb might counter the degeneration of man that he saw as a product of city living, by offering the leisure time for sport, fresh air, and general better health (Low 553). In contrast to Low's view of the upstanding and evolving suburbanites, here they are in fact degenerate; they do not represent religious and civic values, but rather 'Bacchic fury unveiled and unashamed' (*Hill of Dreams* 237–38). Lucian recounts that 'the lurid picture of that fiery street, the flaming shops and flaming glances, all its wonders and horrors, lit by the naphtha flares and by the burning souls, had possessed him' (*Hill of Dreams* 247). Like De Quincey, Lucian is consumed by the suburbs and as a consequence loses self, sanity, and life.

The London suburbs become monstrous for Lucian because of his inability to reconcile the real suburbs and his imagined version, the common inhabitants and imagined pagan denizens – which is reflective of this region that defies logical definition. His last journey into the suburban streets is entirely imaginative. He envisions himself 'wandering through the waste avenues of a city that had been ruined from ages. It had been as splendid as Rome, terrible as Babylon, and forever the darkness had covered it, and it lay desolate forever in the accursed plain' (*Hill of Dreams* 304). This last image is of a dead city, one that collapses greater London – past, present, and future – into a Gothic labyrinth which Lucian can no longer navigate. It is this final vision of the suburbs that Lucian must face before his death. As he drifts in and out of reality, from the safety of his room to this bleak suburban impression, the suburb encloses him, 'ring within ring', echoing the earlier representation of the suburb that encompasses the city (*Hill of Dreams* 304). His last conscious thought is of his 'dismal room', before 'a vapour of the grave entered his nostrils, and he cried out with a loud scream; but there was only an indistinct guttural murmur in his throat' (*Hill of Dreams* 306). While his inability to scream is the literal effect of the drug overdose, the overlaying of suburb and drug is undeniable, suggesting that the combination of the two lead to his demise. As Alex Warwick has suggested, Lucian is 'an inverse of the flâneur, not the man who masters the variety of spectacle, but the one who is mastered by it' (Warwick 136).

This final representation of Lucian as slave to the city translates to his cognitive dissociation from society and even from his writing. After Lucian's death, the manuscript for his great book is discovered, which amounts to sheets 'covered with illegible hopeless scribblings; only here and there it was possible to recognize a word' (*Hill of Dreams* 308). This initially seems ironic, as the reader has spent the duration of the novel reading of Lucian's attempts to write a novel only to find the end-product is indecipherable. Linda Dowling has suggested that the illegible novel represents a solipsistic Decadence which necessitates 'a language so perfected in its private symbolism that it will no longer yield its meaning even to the selected few, but only to the unique reader' (Dowling 160). While the final dissolution of Lucian's text does suggest a fittingly Decadent ending, it also reflects the complete mastering of the suburb over the individual, or a moment of hysteria. Kelly Hurley argues that 'to assert that something is too horrible to be spoken of is the privileged utterance of the Gothic, but it is also the privileged utterance of the hysteric' (Hurley 48). Lucian's inability to write coherently can be seen as an hysterical moment precipitated by his suburban anxiety. *The Hill of Dreams* ultimately presents suburban anxiety as a product of an area that resists any definition, spatial, temporal, or otherwise.

Works Cited

Crosland, T. W. H. (1905), *The Suburbans*, London: John Long

De Quincey, T. (1986), *Confessions of an English Opium Eater*, Harmondsworth: Penguin

Dowling, L. (1986), *Language and Decadence in the Victorian Fin de Siècle*, Princeton: Princeton University Press

Freud, S. (2001), 'Delusions and Dreams in Jensen's *Gradiva*', in *Standard Edition of the Complete Works*, volume. 9, London: Vintage, 3–95

Hurley, K. (1996), *The Gothic Body: Sexuality, Materialism, and Degeneration at the Fin de Siècle*, Cambridge: Cambridge University Press

Hutton, L. (1889), *Literary Landmarks of London*, London: T. Fisher Unwin

Low, S. J. (1891), 'The Rise of the Suburbs: A Lesson of the Census', *Contemporary Review*, 60, July-December, 545–58

Luckhurst, R. (2005) (ed.), *Late Victorian Gothic Tales*, Oxford: Oxford University Press

Machen, A. (1895), *The Great God Pan*, London: John Lane

Machen, A. (1907), *The Hill of Dreams*, London: E. G. Richards

Machen, A. (1923), *Things Near and Far*, New York: Alfred A. Knopf

Moncrieff, A. R. H. (1902) (ed.), *Black's Guide to London and its Environs*, London: Adam and Charles Black

Pope, G. (2008), 'Deep in South London', *Literary London: Interdisciplinary Studies in the Representations of London*, 6(1), accessed 1 November 2009 http://www.literary-london.org/london-journal/march2008/pope.html

Stead, W. T. (1885), 'The Maiden Tribute Of Modern Babylon', *Pall Mall Gazette*, 6–10 July

Thomson, J. (1880), *The City of Dreadful Night and Other Poems*, London: Reeves and Turner

Warwick, A. (2006), '"The City of Resurrections": Arthur Machen and the Archaeological Imagination', in R. Pearson (ed.), *The Victorians and the Ancient World: Archaeology and Classicism in Nineteenth-Century Culture*, Newcastle: Cambridge Scholars Press, 124–38

Wilde, O. (1891), *The Picture of Dorian Gray*, London: Ward, Lock

Chapter 5

An Occult Gazetteer of Bloomsbury: An Experiment in Method

Roger Luckhurst

Cultural theorists have long been trained to be suspicious of maps and exercises in mapping. The map is panoptic and totalizing, the impossible perspective of the cartographer entirely detached from the everyday experience of traversing the territory. The map, Michel de Certeau proclaimed, was a strategy of control, one of the 'proper places in which to *exhibit the products* of knowledge, form tables of *legible* results' (de Certeau 121). Others have investigated the intimate links between mapping and empire, 'cadastral possession' of a terrain equating to its conversion into information for the archive-state (Richards 14). To resist the map, there has been a long-term obsession with the avant-garde counter-urbanism of the Situationist International that offered, between the late 1950s and early 1970s, tactics for the derangement of the ordered city by psychogeography, drift and *détournement*. For a while, it became common to expect texts and essays on London to be about exactly what evades the map, the attempt to track the 'absent, secret, invisible, hidden, intangible, tacit, forgotten, unfathomable' (Pile 203). Interest was absorbed by the 'excess beyond comprehension which is the modern city of London' (Wolfreys 6): the city of disappearances, of vanishings, explored in an all-consuming language of hauntings.

Of late, however, Franco Moretti has revived mapping as an analytic tool for literary study, embracing the map's positivism as a place where 'one can make exact experiments upon uniform diagrams' (Moretti 4). Moretti suspects that novels, too, schematize chaotic city experience into meaningful maps of social and psychic significance and that their imaginative acts of geography might reveal much if we pursue their plotting with a dogged literalism, a London *A-Z* in hand. Consequently, Moretti sets out to chart the distribution of London crimes in Sherlock Holmes stories, or track the innovative progress of Dickens' characters across the class fractures of Victorian London. Moretti's method has partly inspired others to explore the urban concentrations of English

Modernism, the houses, cafés and restaurants where manifestos were signed and aesthetic alliances secured (see Brooker and McCracken).

I want to explore whether it is possible to combine these competing methods and attempt to map what is claimed to be unmappable. Can you gazetteer the ghost? Can you map fugitive instances of supernatural phenomena or secret occult rituals, chart the oneiric pathways of the London Gothic? Isn't the allure of these modes precisely in their refusal to be converted into positive knowledge? What does mapping do to them?

The experiment will take Bloomsbury as its focus, because it seems to me that there has been a striking geographical concentration of these kinds of marginal or subjugated knowledges in this area. The first half of this chapter is therefore distressingly empirical: it is largely an accumulation of details, placed in a roughly circumscribed grid of Bloomsbury. In the second half, I'll reflect on whether this geographical concentration has anything significant to tell us: whether the act of mapping, to follow Franco Moretti, can do more than be an ornament to cultural study and become an analytical tool to illuminate the supernatural in new ways.

Bloomsbury was only substantially developed as a residential area in the early nineteenth century after the intensive buildings of squares and speculative housing projects by the builders James Burton and Thomas Cubitt. It was associated with populations of lawyers from the nearby Inns of Court, but also with the specialist hospitals that emerged around Queens Square in mid-century, a supplement to the great reforming hospital at University College founded in 1834. These professional knowledges were soon shadowed by Spiritualism, which developed in Britain from the 1850s and found one of its metropolitan centres in Bloomsbury. Mrs Marshall, one of the very first professional, paid mediums in London, took rooms in Red Lion Square. In 1863, James Burns set up the Progressive Library and Spiritual Institute at 15 Southampton Row, just off Bloomsbury Square. This became an important centre for a variety of heterodox activities, including séances, lectures, and the publication first of the journal *Human Nature* and then, more significantly, the weekly *Medium and Daybreak*. The Institute also reported on conferences, lectures and Spiritualist demonstrations at the Old Conference Rooms in Gower Street. In *Mystic London,* a compendium of strange institutions and beliefs in the metropolis, the Reverend Charles Maurice Davies reported on a Monday night mesmeric séance at the Progressive Library. Tuesdays were devoted to phrenology, but the big guns were kept for the Friday night shilling séance, where star mediums appeared. When 'dark' séances developed in the 1870s, they cost two shillings, probably because these came with the promise of seeing a full scale materialization of a spirit.

Class was crucial in the geographical distributions of Spiritualist belief. Proletarian versions were associated with the industrial cities of the north of

England and with the metropolitan poor. In an earlier report, Davies commented that one sixteen-year-old medium 'lives on the outskirts of London, as Spiritualists always seem to do' (Davies 1873 338). Yet Davies saw a significant geographical migration in 1870s London: 'The great fact I notice about Spiritualism is, that it is obeying the occult impetus of all great movements and steadily going from east to west. From Hackney to Highbury it gravitates towards Belgravia and Tyburnia. I left the wilds of Hackney, and neared Hyde Park . . .' (Davies 1875 343). Bloomsbury seems to be conveniently half way in this migration, the Spiritual Institute a beachhead to the West. 'It does seem remarkable', Davies said, nevertheless, 'that such things should be going on amid the very roar of Holborn in this nineteenth century' (Davies 1875 321). The same thing was being said in 1925, when Edward Lovett of the Folk-Lore Society, expressed defeat in searching for 'the reason why these remarkable beliefs in magic still exist in Modern London' (Lovett 7). Perhaps this was why the Christian mystic Charles Williams situated his occult novel *All Hallows' Eve* about a Satanic magician attempting to breach the border of life and afterlife in the backstreets of Holborn. Amidst the rubble of the Blitz that killed his wife, the grieving Richard glimpses her just where the boundaries have most thinned: 'They stood on either side of that Holborn by-way, and gazed' (*All Hallows Eve* 47).

From 1870, Spiritualist activity exploded in these streets. At 61 Lamb's Conduit Street, the mediums Herne and Williams set up shop. Their dark séances were sensations, with *Medium and Daybreak* reporting that 'hundreds of influential visitors to the metropolis have sat with them' (*Medium and Daybreak* 29 December 1871 421). Herne could get spirits to play musical instruments and deliver apports (physical gifts for sitters from spiritual sources), such as flowers and fruit. He was also good at levitating in his chair (you could hear his head bump on the ceiling). For his part, Williams was sufficiently famous to be hired by Erasmus Darwin in January 1874 for a private sitting at his house at the considerably more fashionable address of 6 Queen Anne's Street. This séance included his brother Charles Darwin, his cousin Francis Galton, and George Eliot and her partner, G. H. Lewes. Eleven days later, Darwin's ideological bulldog, T. H. Huxley was dispatched to attend a séance in order to calm Darwin's unease at being confounded by Williams. His written report was contemptuous of the trickery he thought he had confidently detected (see Luckhurst 2003).

In one famous (much mocked) incident in 1871, another prominent medium, Mrs Guppy, was minding her own business writing her shopping list in Highbury Hill only to enter a trance state and apparently vanish. At a Lamb's Conduit Street séance being conducted by Herne and Williams at the same time 'an object was felt to come upon the table, and when the light was struck, their visitor was found to be Mrs Guppy'. Mrs Guppy had astrally travelled across a mile and a half across London, her ample frame thumping materially onto the table in midst of writing 'onions' (*Medium and Daybreak* 9 June 1871). Another Guppy séance prompted the headline: 'REMARKABLE SEANCE /INSTANTANEOUS TRANSFERENCE OF A SCEPTICAL GENTLEMAN /FROM WITHIN

A LOCKED ROOM/TO A DISTANCE OF ONE MILE AND A HALF' (*Medium and Daybreak* 5 December 1873 562).

Meanwhile, at the townhouse of the Serjeant-at-Arms Edward Cox, at 36 Russell Square, some very strange experiments were being conducted. The sudden rise to prominence of Spiritualism in London had resulted from a number of significant converts from science, most notably Alfred Russell Wallace, Darwin's co-theorist of natural selection. In 1869, the influential London Dialectical Society began an investigation of Spiritualistic phenomena, and delivered a deeply ambiguous report on the evidence, despite submissions from contemptuous men of science like Huxley and Lewes. In 1870, the chemist William Crookes announced that he would scientifically settle the claims of Spiritualism once and for all. After twelve months of researches with Edward Cox and others, Crookes announced, to the bewilderment of the fragile new scientific establishment, that his experiments 'appear conclusively to establish the existence of a new force, in some unknown manner connected with the human organization, which for convenience may be called Psychic Force' (Crookes 9). The term 'psychic force' had been coined by Edward Cox to avoid assuming the spirit hypothesis and suggest a neutral scientific terminology, and it is from Cox we get the terms psychism and psychics. Cox set up the first Psychological Society of Great Britain, which gave its address as 11 Chandos Street, Cavendish Square. Many of the séances took place at his home in 36 Russell Square, however. It was in Cox's house as well as in his laboratory that Crookes linked young women mediums into electrical circuits or used improvised mechanisms to measure the weights psychic force could push: a miraculous new force measured in pounds per square inch. Sometimes, as Williams Crookes' research notes detail, the eminent scientist Francis Galton was scrabbling around on the floor, checking the integrity of the knots and circuits that bound the mediums.

It was to 36 Russell Square that the pioneering anthropologist Edward Tylor came in 1872 from Oxford, when he undertook his one and only field trip – to the Spiritualists of Bloomsbury. Tylor had published *Primitive Culture* in 1871, where he had confidently asserted that 'modern spiritualism is a survival and revival of savage thought, which the general tendency of civilization and science has been to discard' (Stocking 90). His field notes report an evening at the Progressive Library, where he was upset by the over-familiarity and class mixture of the circle, a common reaction. At 36 Russell Square, with a more select grouping, he sat with Mrs Olive, who was possessed successively by an Indian and then Negro child-spirit – perhaps in deference to the great ethnographer? – before impressively bringing on the ghost of Franz Anton Mesmer, the controversial discoverer of animal magnetism as a tool for healing, who had died in 1815. Tylor was disgusted, although more impressed by the highly respected inspirational Spiritualist preacher, Stainton Moses, who also gave him a sitting in Russell Square when the famed medium Williams failed to turn up. Tylor soon moved further West, into the more middle class circles of William and Mary Howitt in Notting Hill. Their gentle Christian Spiritualism was perhaps more amenable to Tylor, less proletarian and less aggressively dissenting. Although the field work reinforced Tylor's scepticism, he did get a lesson in the dangers of participant-observation, recording that in one séance towards the end of his investigations that he himself began to enter a light trance state, 'a drowsy influence', something he speculated might be 'hysterical simulation' (Stocking 100).

The threat to the new scientific naturalism posed by Spiritualism in the 1870s resulted in a key incident in 8 Upper Bedford Place in October 1876. The evolutionary biologist, Edwin Ray Lankester, had been incensed by machinations that had led to a paper on séance 'research' being reported at the British Association for the Advancement of Science meeting in September. He set out to expose a medium, and chose one of the most famous visiting mediums of the era, the American Henry Slade. Slade had taken rooms in Bedford Place to break his travel from America to St Petersburg, where he had been invited by aristocratic supporters. Lankester posed as a grieving husband, which allowed Slade to perform his trick. The medium allegedly received messages from the dead which were communicated on sealed slates. Satisfied that this was a simple conjuring trick, Slade returned with the society doctor Horatio Donkin, seized Slade in the middle of his sleight of hand, and had him arrested under the Vagrancy Act for illegal fortune-telling. The trial of Henry Slade became a major public event, each day's proceedings reported in detail by the press. Although Slade was found guilty, the trial backfired for Lankester: it was considered heavy-handed and illiberal and Slade was allowed to leave the country before the sentence was imposed (for more detailed commentary, see Luckhurst 2002 44–47).

Scientists remained fascinated by figures who hovered uncertainly between claims of supernatural powers and good old-fashioned stage conjuring. In 1881, in Bedford Square, the famous American mind-reader Washington Irving Bishop, performed before an august body of investigators including Lankester, Galton, the alienist Daniel Hack Tuke and the Queen's physician, Andrew Clark. In Galton's notebooks on his psychological experiments, preserved in University College library, a clipping of this event from the evening *Standard* is carefully preserved. Bishop was so consistently able to hit the mark that 'scepticism began to give way, if not to faith, at least to something approaching sympathetic curiosity' (*Standard* 10 May 1881). This was part of an era of competitive public performances around London by Bishop and his rival Stuart Cumberland.

The new confidence of London's Spiritualist movement was reflected in the founding of the British National Association of Spiritualists in 1873. They took offices at 38 Great Russell Street, following a conference of interested groups in Lawson's Rooms in Gower Street. The National Association of Spiritualists, however, was an unstable organization, since it was trying to unify different class and doctrinal factions of the movement. When Captain Richard Burton lectured on Oriental Spiritualism in Great Russell Street in December 1878, the protests were vocal: despite his wife's very evident Spiritualist beliefs, *Spiritual Notes* complained that Burton, already a scandalous figure, was not a proper believer. 'Like other scientific men and materialists, he believes in a natural force which has no name, which he calls zoo-electricity, but he does not mean the ghosts that real believers are said to see' ('Editorial' *Spiritual Notes* Jan 1879 93).

It was on these premises, too, that a conference was organized by the physicist William Barrett in 1882, which led to the formation of the Society for Psychical Research (SPR). The discussions also took place in the townhouse of Hensleigh Wedgwood in Gower Street. Wedgwood was a cousin of Charles Darwin who had become a firm believer in Spiritualism. The SPR was soon controlled by the Cambridge agnostics surrounding Henry Sidgwick and Frederic Myers. They sought to distance the new Society from the lower class and religious aspects of the Spiritualist movement by claiming to be rigorous scientific sceptics of as-yet inexplicable phenomena. They deliberately antagonized Spiritualists by suspending the 'spirit hypothesis' in their early years in order to establish their sceptical credentials. This was also reflected in their London addresses: they had an office at 19 Buckingham Street, in the Adelphi off the Strand, but also conducted their main meetings in Dean's Yard in Westminster, where it was easy for leading politicians like Gladstone to attend. Their meetings met in the same rooms as the nascent socialist group, the Fabian Society, and there was considerable movement between the memberships (Frank Podmore was an active member of both groups and George Bernard Shaw remembered moving from one meeting to another). This reflected the SPR's attempt to ally psychical research with centres of power, rather than remain a marginal, dissenting religious belief. The SPR soon moved West, into Kensington. Early on, they were trying to find corroboration for the appearance of an astral double at 77 Elgin Crescent, by firing off a telegram from the Parliament Street telegraph office: 'Olcott to Damodar, Adyar, Madras. Have you visited London lately? Write Myers full details' (*Journal of the Society for Psychical Research* I 1884 76).

The SPR maintained its allegedly sceptical, impartial stance. In 1960, G. W. Lambert published 'The Geography of London Ghosts', a study of the one hundred or so records of haunting in the SPR archive. Incidents chosen were traced on London maps (areas sampled did not include Bloomsbury). Lambert's thesis was that these supernatural events traced the path of London's lost rivers, the Tyburn through Marylebone, the Wesbourne through Marble Arch, in particularly notable clusters for reports of psychical disturbance. Essentially, Lambert argued, these hauntings were not psychical but likely to be the products of bad drains on rainy days.

Bloomsbury spiritualism and psychical research is complemented by a significant magical concentration. In October 1901, another trial exposed this world to a bemused public. Frank and Editha Jackson were tried for obtaining money under false pretences and the immoral procurement of three young women. The women had been initiated into The Order of Theocratic Unity, whose temple was based at 99 Gower Street. This initiation largely appeared to involve ritualistic sex magic with Frank, or Theo Horus, as he preferred to be known. There were sensational claims that magicians of the order exerted immense mesmeric power and could send malign influences across great distances. Although reported in comic terms by the *Evening News* and other London newspapers, the trial dragged into public light the now well-known world of the Hermetic Order of the Golden Dawn. The Golden Dawn had been set up in 1888 by the coroner and occultist William Wynn Westcott (who lived in Camden Road). It attracted significant supporters, including Annie Horniman, Florence Farr, William Yeats and, briefly, the Gothic novelist Arthur Machen. The Order was blown apart by the arrival of Aleister Crowley, in 1898, who worked his way up the hierarchy of magical skills quickly before staging a coup in 1900 (see Gilbert). He was soon claiming to be the most powerful magician in England, the Beast, the Anti-Christ. Temples of the Order were improvised in various spaces, but the Second Order was initially situated in Thavies Street, just off Holborn, before moving west to Blythe Road in Kensington. Many of these self-mythologizing occultists spent time in Bloomsbury. Yeats lived in Woburn Walk from 1896 to 1919, where many magical and literary soirées were held in his rooms. Arthur Machen lived in misery in Gray's Inn Road and Rosebery Avenue between 1895 and 1899, a time of painful solipsism recorded in his novel, *The Hill of Dreams* (1907) a study of writer's block measured out by walking dusty streets. The itinerant Aleister Crowley in 1898 took on the pseudonym of Count Vladimir Svareff to occupy a flat at 67 Chancery Lane, where he conducted two months of intensive visionary magical rituals (see Owen 2004). Although Anthony Powell's twelve novel sequence *A Dance to the Music of Time* is the great novel of Fitzrovia, not Bloomsbury, it is striking to note that one of the recurring figures who helps structure and pattern the novel is the occultist, Dr Trelawney, plainly modelled on Crowley. Trelawney appears in *The Kindly Ones* conducting 'a centre for his own peculiar religious, philosophical – some said magical – tenets, a cult of which he was high priest, if not actually messiah' (*The Kindly Ones* 502). He is regarded as an eccentric, with 'too much abracadabra' about him, involved with 'all sorts of mystical nonsense, transcendental magic' (505), and reappears in progressively reduced and marginal circumstances through the series. Yet in many ways, Powell resorts to magical sympathies for the rhythms of chance and significant conjuncture woven into *Dance*.

The boundaries of occultism are hard to determine: in the early twentieth century, it was often considered co-terminous with other fringe knowledges. Bloomsbury intellectual circles were interested in the new dynamic psychology emerging on the continent, from the psychotherapeutics associated with the Nancy School in France to the psychoanalysis of Sigmund Freud in Vienna. The Medico-Psychological Clinic was founded in 1913 in Brunswick Square by two women who had been medically trained in France, Jessie Murray and Julia

Turner. The Clinic was part funded by May Sinclair, the Modernist writer and psychical researcher who was publishing the ghost stories that made up her *Uncanny Stories* at about the same time. Sinclair was a psychical researcher and fascinated by emergent forms of psychological therapy. A rival centre, the Tavistock Square Clinic, opened in 1920. As Sally Alexander points out, the Clinic twice had to deny in letters to *The Lancet* that its range of methods included 'occultism' (Alexander 138). This was a common association. The *Saturday Review* sarcastically reported in 1921 that 'the far-seeing occultist has abandoned the necromantic arts, and now poses as a psycho-analyst' (129).

Another permeable border was between certain strands of Modernism and the occult. A. R. Orage founded the journal *The New Age* in 1908, which became a crucial passageway between the worlds of the mysticism, the occult and literary Modernism. Orage ran their weekly editorial meetings in a dingy A.B.C. café on Chancery Lane, the chain of London tea-shops that has an insistent presence in London Modernism, as Scott McCracken has observed. It was partly through Orage that those on the fringes of the Bloomsbury Group became interested in these occult concerns. In the last months of her life Katherine Mansfield pursued the mystical training offered at Gurdjieff's Institute for the Harmonious Development of Man in France. Very soon after Mansfield died in January 1923, her husband John Middleton Murry, another important Modernist journal editor, had a mystical experience that prompted him to pursue a decidedly odd personal theology. It all prompted Virginia Woolf to complain that 'there is a great deal of mystic religion about' (Owen 2006 159). Yet her aesthetic of epiphany and her interest in dissociated states prompted by the urban phantasmagoria in *Mrs Dalloway* or her essay 'Street Haunting: A London Adventure', were closely allied to the psychical or mystic experiences being explored in these adjacent registers.

With more space, a mapping of the Bloomsbury occult might also include more detailed consideration of the Swedenborg Society, based in rooms at 36 Bloomsbury Street in 1870, before moving to its current hall in Bloomsbury Square in 1925. A swift walk passed Nicholas Hawksmoor's St. George's church, subject to much psychogeographical occult theorizing, leads to Museum Street, where the famous occult bookshop, Atlantis, survives, an address that figures in one of the finest occult novels of recent years, M. John Harrison's *The Course of the Heart (1992)*. Odd occult archives in the area include the Harry Price Library of psychical and magical material lodged in the University of London Library and the Warburg Institute, with its famous collections of magical arcanae, including some of Crowley's papers. The Magic Circle library is on the fringes of Bloomsbury, in Stephenson Way, just over the border of the Euston Road. But this is enough accumulation: what to do with this information?

Why Bloomsbury? Perhaps the occult mapping of this concentration demands different ways of moving across the rational, panoptic, planar grid of the map.

We could reach for a Fortean explanation, perhaps. Charles Fort (who lived for some time in Marchmont Street in Bloomsbury) wanted to collect together what he called in 1919 'a procession of the damned. By the damned, I mean excluded. We shall have a procession of data that Science has excluded' (Fort 3). Fort worked merely by the mass *accumulation* of weird and supernatural details to argue for the significance of phenomena that science refused to accept. Might it be then that my own accumulation becomes evidence that Bloomsbury is a sort of *genius loci* of these marginal knowledges? Peter Ackroyd isolates this slightly to the south of Bloomsbury in Seven Dials, which he suggests is a sort of transhistorical locale for astrologers, quacks, Theosophists and magi. 'Here again', he intones in his vatic mode, 'may be another example of that territorial imperative, or *genius loci,* which keeps inhabitants and activities in the same small area' (Ackroyd 141). Ackroyd's way of grasping London invokes an unchanging mythic structure that runs beneath its modernity. To reach this alterity, he offers a populist version of the favoured form of urban exploration, psychogeography. This mode has preserved the Surrealist appropriation of occultism to derail the utilitarian and administered spaces of the planned city. Thus, we explore what Christine Boyer calls the counter-memorial city. 'Our memory crisis', she suggests, 'seems to be based on our need to establish counter-memories, resisting the dominant coding of images and representations and recovering differences that official memory has erased . . . We are compelled to create new memory walks through the city, new maps that help us resist and subvert the all-too-programmed and enveloping messages of our consumer culture' (Boyer 28–29). Might occult traces mark out a counter-territory? This is certainly how Stewart Home used the language of occultism for his explosive missives sent from the London Psychogeographical Association, collected together in 1997.

There are evident problems with this approach: the method repeats its object, never escaping the occult presumption that secret sympathies are meaningful rather than effects of its own belief system. I am not sure, either, that occult discourse, which is intrinsically hierarchical and anti-democratic, is automatically subversive. Instead, I want to suggest something slightly more materialist than this emphasis on uncanny, transhistorical repetition or inherently avant-garde occultism. Franco Moretti's empirical mapping of the spaces of the nineteenth-century novel insists that spatial distributions can sharpen analytic insight. In the instance of Bloomsbury, Moretti offers some suggestive observations about the emergence in the mid-nineteenth century of liminal zones between the aristocratic West End and the plebeian East, '*a third London*: a sort of wedge that holds the two extremes together' (Moretti 116). Might Bloomsbury's shifting economic and class status make it the quarter for transitional or marginal knowledges? Just as The Spiritual Institute opened its doors in Southampton Row, *Punch* satirically reported that 'There is the most awful commotion in what used to be thought the Genteel District all round the British Museum. All the inhabitants are moving'. This was because *The Times* had pronounced that

Bloomsbury was no longer 'the splendid quarter of legal eminence and mer-
cantile wealth', but had been socially downgraded to 'the economical quarter
for Trading Respectability' (*Punch* 17 October 1863, cited Ingleby 2009). This
significant shift in status offers one persuasive lead for thinking about this
clustering of modern occultisms: Bloomsbury is a newly liminal zone.

Another route is to ask what this concentration of occult events is grouped
around? One answer is the presence of University College, bastion of dissenting
secularized knowledge, set up to counter the orthodox Christian institutions of
Oxford and Cambridge in the 1830s. Another obvious answer is the British
Museum, emblem of the total archive that opened its current neo-classical
building designed by Sir Robert Smirke on Great Russell Street in the 1850s.
From this point, it became a centre of calculation receiving arcane materials
from around the world and processing them into developmental narratives
of progress and decline. The British Museum was one of the models for the
'universal survey museum' designed to educate the ignorant mob and help
transform them into rational citizens (see Duncan and Wallach 1980).

This temple to the Enlightenment of course attracted its share of occultists
inside its walls. The Reading Room was where Yeats, Samuel Liddell Mathers,
Mina Bergson, A.E. Waite and others met and exchanged magical arcanae
mined from the depths of the library's collections. There is even a fine short
story by Amy Levy called 'The Recent Telepathic Occurrences at the British
Museum' (1888) in which an apparition of a woman disturbs a dysfunctional
professor in the Reading Room with its 'rustle of feminine skirts' (Levy 432).
The professor only realizes belatedly that this is a vision of a potential lover he
has ignored and notices only at the moment of her death, when in her psychic
agony she projects what the SPR would have defined as a telepathic phantasm.
The British Museum also housed a cursed mummy case in the Egyptian Rooms,
a story that first surfaced in London in 1904. Object 22542, a coffin-lid painted
with an image of a priestess of Amen-Ra, had been donated to the Museum in
1889, after thirty years of allegedly bringing misery and death on the family that
had bought it illegally from Arab traders in Egypt. One psychic investigator,
Elliott O'Donnell, declared in his *Haunted Houses of London* in 1909 that whilst
in the Oriental Department, some malign elemental 'had passed through the
glass frame containing the mummy case and had planted itself by my side.' He
continued to see her 'long and glittering eyes' menacing him for over two weeks
in every corner of London (O'Donnell 92). Wallis Budge, keeper of Egyptian
and Assyrian Antiquities, revealed that the journalist and occultist William Stead
had requested permission to 'pass a night in the mummy rooms' that he and
others 'might converse with the souls' of the Egyptian departed (Budge 391).
Budge refused the request, although his affair with the writer Edith Nesbit
partly inspired her to write *The Story of the Amulet* (1906), which includes an
episode where the Queen of Babylon arrives in modern-day London to demand
the return of her treasures from the British Museum. As her plundered posses-
sions dance magically down the steps of the Museum, Nesbit has the tabloid

press report: 'IMPERTINENT MIRACLE AT THE BRITISH MUSEUM' (*The Story of the Amulet* 147). Long into the 1930s, rumours about the menacing mummy continued. One theory about the closure of the British Museum underground station on the corner of Great Russell Street and Bury Place was that a secret tunnel linked the Egyptian Rooms to the platform, thus allowing the mummy to enter the underground system at night and spread her malign influence. This has remained a spooky station-stop ever since: it features again in the great London horror film *Deathline* (1972).

Less than ten years after the British Museum reopened in Smirke's building in Great Russell Street, the Spiritual Institute helped cluster one key aspect of London spiritualism in the shadow of that neo-classical portico. This might be readable as a tactic of legitimation by insisting on a spatial proximity to the knowledge-machinery of the institution. Bloomsbury thus becomes a centre for marginal knowledge, crowded on the edges of the secular university and the universal museum. Yet because they *remained* peripheral, on the streets outside the gates, the marginality of occult knowledge was also ultimately confirmed. These new institutions of rational modernity policed the boundaries of legitimacy very strictly: the model for this was the way in which University College authorities dealt with demonstrations of Mesmeric treatments by Professor Elliotson in 1838. After claiming that certain of his lowly Irish women patients had preternaturally acute perceptions of otherwise invisible effluvia of animal magnetism, thus contesting professional medical diagnoses, Elliotson was forced to resign. The science of Mesmerism was forcefully shunted into marginal and amateur cultural practice for over fifty years (see Winter 1998). Edward Tylor's denunciation of primitive superstitions around fetish objects was similarly conducted within the walls of the British Museum by Wallis Budge, refusing to countenance persistent beliefs that his Egyptian antiquities carried supernatural curses.

Whilst mapping out these controversies spatially does help to differentiate different kinds of legitimacy and knowledge-claim, we might also end by noting another kind of logic. Boundaries are permeable, difficult to police: Mesmerized women disorder university hospital wards; the Reading Room teems with weird men and women pursuing occult secrets; the artefacts take secret passageways that lead under the walls. When Lord Carnavon died in 1923, the bestselling author Marie Corelli observed: 'According to a rare book I possess, which is not in the British Museum . . . the most dire punishment follows any such intruder into a sealed tomb' (Frayling 43). Hermetic wisdom, occulted truths, marginal knowledges, begin to accrue value by their very absence from the total archive, existing instead in the private collections, secret libraries, and whispered initiations taking place in the dusty backstreets. What this demonstrates then, is what I have sometimes called the *supplemental occult*, the sense that wherever secular modernity exerts its power, a reserve of supernaturalism emerges with it. I've thought this conceptually and discursively before

(Luckhurst 2003), but further insights accrue through an exercise in gazetteer-ing the occult across the map of Bloomsbury.

Works Cited

Ackroyd, P. (2000), *London: The Biography*, London: Chatto and Windus

Alexander, S. (1998), 'Psychoanalysis in Britain in the Early Twentieth Century: An Introductory Note,' *History Workshop Journal* 45: 135–43

Boyer, M. C. (1996), *The City of Collective Memory: Its Historical Imagery and Architectural Entertainments*, Cambridge, Mass.: MIT Press

Brooker, P. (2004), *Bohemia in London: The Social Scene of Early Modernism*, Basingstoke: Palgrave

Budge, E. A. W. (1920), *By Nile and Tigris: A Narrative of Journeys in Egypt and Mesopotamia on behalf of the British Museum Between the Years 1886 and 1913*, 2 volumes, London: John Murray

Crookes, W. (1874), *Researches into the Phenomena of Spiritualism*, London: J. Burns

Davies, Rev. C. M. (1873), *Unorthodox London: Or, Phases of Religious Life in the Metropolis*, London: Tinsley Brothers

Davies, Rev. C. M. (1875), *Mystic London: Or, Phases of Occult Life in the Metropolis*, London: Tinsley Brothers

De Certeau, Michel (1988), *The Practice of Everyday Life*, trans. Steven Rendall, Berkeley: University of California Press

Duncan, C. and Wallach, A. (1980), 'The Universal Survey Museum', *Art History*, 3(4), 448–69

Fort, C. (1974), *The Complete Books of Charles Fort*, New York: Dover

Frayling, C. (1992), *The Face of Tutankhamun*, London: Faber

Gilbert, R. A. (1997), *Revelations of the Golden Dawn: The Rise and Fall of a Magical Order*, London: Quantum

Harrison, M. J. (1992), *The Course of the Heart*, London: Gollancz

Home, S. (1997), *Mind Invaders: A Reader in Psychic Warfare, Cultural Sabotage and Semiotic Terrorism*, London: Serpent's Tail

Ingleby, M. (2009), 'Encountering the Bloomsbury Barrister's Wife: A Phenomenon of Local Literary History', paper at the 'Bloomsbury People' conference, University College London, 16 June 2009

Lambert, G. W. (1960), 'The Geography of London Ghosts', *Journal of the Society for Psychical Research*, 40, 397–409

Levy, A. (1993), *The Complete Novels and Selected Writings of Amy Levy 1861–1889*, Gainesville: University Press of Florida

Lovett, E. (1925), *Magic in Modern London*, Croydon: Advertiser

Luckhurst, R. (2002), *The Invention of Telepathy*, Oxford: Oxford University Press

Luckhurst, R. (2003), 'Demon-Haunted Darwinism', *New Formations* 49, 124–35

McCracken, S. (2007), *Masculinities, Modernist Fiction and the Urban Public Sphere*, Manchester: Manchester University Press

Moretti, F. (1998), *Atlas of the European Novel 1800–1900*, London: Verso

Nesbit, E. (1996), *The Story of the Amulet* (1906), London: Puffin

O'Donnell, E. (1909), *The Haunted Houses of London*, London: Eveleigh Nash

Owen, A. (2004), *The Place of Enchantment: British Occultism and the Culture of the Modern*, Chicago: Chicago University Press

Owen, A. (2006), 'The "Religious Sense" in a Post-War Secular Age', *Past and Present Supplement* 1, 159–77

Pile, S. (2002), '"The Problem of London", or, How to Explore the Moods of the City', in (ed.) N. Leach, *The Hieroglyphics of Space: Reading and Experiencing the Modern Metropolis*, London: Routledge, 202–16

Porter, R. (2000), *London: A Social History*, Harmondsworth: Penguin

Powell, A. (1962), *The Kindly Ones, A Dance to the Music of Time*, volume 2, London: Arrow

'Psycho-Analysis à la Mode', *Saturday Review*, 21 February 1921, 129

Richards, T. (1993), *The Imperial Archive*, London: Verso

Stocking, G. (1971), 'Animism in Theory and Practice: E. B. Tylor's Unpublished "Notes on Spiritualism"', *Man*, NS 6, 88–104

Tylor, E. (1871), *Primitive Culture: Researches into the Development of Mythology, Philosophy, Religion, Art, and Custom*, 2 volumes, London: John Murray

Williams, C. (1945), *All Hallow's Eve*, London: Faber

Winter, A. (1998), *Mesmerized: The Powers of Mind in Victorian Britain*, Chicago: Chicago University Press

Wolfreys, J. (1998), *Writing London: The Trace of the Urban Text from Blake to Dickens*, Basingstoke: Palgrave

Part Two

Contemporary Prose Narratives

Chapter 6

'This Light was Pale and Ghostly': Stewart Home, Horror and the Gothic Destruction of 'London'

Alex Murray

The idea of London Gothic is a pathetic fabulation of tourist operators, a deluded illusion of novelist and film-makers, the preserve of capitalism in its most vulgar and insubstantial forms. Its persistence is no doubt testament to the entwined stupidity of consumers and the greed of cultural producers. Yet there is a temptation to see in London Gothic the idea of an inherent alterity, an ontology of difference, a politics of dispersed and deferred identity that destabilizes the idea of the city itself. Here a haunted London reveals the manifest layers of voices, the polyphonic and echolalic city that will forever be in debt to its own ghosts. The ethical challenge of London past and present, delivered through the medium of a hauntology is no doubt powerful as a means of redressing the kitsch Gothic of the tourist industry and television, yet for all that the two forms of London Gothic are not as dissimilar as they may appear, with both wanting to leave intact the idea of a London that can be marketed and sold, a mythical space. In what follows I would like to explore Stewart Home's novel *Down and Out in Shoreditch and Hoxton* (2004) as an exploration of the Gothic that leaves nothing of London. By the novel's bizarre Lovecraftian climax there is nothing left of the city at all, exposing it as a degraded placeless phantasmagoria of capitalism. In so doing Home has, I will suggest, provided us with a destruction of both London and the Gothic, offering instead something like an ontological horror that calls us beyond the separation and estrangement of capital.

Ghosts of London

A considerable amount of ink has been spilt outlining the contours of the London Gothic in general, and the contemporary in particular. From Julian Wolfreys' Derridean investigation of alterity and ghosting, to Roger Luckhurst's critique of the 'spectral turn' there has been a repeated attempt to outline the Gothic as an important and contested genre in readings of the contemporary city. The debate centres around, on the one hand, the ability of deconstructive accounts of the spectral to deal with the ethics of a text, to remain alive to the polyphony of voices that haunt every text and, on the other, the (non)ability of these deconstructive accounts to grasp the specificity of London literature, to pay adequate attention to that singular political, social and cultural context that marks the city's literature. In both there is still an acceptance of the Gothic as a privileged model for dealing with the city's history, and the 'echolalic' presence of that history in the contemporary.[1]

Julian Wolfreys' ever-growing body of work on London has been of obvious importance to the development of 'Literary London' as a field. His three-volume study *Writing London* has dealt with the canonical literatures of the city, but has also been influential in cementing the canon of London Literature, writing on Blake, Dickens, the Romantics, T. S. Eliot, Iain Sinclair, Peter Ackroyd, Elizabeth Bowen, Maureen Duffy and Richard Marsh, with the three volumes devoted to covering the Romantics and High Victorians (I), The fin de siècle and Modernism (III) and The Postwar Period (II) – a rough approximation. The approaches taken here have developed and shifted, yet the influence of deconstruction (in varied forms) remains consistent. Wolfreys has also elsewhere written at length about the Victorian Gothic, and routinely brings the Gothic and London together. Wolfreys is insistent upon the fact that his Derridean reading of London is not just apposite, but necessary. Against the charges of universality that we will see from Luckhurst below, Wolfreys argues that the Derridean approach to reading can be found at work in the city itself:

> The constant return to Derrida and to his writings is also a response dictated coincidentally enough by the very nature of London. . . . Derrida teaches us to await the event of reading, the unpredictable in the text. Writers in the nineteenth century understood the event of London, and responded in their writing of the capital by writing of the city's very unpredictability. (Wolfreys 1998 17)

It is important to note that Wolfreys' exploration of the ways in which Derridean modes of engagement can be utilized in reading London is not always a recourse to the Gothic. As any good Derridean knows (and Wolfreys is one of the best) those Derridean practices, which appear under a number of names (*différance*, the trace, writing-in-general, etc) are never concepts, always maintaining a polysemy as they refuse to become ossified in a standardized critical fashion, and this is key to Wolfreys' work, giving it a perpetual terminological restlessness. To treat the language of 'hauntology' as a stable concept, as Luckhurst and others do, is to misunderstand the very practice of criticism that Derrida instantiated and Wolfreys remains attuned to. Yet it is worth paying attention to those instances in which Wolfreys does explore the ethical call of the other through the hauntological.

Wolfreys' most sustained elaboration of the hauntological is in *Victorian Hauntings: Spectrality, the Uncanny and Literature*. It is here that he utilizes Derridean ghosting and spectrality to explore the 'powerful form of displacement' the 'trace of non-identity within identity' which characterize alterity (Wolfreys 2002 1). Wolfreys is clear here that he invokes Derrida not because of some pleasant confluence between theory and object, but because the question of 'what constitutes the textual as being haunted' is of vital importance. Its importance is, ultimately, that it 'resists conceptualization and one cannot form a coherent theory of the spectral without that which is spectral having always already exceeded any definition' (Wolfreys 2002 ix–x). It is as a reading practice that Wolfreys turns to spectrality, not as a thematic device. This is an important distinction to my mind and one that I will seek to elaborate, albeit along a very different path. The perpetual displacement that underpins spectrality will be mirrored in a displacement of London itself.

Roger Luckhurst's intervention in the debate around the London Gothic is an attempt to move away from what he sees as a universalizing or flattening effect of the deconstructive position. It is important for Luckhurst that the Gothic is a contested term for contemporary literary practice. This is precisely because the Gothic and the 'postmodern' make all too easy bed-fellows. As Punter and Byron state:

> The postmodern, one might suggest, is the site of a certain "haunting", and in this sense is never free itself from the ghosts of the past, even as if it takes as its task the constant (and constantly dubious) reconstruction of the past. (Punter and Byron 53)

Luckhurst then takes issue not just with the critical practice of hauntology, but with the ways in which forms of contemporary genre fictions can return to the serious concerns of the Gothic with all the frivolity of the postmodern: 'Is this Gothic revival and its fascination with its own generic past anything more than self-referential involution – a kind of return of "return of the repressed" as empty postmodern pastiche?' (Luckhurst 530). For Luckhurst this Gothic revival is not the whole story, and there are more serious textual practices that require more serious critical approaches.

The main target though, as I suggested, is not the Gothic as empty cultural production, but the 'spectral turn' in criticism and theory. As he states:

> the critical language of spectral or haunted modernity that has become a cultural-critical shorthand in the wake of *Spectres of Marx* can go only so far in elaborating the contexts of that specified topography of this London Gothic – that, indeed, the generalized structure of haunting is symptomatically blind to its generative loci. (Luckhurst 530)

For Luckhurst it is the very particular context of London and its government that is at the root of its contemporary insistence on the Gothic: no other genre is able to do justice to the ways in which London is haunted by the 'tyranny and farce' that characterize politics in the city. Luckhurst turns to the usual suspect – Iain Sinclair – along with Christopher Fowler to briefly trace this more politicized Gothic. While there is a certain political and critical force in this return to historical and contextual specificity over a generalized 'spookiness', I don't think Luckhurst goes far enough, or rather not in the right direction. In his insistence upon the place-based specificity of the cultural production of the city he ends up perpetuating an idea of place, and it is place that remains at the 'limit' of the Gothic, not some sort of universalisable alterity. In short Luckhurst, in rejecting the deconstructive hauntology of Wolfreys and others has reinstated a conservative idea of place by claiming the singularity of London Gothic.

The argument I want to follow here proceeds out of an understanding of something like a 'cultural cartography'; the rather obvious idea that place is culturally contingent and inessential, a fact which must be obfuscated in an attempt to make each manufactured locale appear specific and singular. Literary and other forms of cultural production are often complicit in an attempt to construct organic myths of place, myths that tend to cover over the politics at work in privileging a 'generative loci'. 'London Gothic' doesn't work. If Gothic is able to work to destabilize and undermine those solid identities that are tied to such notions as place, it ought not work to reproduce the logic of continuity and essentialism that is at work in the idea of a 'London Literature'. It is precisely this argument that, I will demonstrate, underpins Stewart Home's *Down and Out in Shoreditch and Hoxton*. But for Home there is nothing left of the Gothic, or an idea of a London literature worth recuperating. Instead his novel uses a drastic form of Horror, or Weird to destroy the saccharine image of London produced for us by the Gothic.

From Gothic to Horror to Weird

In order to outline Home's critique of the Gothic, and his attempt to develop a Weird destruction of place, it is worth looking, however briefly, at the contested nature of Gothic and its others. The proliferation of academic work on the Gothic reveals a curious double-bind. There is something deeply attractive about the Gothic, both past and present, yet there is a constant anxiety that the 'Gothic' is a thoroughly exhausted critical framework and perhaps worth jettisoning altogether. For David Punter academic criticism has reached the point at which the Gothic and our critical paradigms for examining it have achieved a 'peculiar confluence':

> The Gothic speaks of, indeed we might say it attempts to invoke, spectres: Derrida, in, for example, *Spectres of Marx*, chooses the same rhetoric to talk about what we might term the 'suppressed of Europe'. Gothic has to do with

the uncanny: the uncanny has come now to form one of the major sites on which the reinvestigation of Freud and the institutions of psychoanalysis can take place. . . . we need to be very careful about the implications of this curious collocation, as we need to be when any mode of criticism appears to get too close to its subject matter and finds itself losing the critical distance of alienation. (Punter xi)

As the brief survey above has revealed this is nowhere more obvious than in the case of a London Gothic in which we either have a proliferation of Gothic frameworks for exploring its literature, or the opposite extreme of a critical apparatus that denies the Gothic its disruptive power. To move beyond a London Gothic I'd like to start at the beginning, with that strange enmity between the Gothic and its cheap twin, Horror.

One could be forgiven for thinking that 'Gothic' and 'Horror' are inter-changeable. Many contemporary studies will flip-flop between the two, or see one as an essential component of the other. Take Clive Bloom, for example, who states:

horror is the usual but not necessarily the main ingredient of gothic fiction and most popular gothic fiction is determined in its plotting by the need for horror and sensation. It was gothicism, with its formality, codification, ritual-istic elements and artifice . . . that transformed the old folk tale of terror into the modern horror story. (Bloom 2–3)

The idea of horror as an ingredient in the force of Gothic works in many ways to obscure the tension between terror and horror as two very distinct modes of the Gothic. The most well-known definition is from Anne Radcliffe's essay 'On the Supernatural in Poetry'.

'They must be men of very cold imaginations,' said W—, 'with whom cer-tainty is more terrible than surmise. Terror and horror are so far opposite, that the first expands the soul, and awakens the faculties to a high degree of life; the other contracts, freezes, and nearly annihilates them. I apprehend, that neither Shakespeare nor Milton by their fictions, nor Mr. Burke by his reasoning, anywhere looked to positive horror as a source of the sublime, though they all agree that terror is a very high one; and where lies the great difference between horror and terror, but in the uncertainty and obscurity, that accompany the first, respecting the dreaded evil?' (Radcliffe 168)

Here Radcliffe's separation is one maintained on the positive, transformative effect of the terror associated with Gothic and the rather less refined abject hor-ror. There is also an important moral dimension – terror will always attempt to develop a heightened moral state in the reader whereas horror's 'obscurity' in regard to Evil means that it maintains an ambivalence. The distinction that

Radcliffe drew is, so far as most commentators are concerned, no longer so clearly demarcated, if it exists at all. Angela Wright describes the distinction as 'haunting' Gothic criticism, largely because of the heterogeneous and fluid nature of the two terms, 'because underneath the arch of "Gothic" we continue to assemble a disparate collection of texts which share a fascination with persecuted heroines, gloomy villains, castles and monasteries' (Wright 36). If one was to make a meaningful distinction for the contemporary it would be that Gothic is far more often about atmosphere, allusion and an uncannyness, whereas Horror is graphic, gory and lacking in any subtlety. Horror may use Gothic tropes, but will do so with a complete lack of subtlety, rolling them out as a set of stock motifs but without the more deeply unsettling implications that the 'higher' art of Gothic could induce.

However rather than attempting to align Stewart Home's novel with one or the other of these critically uncertain terms, I'd like to instead investigate his work as being part of the Weird tradition which destabilizes the already confused distinction between Horror and the Gothic and, as I will explore below, is utilized in *Down and Out* to destroy both 'London' and the Gothic. Horror is regarded as undergoing some sort of transformation in the late nineteenth- and early twentieth-century as the genre of 'weird' fiction developed, exponents including H. P. Lovecraft, William Hope Hodgson, Arthur Machen M. R. James and Algernon Blackwood and other writers, some of whom published in the magazine *Weird Tales*. Despite the proliferation of novelists grouped under the moniker 'weird' it is Lovecraft whose fictional and critical practice dominates how we think of the weird. Lovecraft famously defined the critical practice of Weird in his 1939 extended essay *Supernatural Horror in Literature*. It still provides an instructive demarcation of Weird, though one that is certainly contestable in the genre today. Importantly for Lovecraft it is the atmospherics of the fiction and its existential effects that are of vital importance. As he states:

> The true weird tale has something more than secret murder, bloody bones, or a sheeted form clanking chains according to rule. A certain atmosphere of breathless and unexplainable dread of outer, unknown forces must be present; and there must be a hint, expressed with a seriousness and portentousness becoming its subject, of that most terrible conception of the human brain – a malign and particular suspension or defeat of those fixed laws of Nature which are our only safeguard against the assaults of chaos and the daemons of unplumbed space. (Lovecraft 15)

The primary distinction to my mind is that of affect over convention. Horror can be found anywhere, but not necessarily in the stock symbols and metaphors that have come to stand in for the experience themselves. This is an important distinction as we proceed where Home will create a 'certain atmosphere' that works to destabilize the 'rule' of London Gothic, but will ultimately work to destabilize any recourse to a Lovecraftian atmospherics as well.

In weirding Lovecraft, Home can be aligned with some of the Weird fiction that is now an important element of contemporary horror with exponents such as Thomas Ligotti and Ramsey Campbell. Whereas Gothic might want to raise moral questions, Weird fiction is far more existential. Writers like Ligotti are unapologetically nihilistic and bleak, forcing readers to ask fundamental questions about the nature of existence, rather than trying to return them to some moral status quo. Thomas Ligotti, for instance, argues that the human race will manage to kill itself off before it might, with one voice cry out 'Enough of this error of conscious life. It shall be passed down no longer to those innocents unborn' (Ligotti 258). Ligotti's condemnation of the human as conscious animal is far removed from the rather more placid conventions of the Gothic, and readers of Ligotti's work will be familiar with a horror that refuses to conform to convention. Recently China Miéville has categorized the differences between the Gothic and Weird fiction:

> The weird then is starkly opposed to the hauntological. Hauntology, a category positing, presuming, implying a 'time out of joint', a present stained with traces of the ghostly, the dead-but-unquiet estranges reality in an almost precisely opposite fashion to the Weird: with a radicalised uncanny – 'something which is secretly familiar, which has undergone repression and then returned from it' – rather than an hallucinatory nihilist novum. . . . The Weird is not the return of any repressed: though always described as ancient and half recalled by characters from spurious texts, this recruitment to invented cultural memory does not avail weird monsters of Gothic's strategy of revenance, but back-projects their radical unremembered alterity into history to en-Weird ontology itself. (Miéville 112–13)

To my mind Miéville's distinction, and his identification of a possible reunification of the hauntological and the Weird are important in thinking about how we might think beyond the neo-liberal Gothic of contemporary London. For Miéville the separation between hauntology and Weird is one that is indicative of the separation of capital, and if horror fiction is to act as an agent of critique it must be Weird. The Gothic's obsession with revenance and the sins of the past has a very problematic relationship to the heritage industry and associations of gentrification, as Home explicitly and repeatedly details. Home's own 'hallucinatory nihilist novum' works precisely in order to destabilize the relationship between revenance, commodification and London.

Stewart Home's London

Stewart Home's fictional works are some of the most unusual in contemporary literature. In equal measures of vulgarity and pretension they provide a self-reflexive critique of the role of fiction in today's cultural economy, demonstrating an allusive range that makes no concessions to its readers. Part hardcore pornography, part hard-left diatribe, Home's books are designed to outrage, appal and frustrate yet do so in such a way that underpins any critical position – whether moralizing or aesthetic – we may desire to take in response. Home's first novel, *Pure Mania*, was published in 1989 by Polygon. A tale of East London council estate skinheads, filled with sex, violence and ruminations on politics and art it set the tone for much of Home's fictional production throughout the 1990s. It wasn't, however, until the publication of *69 Things to do with a Dead Princess* (2002) that Home's work was increasingly noticed by academics and more broadly reviewed in the literary press. This is no great surprise as its self-reflexive pastiche of postmodernism is the sort of thing academics love – the layers of irony and critique are so densely woven it is impossible to provide any stable reading. Yet that in itself is an irony as it is written with an eye to destabilizing the jargon of the academy and the pretension of its readers.

Home's status as a 'London' writer is certainly contestable. Many of his novels, in particular the early skinhead genre-bending novels, are set on the council estates of East London with later works such as *Tainted Love* (2005) exploring the London of the 1960s. Yet *69 Things* is set in Aberdeenshire and his most recent novel, *Memphis Underground* (2007), is primarily set in a remote Scottish community. However Home's fictional and critical practice is deeply linked to the tradition of the London underground, with which Home has been associated since the 1970s. Many of Home's references are to London avant-garde writers, punk music and artists and he has himself been involved in (or the sole exponent of) London art 'movements' like Neoism. While Home is certainly a chronicler of the London avant-garde and has spent the majority of his life living in the capital, he is painfully aware of the dangers of authenticity that come with the moniker 'London writer'. In the biography on his website Home satirizes the cockneyer-than-thou tendencies of many 'London' writers stating 'He lives in London. Thames water, rather than blood, is said to run through Home's veins.'[2]

During the course of the 1990s Home became more regularly identified as a 'London' writer through being reviewed and interviewed by Iain Sinclair, first in the *London Review of Books* in 1994, then in *Lights Out for the Territory* (1997) and more recently *Hackney, That Rose Red Empire* (2009). Sinclair's inclusion of Home into his now familiar pantheon of excoriated London visionaries is indicative of a mode of Gothic fabulation that I will suggest is anathema to Home's work:

> What was Home's background and how did he come to achieve such a grip on the Matter of London? . . . Home simply had to open his windows and plug in his word processor. The books wrote themselves. They were anonymous, mediumistic, so rapidly produced that no single press could keep up with them. Other voyants have equalled Home for pace, usually with the aid of performance-enhancing substances. Home had something better. Home had Hackney. (Sinclair 217)

Sinclair's language here is almost explicitly that of the Gothic, one that attempts to give the city a spiritual energy that is accessible to only the most in-tune of visionaries. Home is thus turned into a shamanic figure who can be mythologized into Sinclair's Gothicized London. As Sinclair is so keen to remind us his counter-mythography of the city is in contradistinction to that of the banal images of gaslight and fog that feature in marketing of literary London, yet that is not to say that it does not suffer the same fate as its more compromised counterpart. As Home so satirically demonstrates it is almost impossible to undertake avant-garde cultural production that isn't on the verge of being dragged back into mainstream commodification. It is perhaps only the Weird, a fiction of banal pornography intersecting with Marxist rants and ending in a cosmic apocalypse that is able to escape the nauseating production of London Gothic.

Transgression and the Logic of Capital

Perhaps the most important feature of Home's writing, and one that is often overlooked in reviews and commentary, is the complex critique of cultural production under capitalism. *Down and Out in Shoreditch and Hoxton*, like all of Home's work, is marked by an experimentation with genre, crossing from high-brow to the lowest forms of erotica and violent pulp fiction in order to subvert notions of cultural value, reader expectations, and destabilize the novel form, which Home regards as effectively dead. In addition every paragraph is exactly 100 words long, a feature of which Home states 'this was a way of forcing myself to write differently and simultaneously of self-consciously signifying to readers how distinctions between poetry and prose don't really work. This book is both poetry and prose.'[3] Home here identifies the paradox of form: it simultaneously guides us by providing a set of generic conventions, yet those conventions are largely arbitrary. In making such an arbitrary limit on the construction of his novel, Home demonstrates precisely how formulaic expectations cannot help us alone to construct meaning. Our frames of reference need to instead work beyond the arbitrary illusions of form and genre. Simultaneously our ideas of social relation need, for Home, to stretch out beyond their relation to commodification. It is this set of stylistic and formal features that, I believe, mark Home's work as an important intervention in London fiction and performatively work to maintain the critique of gentrification that the book explicitly states with the experiments in form tied to his form of critique.

This refuse can be seen at work in the scene in which Alan Abel is fucked to death. The scene consists of passage after passage in which a different girl is brought in and their intercourse is economically summarized in hundred words. There are forty-two such paragraphs, all following a formulaic structure, some even just substituting names as the only difference. The cumulative effect is a boredom far from titillation in which the women, even the spectacularly anachronistic inclusion of Simone De Beauvoir and Melanie Klein, all become one giant monotonous entity. Here the prose enacts the boredom of transgression. Transgression relies on excitement, a novel rupture of a situation. The repetition and forced nature of the prose underpins the fact that transgression is forced, created by a social structure – here class and gender – and perpetuated as a series of encounters that are only palatable in isolation.

As a symbolic gesture the snuff film captures Home's arguments surrounding sex, death and commodification. Scald, as someone who gets off on transgression through commodified sex, wants to simultaneously be titillated, yet to retain a complete sense of control and class boundary. As the narrator states: 'having constituted himself as a bourgeois subject, Scald insisted on projecting his own limitations as a universally valid "human condition"' (*Down and Out* 46). As is often the case in Home's fiction he takes the logic of this bourgeois notion of transgression within a controlling and universalizing centred subject and pushes it to its logical conclusion. Here we see Home's aesthetic working in a sense analogous to Adorno. In *Aesthetic Theory* Adorno stated:

> Capitalist society hides and disavows precisely this irrationality, and in contrast to this, art represents truth in a double sense: It maintains the image of its aim, which has been obscured by rationality, and it convicts the status quo of its irrationality and its absurdity. (Adorno 53–55)

Home's novel is then to be read not as a piece of fabulist fiction, its absurd fantasy and temporal incongruity become not a symptom, but a critique of the illogic of contemporary modes of production, and in particular the production that can turn the brutal deaths of five exploited women into a sanitized marketing exercise.

Gentrification and Jack the Ripper

The plot of *Down and Out* is, for the most part, fairly straightforward: a young female artist, the narrator Eve, has undertaken a performance art project whereby she sets out to become a prostitute in order to maintain the history of the area which is being eroded by gentrification. She markets herself to the true crime customer for those who want to be serviced on the sites of Jack the Ripper murders, and other such unusual fetishes. The book then consists of relating the resultant experiences with her intelligent middle class customers which entails repetitive, graphic sex alongside extended discussions on art and Marxist aesthetics. Forced into the Tower Hamlet's graveyard to continue plying her trade the narration and plot become increasingly odd, entering into the realm of fantasy and supernatural culminating in a bizarre solar eclipse. Yet, as always with Stewart Home, narrative is superfluous.

Down and Out in Shoreditch and Hoxton is awash with the traces of London Gothic. But this is not just any London Gothic, but one that is intrinsically tied to the gentrification of the East End, and in particular to the rusty razor-blade industry surrounding Jack the Ripper. David Cunningham has recently provided an incisive picture of the relationship between gentrification and the New Heritage that has fed the spread of London Gothic. For Cunningham there are two different levels to the Gothic attraction of Jack the Ripper. One is the banal waxworks of the London Dungeon, Madame Tussaud's and Jack the Ripper walking tours. These spectacles are designed primarily for tourists, set in 'an instantly recognizable stage set consisting of a narrow, dark Victorian street, each woman is safely abstracted from the specificities of place' (Cunningham 162). Cunnningham argues that this sort of Gothic spectacle turns the historical incident into myth, with Jack the Ripper 'a figure of "fiction" a Gothic image . . . who belongs within a larger cast of late nineteenth-century characters, including Sherlock Homes, Jekyll and Hyde, Dracula and Dorian Gray, populating an imaginary fog-engulfed city' (Cunningham 167). The placelessness of this mythic London is often seen as opposed to the London of writers such as Sinclair, Ackroyd and Moorcock. Sinclair is particularly scathing of the ways in which an invented Gothic has been utilized to market Spitalfields: 'The dingy streets held residues of Georgian London, cloacal smears from the victims of Jack the Ripper, poverty statistics customized by Arthur Morrison. This was the Gothic imagination tamed by social reformers' (Sinclair and Lichtestein 174). Yet as much as writers such as Sinclair may wish to distance themselves from the world of commodifiable history and cultural capital, the reality is they cannot. Ludovic Hunter-Tilney, in a review of Sinclair's novel *Dining on Stones*, captures this perfectly: 'Just as Sinclair has moved from obscurity to the mainstream, so too have the hidden, unglamorous parts of east London that he writes about, transformed by the city's recent property boom. The anxiety at the heart of his writing is that he is implicated in its gentrification, like a siren voice luring property developers and literary acolytes alike' (Hunter-Tilney 30). The implication of 'alternative' historiography in the new heritage of the East End indeed presents a number of problems for literary London.[1] Cunningham sees, like Hunter-Tilney, a dovetailing of alternative cultural production and gentrification, suggesting conservationism has been replaced with a 'new' heritage, whose 'Gothic' qualities have been appropriated by a new monopoly rent culture: 'In its own Gothic form, capital feasts vampirically off the "negative", recuperating and reforming it to its own purposes' (Cunningham 170). It is this vampiric nature of capitalism and its Gothic mascot that Home confronts in his novel, attempting to think the possibility of critique in this brave 'new' world of gentrified East London.

Throughout *Down and Out* Home refers to 'the new Shoreditch' and the text contains many references to the bars and clubs of the 'trendies' who now populate the area. The arrival of the gentrifying middle classes has of course resulted in the destruction, or at least perversion, of that identity which had always marked the area as other to the wealth and power of the city. The most immediate effect for our narrator Eve, who is also a sometime historian of her most ancient of trades, is that she can no longer ply it as she once had. As the narrator states there is:

> evidence that common prostitutes has plied their trade here for at least 400 years. Now things were changing. Warehouses converted to loft apartments. Kwik Save gone. Hoxton, Shoreditch, Spitalfields would never be the same. I wanted to bring back the image of the dell, the doxie, the bawdy basket to an area that gentrification was trying to sweep clean. (*Down and Out* 7)

The narrator's project is one of cultural memory, trying to keep the spirit of place alive. Yet the gesture is not one of Ackroydian or Sinclairian fabulation. As an artist the narrator now struggles to pay her rent in the spiralling property market in the area. Therefore she needs the money she makes from prostitution to survive. So here the need to provide an alternative history is intricately connected with the economic conditions of the present. Effectively, the marauding middle classes are screwing the area, so Eve, our narrator, is forced to screw them back.

One of Eve's clients, Alfie Cain, is making a film about Jack the Ripper. Indicative of the creative industries' desperation to make a cheap quid he has hit on an ingenious twist – have a Karl Marx look-a-like play the Ripper:

> Alfie insisted this prank would spring him out of the art ghetto. Right wing journalists were bound to fall for a hoax about Marx being a homicidal maniac and the liberal press would ridicule them for believing a man who died before the Ripper murders took place could be a credible suspect. Cain was expecting a publicity bonanza. (*Down and Out* 80)

The cheap opportunism of using the London Gothic as a vehicle for fame and fortune encapsulates the danger of using the motifs of a generic category that can easily shift from being destabilizing to becoming perfectly banal and empty. It also mirrors Cunningham's argument as to the vampiric nature of the new heritage and the blurring boundaries between 'alternative' and mainstream cultural production.

Home's novel works to introduce all the major figures: Dickens, Jack the Ripper, Thomas de Quincey, William Blake, along with some more marginal figures such as Thomas Dekker, etc. Yet as Home makes clear all of these are little more than a marketing tool. While Sinclair uses the Ripper myth as a form of reading the occult history of the East End, Home uses it as the founding myth of the regenerated new East End. This is confirmed as Eve uncovers the true identity of her fellow streetwalker, Amy:

She wasn't really a crack hoe, that was just her cover story. She was actually a marketing consultant who'd been paid to draw gullible trippers into the East End. She'd figured that if murdered prostitutes could be transformed into a money-spinner, then cutting up a few of the men who paid for sex would serve to increase the lucrative trade generated by the Ripper trail. Amy wanted to diversify the appeal of the murder sites by adding a feminist frisson. (*Down and Out* 102)

If the feminist critique of the misogynistic and voyeuristic appeal of Ripperology is to copy its logic for the sake of profit then what can be left, both as a remainder and politically for the London novel?

From London Gothic to Weird Nowhere

Down and Out in Shoreditch and Hoxton identifies the Victorian period as the locus for the creation of the London Gothic. It was in this period that London Gothic begins to develop a stock series of motifs that will be drawn out at any moment. Eve is keen to avoid this clichéd image of a literary London, but is soon drawn into it through her association with Adam Scald: 'I'd been trying to avoid the Victorian period – but thanks to all of its historic resonances, this was what the matter of London always drew the psychohistorian towards, or rather forced her to fight against' (*Down and Out* 65). This battle against the Victorian period rears its head throughout; largely through Jack the Ripper's hold over many of the characters, as well as the pall of Dickensian London. Eve gives over a rather long excursus into the failure of Dickens, particularly in *David Copperfield*, to do anything more than become the celebrant of bourgeois values. But it is not until the novel reaches a Gothic crescendo before the cosmic apocalypse that is the satire of Gothic can be seen in all its power.

After a time the narrator professes herself bored with the task of describing the scene and, after killing Alan, runs outside. At the same time we see a dramatic shift in prose, the entry of a parody of London Gothic:

the stillness of the air grew quite oppressive, and the silence was so marked that snoring and the creaking of old stairs could be heard like a discord in the harmony of nature's silence. . . . Grey, wet clouds, which swept by in ghostly fashion, so dank and damp and cold that it needed but little effort of imagination to think that the spirits of earlier generation were greeting the living with the touch of death. (*Down and Out* 134)

Home is here laying the Gothic motifs on as thickly as possible, reducing atmospherics to a series of clichés. In doing so he signals the impossibility of using the Gothic as a mode of critique in London. Saturated and exhausted Home knows that his reader will retreat into a fictional image of the city which will simultaneously be placed at odds with, but covertly in support of, the gentrification that has transformed the East End.

Home's response is, however, not to return to some sort of 'realism' – which he associates with bourgeois values and the attempt to develop categories of taste: 'The novel is a paradigmatically bourgeois cultural form, so a good novel is inherently reactionary – only bad books can be revolutionary' – instead Home turns the Gothic into its over-driven other, a weird Horror. Home's gesture to Lovecraft is, I would argue, working on two levels. On one it is the level of parody – not hard with a writer as readily identifiable as Lovecraft. On the other I believe that Home salvages some critical position from the remnants of the weird – that of a destroyed London. The novel's critical position is one that is based upon the commodification of a particular image of the city. Home's new London is one in which the brooding light of the Gothic is shattered by the arrival of the Weird:

> There were trampings and a sound like something heavy being laid on the floor, such, for instance, as must have been made when the mummy of the pharaoh was set down for its last journey to the western banks of the Nile. There was a strange play of light. This light was pale and ghostly, though very penetrating and tinged with blue. At first it arose to form a kind of fan or fountain. But what was this that stood at the door now radiating glory? It was Osiris himself, God of the Dead, the Egyptian saviour of the world! (*Down and Out* 138)

The laughable oddness of the arrival of Osiris works to relocate the mythic work of hauntology to an hallucinatory space of destruction. This destruction of the hauntological is also a destruction of revenance as a critical tool. No longer can we think of a haunting of place as a powerful metaphor for alterity. Instead alterity has become ontological rather than identitarian. We have a weirdness of being that works to unwork the categories of identification on which the essentialism of place can rest. There can be no valorization of the Gothic precisely because it has been used to obscure meaningful social relations and replace them with, as Home suggests, an 'obsession with cultural objects'. It is only once the cultural objects of our spectacular age have been destroyed that we can rethink relations anew. And for Home what better place to start than with the destruction of London as a privileged site of literature, and the Gothic as its genre of choice: 'The world turned. London wasn't even a ruin. It had disappeared from the face of eternity and the cosmos' (*Down and Out* 200). This 'hallucinatory nihilist novum' is, to my mind, an improvement on London Gothic.

Notes

[1] I have explored the echolalic model of representing the city at length in (2007), *Recalling London: Literature and History in the work of Peter Ackroyd and Iain Sinclair.* London: Continuum, 21–48.

² http://www.stewarthomesociety.org/biography.htm, accessed 26/11/2009

³ Interview with *Flux*, circa 2004 'DOWN & DIRTY: STEWART HOME SPEAKS TO FLUX ABOUT HEREOS, ANTI-HEROES AND HIS NOVEL *DOWN & OUT IN SHOREDITCH & HOXTON*', http://www.stewarthomesociety.org/interviews/litpol.htm 09/12/2009

¹ I have explored New Heritage's appropriation of the Sinclairian method in the conclusion to *Recalling London*.

Works Cited

Adorno, T. (2002), *Aesthetic Theory*, trans. Robert Hullot-Kentor, London: Continuum

Bloom, C. (ed.) (2007), *Gothic Horror: a Guide for Students and Readers* (second edn), London: Palgrave Macmillan

Cunningham, D. (2007), 'Living in the Slashing Grounds: Jack the Ripper, Monopoly Rent and the New Heritage', in Alex Warwick and Martin Willis (eds), *Jack the Ripper: Media, Culture, History*, Manchester University Press, 159–78

Home, S. (2004), *Down and Out in Shoreditch and Hoxton*, London: Do Not Press

Hunter-Tilney, L. (8 May 2004), 'Review of Dining on Stones' in *Financial Times, Weekend Magazine*, 30

Ligotti, T. (2008), 'Thinking Horror', *Collapse IV*, 208–60

Lovecraft, H. P. (1973), *Supernatural Horror in Literature*, London: Dover

Luckhurst, R. (2002), 'The Contemporary London Gothic and the Limits of the "Spectral Turn"', *Textual Practice* 16(3), 527–46

Miéville, C. (2008), 'M.R. James and the Quantum Vampire: Weird; Hauntological: versus and/or or and/or or', *Collapse IV*, 105–28

Murray, A. (2007), *Recalling London: Literature and History in the work of Peter Ackroyd and Iain Sinclair*, London: Continuum

Punter, D. (2001), 'Introduction: the Ghosts of History', in *A Companion to the Gothic*, David Punter (ed.), Oxford: Blackwell

Punter, D. and Glennis Byron (2004), *The Gothic*, Oxford: Blackwell

Radcliffe, A. (2000), 'On the Supernatural in Poetry', in E. J. Cleary and Robert Miles (eds), *Gothic Documents: a Sourcebook, 1700–1820*, Manchester: Manchester University Press, 163–72

Sinclair, I. (1997), *Lights Out for the Territory*, London: Granta

Sinclair, I. and Rachel Lichtestein (1999), *Rodinsky's Room*, London: Granta

Wolfreys, J. (1998), *Writing London: the Trace of the Urban Text from Blake to Dickens*, London: Macmillan

Wolfreys, J. (2002), *Victorian Hauntings: Spectrality, the Uncanny and Literature*, London: Palgrave

Wright, A. (2007), *Gothic Fiction: a Reader's Guide to Essential Criticism*, Houndsmill: Palgrave Macmillan

Chapter 7

'[T]hat Eventless Realm': Hilary Mantel's *Beyond Black* and the Ghosts of the M25

Catherine Spooner

The M25, the orbital motorway surrounding Greater London, may not seem a likely site for the Gothic. Begun piecemeal in the 1970s and finally completed in 1986 under the auspices of Thatcher's government, it is a monument to modern urban planning, the supremacy of the motorcar, and the unremitting spread of the suburbs. 117 miles long and spanning twelve lanes at its widest point, it forms an enormous bypass, directing an incessant stream of congested traffic away from the historically layered, labyrinthine urban centre and its more conventionally Gothic geographies.

Yet the M25 also figures, in its own way, as a Gothic landscape. J. G. Ballard's *Crash* (1973) anticipated the existential horrors of the M25 in its exploration of the non-places of the London road-system via its protagonist's pornographic fixation with car crashes. *Crash* has been variously described by Melissa Iocco as deploying 'familiar Gothic tropes and effects' (Iocco 46) and by Jim Byatt as an inverted ghost story in which the living haunt the dead (Byatt). More directly, Iain Sinclair's non-fictional account of his walks around the M25, *London Orbital* (2002), traces the motorway's occluded histories and occulted geographies, including those of Carfax Abbey, where Bram Stoker located Dracula's English residence, and the nineteenth-century asylums for the mentally ill that ring the capital. For Sinclair, the M25 is 'The point where London loses it, gives up its ghosts' (Sinclair 3). Sinclair captures the M25's ambivalence: the point where London stops being London is the point where the city's ghostliness is exhausted, comes to an end; but also the point where ghosts are made visible, are released.

The narrative that draws most overtly on a conventional Gothic vocabulary, however, is Hilary Mantel's *Beyond Black* (2005), the tale of a professional spirit medium, Alison Hart, who lives and works in the zone that buffers London from the provincial hinterlands. Mantel's satirical novel presents the outer suburbs as, against the odds, a haunted landscape; a landscape in which the living have become indistinguishable from the dead. Covering much of the same geographical territory as Sinclair, and similar reference points (in *London Orbital*

Sinclair notes a sign for a 'PSYCHIC FAYRE' as he leaves Potter's Bar, and tarot readers in barges along the Grand Union Canal), Mantel ultimately presents a very different vision of the M25; a comic and partially affirmative one that accommodates the domestic, interior and private. As Alison and Collette 'strike out east beyond the Thames barrier', Alison notes:

> The world outside the glass is the world of masculine action. Everything she sees is what a man has built. But at each turn-off, each junction, women are waiting to know their fate. They are looking deep inside themselves, into their private hearts, where the foetus forms and buds, where the shape forms inside the crystal, where the fingernails click softly at the backs of cards. (*Beyond Black* 237–38)

In contrast to Sinclair's exploration of the world outside the glass, his deconstruction of the masculine architecture of the city's hinterlands, Mantel explores the interior spaces that overlie the exterior ones. Her M25 is not, like Sinclair's 'Endless Landscape', a chain of suggestively interchangeable pieces, but rather a series of overlapping worlds (Sinclair 162).

Beyond Black poses the question: what does it mean to be haunted in a culture with no history? If a society has no interest in its personal and collective past, then in what form can that past return? If ghosts, moreover, have traditionally been associated with locations with a dense historical charge – castles, abbeys, stately homes, places that have seen decades or even centuries of human use – then how can they manifest in what Marc Augé (1995) has called the 'non-places' of supermodernity – the motorways, shopping malls, and gated communities symptomatic of contemporary culture? Mantel's novel conjures a specific time and place, 'the conurbations that clustered around the junctions of the M25, and the corridors of the M3 and M4' in the final years of the millennium (*Beyond Black* 10). At the same time, it uses the metaphor of the spirit world, as revealed to Alison, to suggest that the space tracked by the London Orbital is 'beyond geography and history' (*Beyond Black* 44), a dead zone in which community is fragmented and memory lost, swallowed by an affectless consumer culture.

Mantel's novel can be set against an earlier tradition of supernatural narrative, one in which ghosts are historically rooted in particular communities and locations. According to Michel de Certeau, it is the presence of 'the stories and legends that haunt urban space' that makes a place habitable. As he writes in *The Practice of Everyday Life*: 'It is through the opportunity they offer to store up rich silences and wordless stories, or rather through their capacity to create cellars and garrets everywhere, that local legends . . . permit exits, ways of coming out and going back in, and thus habitable spaces' (de Certeau 106). He is not referring only to ghost stories; indeed if anything the trope of haunting stands, in his text, for a much broader register of narrative traces on a given environment. Nevertheless, his argument is suggestive in relation to Mantel's novel; the inhospitability of the outer suburbs to local stories and legends paralyses both their living and dead inhabitants, sending them 'round in a ring' like T. S. Eliot's damned souls, or drivers on the London Orbital. It is the job of Alison, the medium, to narrativize these presences, to unblock the exits and make these hostile spaces habitable.

Jennifer Westwood and Jacqueline Simpson, writing about English folklore and local legends, suggest that:

> On one level, many [stories] grow out of a community's natural curiosity about itself and its surroundings . . . On a second level, they echo and enhance the community's pride in its own identity, highlighting some striking event which its neighbours cannot match. (Westwood and Simpson viii)

Ghosts, in common with other kinds of folklore, are thus both a means of interpreting a place, and a source of identity. The ghost-story writer Vernon Lee insisted that place was crucial in conjuring the presence of fictional ghosts: 'Do not these embodied ghosts owe what little effect they possess to their surroundings, and are not the surroundings the real ghost?' (Lee 311). The conventional expression, 'spirit of place', has an attractive etymological proximity to the ghostly. Ghosts are both defined by place and define places.

While ghosts have always appeared in Gothic fictions, and indeed in other forms of literature before that, the ghost story as a specific literary form arose in the mid-nineteenth century, coincident with both the rise of spiritualism and the emergence of folklore studies. The ghost story was marked by a tendency to relocate the exotic European settings of earlier Gothic novels to a British landscape characterized as remotely rural, or to historic urban centres such as London, Edinburgh and Dublin. During the same period, folklorists tended to collect their data in what they perceived to be the most remote regions of the UK, so that large cities and their swiftly expanding suburbs are relatively absent from their accounts. Westwood and Simpson, whose book *The Lore of the Land* draws on folklore archives in order to construct a supernatural cartography of England, attribute this in large part to the presumptions of those gathering the data: 'In particular, it was taken for granted . . . that the counties closest to London would have lost much of their traditional lore because of industrialization and the movement of population, whereas remote rural communities would be more rewarding' (Westwood and Simpson viii). Their map of London confirms this thesis; there is a very dense cluster of phenomena in the centre of the city, with a couple of peripheral clusters at Highgate and Hampton Court, but otherwise the vast expanses of the suburbs are mostly devoid of legend, the most striking empty expanse to feature on any of the maps in the book. While their own survey is not conducted according to strict scientific principles and involves a degree of authorial selectivity, if anything this further confirms their argument; they too find the dichotomy of urban centre and rural outposts the most effective means of structuring ghostly geographies, and the most promising environments for supernatural narrative.

Mantel is not the first writer to place ghosts in this supernatural no-man's-land; in the nineteenth century a number of writers, most prominently Charlotte Riddell, published suburban ghost stories. However, while these earlier suburban ghost stories tend to focus on the uncanniness of domestic space, Mantel's reinvention of ghostly geographies maps the dislocation of an entire society. By relocating the historically rooted urban and rural ghosts of folklore and Gothic narrative into the suggestive non-place of the outer suburbs, Mantel blocks, or reverses, the traditional function of hauntings. In Gothic texts, ghosts are conventionally a manifestation of the past returning: they offer confirmation of history, albeit often a mythical or fantasized one; they allow people to remember, and trauma to be worked through. So, to give a London-based example, in Dickens' tale 'To Be Taken With a Grain of Salt', the ghost of a murdered man appears in order to convict his killer, and only vanishes once justice has been done and the historical record made straight. In Mantel's novel, however, only Alison herself is allowed this means of resolving her past through coming to terms with haunting – for the population at large, hauntings indicate not the presence of history, but its erasure. Moreover the manifestation of ghosts does not deliver a sense of place or enhance communal identity, but rather illustrates its fragmentation. If, according to sociologist Avery Gordon, the ghost is a 'social figure' (Gordon 8) that marks the presence of something missing or lost, then the swarm of ghosts inhabiting the 'marginal land' flanking the M25 seems to indicate an entire culture adrift (*Beyond Black* 1).

The novel begins with a lyrical evocation of driving on the M25, a liminal, twilit space peopled by 'outcasts and escapees' (*Beyond Black* 1), poised on the hinge between winter and spring, 'the time of Le Pendu, the Hanged Man' (*Beyond Black* 2). Implicitly evoking Eliot's *The Waste Land*, Alison and her business partner Colette circle the capital like a latter-day Dante and Virgil, picking their way amongst the damned souls. Yet this is not entirely metaphor; as a professional spirit medium, Alison is a kind of millennial Madame Sosostris, and the spirits of the dead she encounters have an all too material presence. The M25 constitutes a literal borderland, a zone in which the membrane between worlds is thin. As Mantel writes of Alison, 'the space the road encloses is the space inside her: the arena of combat, the wasteland, the place of civil strife behind her ribs' (*Beyond Black* 2). Inner and outer space are interpenetrable, Alison's ghosts manifesting physically in the landscape she inhabits.

As the novel progresses, the paralleling of the world of the dead with the blank spaces of the London Orbital becomes increasingly explicit. Questioned about the spirit world, Alison describes it as an 'eventless realm, neither cold nor hot, neither hilly nor flat, where the dead, each at their own best age and marooned in an eternal afternoon, pass the ages with sod all going on' (*Beyond Black* 43). The interpenetration of the two worlds comes as no surprise; each is as boring as the other. The spirits themselves are just as banal as their living counterparts, passing on messages about dieting and kitchen fittings. As Alison points out, 'they give trivial messages, but that's because they're trivial people. You don't get a personality transplant when you're dead. You don't suddenly get a degree in philosophy' (*Beyond Black* 98).

The inhabitants of the commuter belt are simultaneously hungry for signs from the past, and blissfully ignorant of them. In a scene where Alison is frustrated by a teenage punter who insists that she has no grandmother, Mantel notes that:

> It was not uncommon to find family memory so short, in these towns where nobody comes from, these south-eastern towns with their floating populations and their car parks where the centre should be. Nobody has roots here; and maybe they don't want to acknowledge roots, or recall their grimy places of origin and their illiterate foremothers up north. (*Beyond Black* 16–17)

Again, a deliberate parallel between the living and the dead is constructed. The rootless inhabitants of the centreless towns Alison works, like their counterparts in the afterlife, 'have no sense of time, no clear sense of place; they are beyond geography and history' (*Beyond Black* 44) and cut loose from the origins that once might have delivered identity. In a short essay entitled 'Revering the Gone-before', included at the end of the Harper Perennial paperback edition, Mantel writes that this scene was based on a real-life incident she witnessed at a spirit-medium demonstration that inspired the novel as a whole: 'The thing that frightens me most is the confiscation of history. If you don't own the past, and can't speak up for it, your past can be stolen and falsified, it can be changed behind you' (*Beyond Black* 13).[1]

This spiritual malaise linked to loss of historical narratives is specifically that of the white middle classes; Alison doesn't work the inner cities, partly because the number of spirits becomes too much to bear and partly because the convoluted spirit beliefs of the multicultural populations give her a headache. Alison's own ignominious background is another matter, and the belching, farting spirit guide who disrupts her comfortable, tastefully co-ordinated home plays the role of the inappropriate, unwelcome relative of the *parvenu* – the haunting of the recently middle class by their lower-class upbringing. The territory of Middle England is turned inside-out so that it is no longer middle as in central, or even as in average, but rather as in in-between – a kind of liminal zone or place of passage.

If Alison's clients are dislocated from their recent, family histories, they are also dislocated from a collective past. We learn that, 'It was in the week after Diana's death that Colette felt she got to know Alison properly. It seems another era now, another world: before the millennium, before the Queen's Jubilee, before the Twin Towers burned' (*Beyond Black* 140). Although, of course, Diana Princess of Wales died in 1997, less than 10 years before the novel was published,

it already seems 'another era . . . another world'. History is not so much accelerated as truncated. Owen Davies demonstrates how the historical knowledge of
any given community determines the ghosts that it sees, with nineteenth and
early twentieth-century ghosts, for example, almost always reflecting 'the popular histories that made up the Victorian school curriculum', and virtually all
sightings of Roman legionnaires post-dating the popularity of sword-and-sandal
epics (Davies 42). Similarly, Alison explains to Colette that while she frequently
encounters 'spirit-impostors' (Mantel 150), the other-worldly equivalent of
look-alikes and body doubles, their range of historical reference has narrowed:
'In Mrs. Etchells' day, she explained, people still thought they were Napoleon.
They were better educated then, she said, they still knew dates and battles'
(*Beyond Black* 150). The spirits, like the living, have impoverished historical
imaginations.

   Alison herself, all too aware of the spirits congregating in any given place,
actively seeks out places that are devoid of history. The corporate hotels and
new-build housing developments of south-east England are her ideal environment, their lack of identity a benefit rather than a drawback. As Mantel states,
'What Alison prefers is somewhere new-built and anonymous, part of some
reliable chain. She hates history: unless it's on the television, safe behind glass'
(*Beyond Black* 41). Her description recalls Sinclair's visit to the ibis [*sic*] hotel
chain in *London Orbital*, which leads him to conclude that 'The M25 . . . was
about erasure' and note how women in particular seek out the 'elective amnesia,
retreat and renewal' the featureless hotel provides (Sinclair 511). Non-places
are liberating to Alison; they enable her to escape the weight of histories not
her own. She is attracted to the house she buys on a Surrey new-build estate
because 'It's not even on a map' (*Beyond Black* 221). Yet this is no guarantee of
spectral tranquillity. The unmapped territory of the housing estate soon
becomes subject to a series of apocalyptic urban myths, while the badlands of
the M25 are presented as swarming with spectral activity:

> They tried to avoid the high streets and shopping malls of the denatured
> towns, because of the bewildered dead clustered among the skips outside the
> burger bars, clutching door keys in their hands, or queuing with their lunch
> boxes where the gates of small factories once stood, where machines once
> whirred and chugged behind sooty panes of old glass. There are thousands of
> them out there, so pathetic and lame-brained that they can't cross the road to
> get where they're going, dithering on the kerbs of new arterial roads and
> bypasses, as the vehicles swish by: congregating under railway arches and
> under the stairwells of multi-storey car parks, thickening the air at the
> entrance to underground stations. (*Beyond Black* 265–266)

According to Marc Augé, one of the most distinctive new kinds of 'non-place'
is that created by new kinds of transportation – motorway, rail, and air links –
that isolate individuals and encourage a particular kind of solitude. Mantel's lost

spirits appear stymied and frustrated by modern transport links; unable to cross the roads, congregating in the empty pockets of space created by railway bridges and car parks, hovering at the entrance to tube stations but not going inside. They are disoriented by modern urban planning, trying to move on but stuck in a kind of spiritual traffic jam.

A further point of interest about this passage, recalling Michel de Certeau's theory of walking in the city, is the way that ghosts *use* space, what we might play-fully call the 'practice of everyday death'. For de Certeau, walking resembles a speech act, a form of communication, a means of narrating the city. Walking also provides 'a substitute for the legends that used to open up space to some-thing different' (de Certeau 106–07); it enables the exits and entrances that make places habitable. The ghosts described in the above passage are attracted to exits and entrances, but appear unable to cross thresholds – queuing at gates, dithering at kerbs and clutching keys in stairwells. This is the opposite of how de Certeau's haunted urban space is supposed to work – the ghosts' entrances and exits are blocked, preventing the free flow of the (ghostly) pedestrian through the city. This appears to be a deliberate inversion on Mantel's part. Without narrative, without history, (sub)urban spaces become stagnant; ghosts do not walk but cluster, queue, dither, congregate. Moreover in the shadow of the M25, *Beyond Black* presents an environment in which walking has become redundant; both ghosts and living travel exclusively by car. Automobile travel creates a different kind of movement through space, a different means of narrating the environment. As Augé suggests:

> 'Main roads no longer pass through towns, but lists of their notable features – and indeed, a whole commentary – appear on big signboards nearby. . . . Motorway travel is thus doubly remarkable: it avoids, for functional reasons, all the principal places to which it takes us; and it makes comment on them'. (Augé 97)

History is reduced to the text and symbols on road-signs; packaged as leisure and offered in bite-sized, easily digestible pieces.

Haunting in this novel reflects what Brian McHale has described as the postmodern shift from an epistemological dominant to an ontological one (McHale 10). The ghost is no longer a producer of knowledge – where to find buried treasure, what terrible crime was committed, how revenge can be achieved. Rather, it is an inhabitant of worlds – the insalubrious, intermediate places of exchange where Alison's ghosts fester and gather and which she there-fore tries to avoid:

> Nowhere near a racecourse, a dog track, an army camp, a dockyard, a lorry park nor a clinic for special diseases. Nowhere near a sidings or a depot, a customs shed or a warehouse; not near an outdoor market nor an indoor market nor a sweatshop nor a body shop nor a bookies. (*Beyond Black* 221)

Reflecting the 'spatial turn' identified by Fredric Jameson in postmodern culture (Jameson 154), geography is privileged over history, and the places (or non-places) that the ghosts inhabit predominate over their pasts. Haunting has become lifestyle, replete with courses to improve one's supernatural skills and opportunities to pass judgement on one's descendents' interior decor. For the majority of Alison's punters seeking ghostly communications, to be haunted is a solipsistic activity, a means of seeing their own lives reflected and confirmed. The doubling of the worlds of living and dead demonstrates the spiritual poverty, the dislocation, the self-interest of both.

The most distinctive feature of the landscape of *Beyond Black* is its saturation by consumer culture. One of the funniest passages in the novel lyrically describes the different varieties of junk food Alison and Colette consume in the theme pubs, lay-bys, and pedestrian precincts they pause in during their travels. Property values are another prominent theme, preoccupying the other occupants of the posh housing estate Alison and Colette move to. Property, and its provenance and exchange, is one of the foundational concerns of Gothic fiction, from the threatened legacies of eighteenth-century Gothic heroines to Victorian ghost stories' perennial concern with desirable properties rendered suspiciously cheap. Sinclair, meditating on Carfax, adds: '*Dracula* announces the coming age of the estate agent. Nothing in the book works without the Count's ability to purchase, rent, secure property'. For Sinclair, *Dracula* foreshadows the bloodsucking speculations of the modern property developer, the commuter-friendly London Orbital 'the perfect metaphor for the circulation of blood' (Sinclair 487). In *Beyond Black*, the irony is that Alison and Colette's bland, homogenous Barratt-style house should be the antithesis of the haunted home, but its hastily built and shoddily finished architecture readily offers itself up for possession by malevolent spirits. The flaws in planning and construction rapidly become indistinguishable from the depredations of its resident ghosts. Unbridled consumption, whether of food or of material goods, drives the community, but like the nachos of Virginia Water and the Belgian Buns of Broxbourne, none of it has real substance. Conversely, the spirits have too much substance, leaving bad smells and filthy socks around the house in their wake. Again, the borders between the worlds of the living and dead are blurred.

Rational, worldly Colette regards spectral manifestations as a resource, a commodity to be exploited, and tries to update Alison's psychic business to fit these materialist times, attempting to turn her into a brand like McDonald's or Coca-Cola. The spirit world is inevitably mediated through consumption. This is not in itself new – E. J. Clery has explained at length how 'The rise of supernatural fictions must be understood in relation to the rise of consumerism' in the late eighteenth century, as increased literacy and new means of distributing and marketing books enabled the consumption of sensational literature on a hitherto unprecedented scale (Clery 5). In *Beyond Black*, new media platforms, in particular reality television, operate in a similar fashion to disseminate supernatural narratives to an ever wider audience – and, echoing eighteenth-century concerns, to even further sensationalize them. Towards the end of the novel, the rise of TV psychics alters the dynamic between spirit mediums and their audiences, as customer expectations are produced by the representation of ghosts on TV:

> now, when they came to a dem, the TV shows had tuned up their expecta-
> tions, they couldn't wait for their messages. When a sensitive asked, 'Who's
> got a Mike in spirit world?' fifty hands would shoot into the air. They yelled,
> cheered, embraced each other, made faces for the camera even though there
> wasn't one. They shouted, 'Oh my Gahhd!' when a message came through,
> and burst into grating sobs and doggy howls. (*Beyond Black* 320)

In response to the increasing commercialization of their industry, the loose community of psychics to which Alison belongs are forced to come up with ever more inventive ways of marketing themselves, such as psychic hen parties. The economic transaction at the basis of the spirit medium's trade is brought into sharper focus; the vacuity of the consumer culture highlighted by its fiscal relationship with the afterlife.

The indictment of consumer culture Mantel offers in *Beyond Black* does to a certain degree extend beyond London's outer limits to encompass the whole of England, or indeed all Western, post-industrial nations. For a novel about non-places, however, it does evoke a surprising sense of place, an instantly rec-ognizable portrait of England's south-east. As such, it echoes Iain Sinclair's project in *London Orbital* as described by Brian Baker, 'to turn "non-place" back into "place", where life is practised on a daily basis, and where memory and his-tory are *not* divorced from the spaces in which people live' (Baker 153). Whereas Sinclair, however, 'recurrently represents evacuated space', depopulating his landscapes in order to evoke 'alienation and a kind of "spiritual" emptiness' (Baker 141), Mantel overpopulates hers, with the restless and insistent spirits of the dead. The personal journeys of her protagonists are governed by the insistent motif of circularity, of things coming back, doubling the mechanisms of haunting with the cyclic motion of the Orbital. Mantel writes: 'At some point on your road you have to turn and start walking backwards towards yourself. Or the past will pursue you and bite the nape of your neck, leave you bleeding in the ditch' (*Beyond Black* 418). It is no accident that this book set on and around a ring-road ends with its principal characters making this circular movement. The journey through time is, significantly, described in terms of walking and not driving, a return to a more grounded means of transportation. To turn and walk backwards, it should be noted, is to continue in the same direction, only facing the opposite way. Mantel's warning is to seek self-knowledge, not to return to one's origins. One's self as destination is simultaneously located in the past and future – 'beyond history and geography', perhaps. Significantly, Alison asserts earlier in the novel that 'Spirits don't generally go backwards' (*Beyond Black* 248). The ability to change in the light of one's past is a characteristic of living humanity.

In Colette's case, there is a profound ambivalence about what it means to 'turn and start walking backwards'. In life Colette is already ghostly, an intermediate being; she 'had in fact no looks at all, good or bad, yes or no, pro or con. In her school photographs, her indefinite features seemed neither male nor female, and her pale bobbed hair resembled a cowl' (*Beyond Black* 51). When they first meet, Alison imagines her as a Victorian medium's assistant impersonating a spirit. Her existence prior to meeting Alison, marking time through a banal marriage and a faceless corporate job, is a kind of limbo. Her return to her ex-husband Gavin can thus be read as a coming to terms and a renewal, or as a defeat, a capitulation to the banal life she had attempted to leave behind.

Mantel treats Alison more generously, and in some ways more conventionally. For Alison, haunting registers itself physically on the body and its material surroundings, a continuous and distressing disruption of her personal space. Haunting is almost unbearably intimate; her loathsome spirit guide, Morris, appears beside her in the car, in her bed, while she is in the bath. She is eventually forced to face the traumatic repressed memories of her childhood (if, indeed, that is what they are – it is never clear whether the events she recalls actually happened, or whether they are a mixture of memory and invention). In doing so, she banishes the 'fiends' that haunt her, and gains two new, benevolent spirit guides, little old ladies who are mainly preoccupied with cake. She ends the novel how she started, circling London on the M25, but the doom-laden atmosphere of the opening pages has been replaced by one of jollity and fun. Her elderly companions love the novelty of being in a car so much that 'They will never get tired of the Orbital road, no matter how many times they go round it' (*Beyond Black* 449). This celebratory image is perhaps not what we've come to expect from representations of the M25 (and indeed, not from the rest of Mantel's novel), but the shift from a stagnant loop to an image of renewal and even of pleasure, offers belatedly to transform Mantel's vision of the afterlife from an 'eventless realm' to one where there will, at the least, be iced cakes for tea.

Note

[1] The end material is repaginated from 1 in this edition.

Works Cited

Augé, M. (1995), *Non-Places: Introduction to an Anthropology of Supermodernity* (1992), trans. John Howe, London: Verso

Baker, B. (2007), *Iain Sinclair*, Manchester: Manchester University Press

Ballard, J. G. (2008), *Crash* (1973), London: Harper Perennial

Byatt, J. (2009), 'Being (un)dead: the ghost stories of J.G. Ballard', Unpublished conference paper delivered at *The Ninth Biennial Conference of the International Gothic Association: Monstrous Media/Spectral Subjects*, Lancaster University, 21–24 July

Certeau, M. de (1984), *The Practice of Everyday Life*, trans. Steven Rendall, Berkeley and Los Angeles: University of California Press

Clery, E. J. (1995), *The Rise of Supernatural Fiction, 1792–1800*, Cambridge: Cambridge University Press

Davies, O. (2007), *The Haunted: A Social History of Ghosts*, Basingstoke: Palgrave Macmillan

Dickens, C. (2003), 'To Be Taken With a Grain of Salt' (1865), in *The Oxford Book of Victorian Ghost Stories*, (eds) Michael Cox and R. A. Gilbert, Oxford: Oxford University Press, 55–64

Gordon, A. (1997), *Ghostly Matters: Haunting and the Sociological Imagination*, Minneapolis: University of Minnesota Press

Iocco, M. (2007), 'Addicted to affliction: masculinity and perversity in *Crash* and *Fight Club*', *Gothic Studies* 9(1), 46–56

Jameson, F. (1991), *Postmodernism, or the Cultural Logic of Late Capitalism*, London: Verso

Lee, V. (2006) [1880], 'Faustus and Helena: notes on the supernatural in art', in *Hauntings and Other Fantastic Tales*, (eds) Catherine Maxwell and Patricia Pulham, Peterborough, Ontario: Broadview

Mantel, H. (2005), *Beyond Black*, London: Harper Perennial

McHale, B. (1987), *Postmodernist Fiction*, London: Routledge

Sinclair, I. (2003) [2002], *London Orbital: A Walk Around the M25*, London: Penguin

Westwood, J., and Jacqueline Simpson (2005), *The Lore of the Land: A Guide to England's Legends, from Spring-Heeled Jack to the Witches of Warboys*, London: Penguin

Chapter 8

'Where The Evil Is': The London of Derek Raymond

Nick Freeman

Per me si va nella città dolente

Dante[1]

Death, the Police, and Society

'Anyone who conceives of writing as an agreeable stroll towards a middle-class life-style will never write anything but crap' (*He Died* 140). Derek Raymond did not admire British crime fiction. The commercial sensibilities of bourgeois publishers prompted, he maintained, the 'ossification' of the genre, and encouraged the prevalence of formulaic police procedurals (*Hidden Files* 136).[2] 'The depressing result', he wrote, 'has been that the terrain where death, the police and society meet has been rendered harmless' since the escapist nature of the genre makes its characters unconvincing and limits the reader's engagement with them (*Hidden Files* 136). For Raymond, the distinction between the 'detective story' and the 'crime novel' was essentially an arbitrary one made by publishers' marketing departments. In Britain at least, neither mode addressed the true nature of violent death or the horror of its impact. 'What makes certain crime-writers such bad writers', he concluded, 'is that they don't really understand what the word evil means' (*Hidden Files* 208). Crime fiction needed, he felt, an altogether darker, more Gothic sensibility to do justice to its horrific content and indeed, to the existential questions that content raised.

Raymond may have caricatured the work of his contemporaries in order to emphasize the radical nature of his own, but regardless of whether one shares his opinions, the fiction he disparaged remained extremely popular. His response was to formulate the 'Black Novel', which addressed 'the question of turning a small, frightened battle with oneself into a much greater struggle – the universal human struggle against the general contract, whose terms are unfulfillable, and where defeat is certain.' His aim was 'to take people into the vile psychic weather outside their front doors . . . to see what true despair – the small, dark isolated rooms of existence with every exit barred, bricked up – really is' (*Hidden Files* 97–98). This determination to 'banish escapism' and 'any attempt to pretty up reality' (*Hidden Files* 138) was at the heart of Raymond's five 'Factory' novels, published between 1984 and 1993, and ensured him a cult following on both sides of the Channel.[3]

What it does not reveal, however, are the means by which the novelist pursued his aims. Often recalling Colin Wilson's *The Outsider* (1956), Raymond's autobiography was frank in admitting elevated literary and philosophical influences – Shakespeare, Donne, Zola, Victor Hugo, Orwell, Eliot, Dostoevsky and Sartre. It said rather less about Gothic writers (with the exception of his admiration for Edgar Allan Poe) or the ways in which he addressed a question of crucial significance for his work. *'[C]an a detective really establish credible contact with a dead victim in a shabby room?'* he asked. 'And if so, why? Who *is* the detective? *Why* does he care – if he does care – about why someone died?' (*Hidden Files* 217) Answering these questions would lead, Raymond concluded, 'into a new and better world' (*Hidden Files* 217), but philosophical attention to the purpose of his fiction was not, in his autobiography at any rate, accompanied by a similar focus on its literary aspects. In what follows I consider the connections between the 'Black Novel' and older Gothic texts, in particular, James Thomson's *The City of Dreadful Night* (1880), a poem which profoundly influenced Raymond's favourite modern poet, T.S. Eliot. London was a poisoned well for both Thomson and Eliot, and Raymond's fiction is similarly informed by a sense that the English capital is a place of darkness, disease, and despair. This chapter will look therefore at the techniques which Raymond uses to dramatize London as a Gothic space, a realm in which the awful and appalling are as much a part of everyday existence for his protagonist as whisky and cigarettes. Gothic narrative devices such as the 'found' document and the nightmare are important aspects of this evocation, as is a concern with a mode of haunting that is, as Julian Wolfreys says, 'irreducible to the apparition' (Wolfreys 6). Each of these contributes to a wider panorama of degradation and horror, a vision of London which is, while related to those seen in the contemporaneous work of Iain Sinclair and Martin Amis, distinctive and powerful in its own right.

Pathological Pathologists

The rise of the modern pathologist as hero(ine), from Jack Klugman's *Quincy M. E.* (NBC 1976 83) to Patricia Cornwell's Kay Scarpetta (1990-), has seen the dead speak to the living with an almost irresistible loquacity. As the post-mortem becomes a medium for popular entertainment from the BBC's *Silent Witness* (1996-) and *Waking the Dead* (2000-), to the wildly popular *CSI* (CBS 2000-) and the public autopsies of Gunther von Hagens, the corpse has become a ventriloquist's dummy, animated and made to speak by the medical scientist.

The body suffers a double violation in many of these narratives: first at the hands of the enthusiastic amateur who committed the murder, and second at those of the sober and conscientious professional whose investigative procedures stress their objectivity even as they descend into ghoulishness and *grand guignol*. Through the device of the pathologist recounting injuries for the record, the reader/viewer is guided through blasted or butchered remains while at the same time distanced from their horror by the clinical discourse of forensic medicine.[1] The body, toe-tagged but otherwise depersonalized, becomes a site of knowledge and a narrative catalyst with the revelatory possibilities of forensic science solving crimes even as they act as psychological or ethical solvents. Compassion for the victim or an understanding of their life and fate is supplanted by the unblinking objectivity of the microscope, the scalpel, and the DNA profile.

Raymond's Factory novels resisted the movement away from the police officer and towards the scientist that was gathering pace in crime fiction during the 1980s. Although the final novel in the series, *Dead Man Upright* (1993), and his autobiography, *The Hidden Files* (1992), hailed the rise of psychological profiling, Raymond's work generally took a very different approach from those who romanticized the pathologist or the pathologist's charismatic and ingenious adversaries. His nameless sergeant sets out to speak with and for the dead through a compassionate immersion in the minutiae of ruined lives. This determination to take on aspects of the victim's existence presents a notable narrative challenge. If the body was not to be the site of knowledge and any supernatural dimension which might have allowed spiritual congress was to be disallowed by the novelist's unblinkingly materialist ideology, then the dead would have to speak through what they left behind. In this respect the deductive semiotics of Sherlock Holmes offers another narrative model by which science supplanted humanist concerns. The sergeant could employ them to enhance his understanding of a crime's sociological context, but they were unsuited to carrying the weight of his investigations or mediating his sympathy for the victim.

The first Factory novel, *He Died With His Eyes Open* (1984) mixed the boozy milieu and sexual jealousy of Patrick Hamilton's *Hangover Square* (1941) with the existential anguish of Samuel Beckett's *Krapp's Last Tape* (1958). The battered body of Staniland, a failed writer, is dumped in a shrubbery 'in front of the Word of God House, Albatross Road, West Five', a 'ghastly lonely area' (*He Died* 9). As so often in Raymond's novels, 'vile psychic weather' is echoed by actual meteorology; the body is found on a freezing wet night. A disdain for scientific detail is evident from an encounter between the sergeant and a pathologist, who says that his function is to 'establish time and cause of death' rather than to understand 'people's horrible motives' (*He Died* 17).[5] Staniland has been systematically beaten before being dispatched with a blow to 'the frontal lobe of the brain' dealt with 'something like a builder's two-pound hammer' (*He Died* 17), but while the novel does not shrink from the grisly detail of these injuries, it does not fetishize them. Instead they serve to shock the reader into recognizing the level of violence at work in the modern metropolis, even in crimes which are not regarded as a serious threat to the body politic, and as a gateway to the sergeant's engagement with the dead man's life and character.

Staniland has left behind a box of audio tapes; an impressionistic archive that records and dramatizes his successive failures as a parent, a lover, and an artist. 'What do tapes mean in a court of law?' the sergeant asks himself, but it is clear even at this point that 'the law' and 'meaning' are two all-but-incompatible concepts (*He Died* 29). The tapes fulfil a far more important function than merely providing evidence. They allow the dead man to speak for himself and ensure, albeit unintentionally, that his voice is finally heard. These tapes solve the technical problem of the 'back story' and explain how Staniland became entangled with the *femme fatale*, Barbara, who eventually brings about his death. At the same time they allow the reader to draw a distinction between the invasive attentions of the pathologist, who mines the secrets of the body, and the compassion of the detective who listens to Staniland's often lengthy recollections in an attempt to restore to him the individuality that murder, and becoming a statistic, a 'case', has otherwise removed. In a translation of Catullus, Aubrey Beardsley wrote of giving 'the last gifts to the dead' and 'vainly parley[ing] with ashes dumb' (Beardsley 195); Raymond's novels might be read in a similar context of failed conversation and a bestowing of love, respect, and peace that comes too late to provide succour or solace. Iain Sinclair has called the Factory novels 'monologues of erasure' (Sinclair 343), but in many ways they are novels of restoration that attempt to recover the dignity and individuality of the deceased. They also often privilege feelings of loss and anguish above the details of the investigation.

One of the few English writers of detective fiction admired by Raymond in *The Hidden Files* is Wilkie Collins whose novels share his interest in the ways by which documentary evidence enriches, but sometimes threatens to displace, human experience. Straddling the Gothic, sensation fiction and the detective story, Collins frequently drew on the tradition of the 'found' letter, diary, or manuscript, a stock ingredient of earlier Gothic fiction which itself grew out of the epistolary novel. *The Woman in White* (1859–1860) and *The Law and the Lady* (1874–1875) placed a preponderance of material evidence at the service of justice and the narrative, with enigmas being resolved by a faith in such evidence proving explanatory and at last conclusive. Unlike the subjective narrative of Staniland's tapes, these texts *do* have legal power within the novels.

Collins' fiction also exploits readers' complicity in transgressive acts of reading. In a startling episode of *The Woman in White*, the villainous Count Fosco reads and annotates Marian Halcombe's private journal; the sudden shift from the first person of Marian's thoughts to Fosco's smug assessment of them still retains its power to surprise. As Miller (1988) and Gaylin (2003) have shown, the invasion of Marian's privacy prompts unwelcome parallels between the

reader and the criminal, since both have access to personal material even if the
reader gains access by the agency of the narrator, Walter Hartright. Raymond
by contrast licenses the sergeant's eavesdropping through the character's
thoughtful engagement with the tapes and diaries and its necessity for his quest.
Ethically beyond reproach at least where 'innocent' victims are concerned, the
sergeant is able to present intimate material to the reader, discomforting them
with its content rather than their means of access to it.[6]

More radically however, Staniland's audio tapes, Mardy's in *How the Dead
Live* (1986), Dora's journal in the harrowing *I was Dora Suarez* (1990) and even
Jidney's video recordings of his killings in *Dead Man Upright* place the victims in
a limbo signalled by the novels' titles. They are dead, yet their recordings, letters, and haphazard memoirs give them a curious afterlife. Textual spectres
haunt the consciousness of the sergeant and the city they once inhabited – the
dead cannot rest.[7] In his review of *I was Dora Suarez*, Chris Petit notes parallels
between Raymond's world and the corporeal claustrophobia of Jacobean
tragedy, observing that 'the dead live and the living are in a sense dead . . .
Raymond's detective now seems more at ease as a medium for the dead than in
communication with the living' (Petit 21). The psychic residue of the murder
victims' experiences can still be detected by those sensitive to them, so while the
sergeant is not a literal medium he is nonetheless a conduit between the world
in which the dead lived and suffered, and the present, in which the processes of
justice can begin an uncertain expiation. In *The City of Dreadful Night*, James
Thomson observes that he does not write for 'the hopeful young', 'pious spirits'
or 'those who deem their happiness of worth' (Thomson 551), but seeks to
commune instead with 'some weary wanderer / In that same city of tremendous
night' who will 'understand the speech, and feel a stir / Of fellowship in all-
disastrous fight' (Thomson 552). Likewise, the act of communion is far more
profound than the act of detection, the application of traditional police methods and a network of informers and contacts by which the sergeant solves his
cases. What is important is less the discovery of the criminal or solving an elaborate puzzle, than the focus on sympathy and understanding. Having arrested
the owner of the club where Dora worked, the sergeant has a sudden vision of
her in 'a space inside my head' (*Dora Suarez* 131) and is seized with love – he
had kissed her hair when he found her body (*Dora Suarez* 41). He is sure that
her eyes would now reveal 'a meaning that on earth I could only guess at' (*Dora
Suarez* 131) but his epiphany is fleeting and jostles with a memory of her shattered body in 'the freezing room where I had found her' (*Dora Suarez* 131).

Dora's Journal, like Staniland's tapes, addresses the sergeant and the reader
with an apparently unmediated directness. One of Staniland's tapes announces:
'Most people live with their eyes shut, but I mean to die with mine open' (*He
Died* 83) and elsewhere in the novel entire chapters consist of uninterrupted
extracts from his recordings. Dora's murder, seen from the killer's perspective
and by a rationalizing narrator – perhaps the sergeant engaging in an imaginative

reconstruction of events – occurs in Chapter 1. Her journal is only discovered at the end of the third chapter and a quotation from it opens the fourth:

> Suarez.
> I read: 'Once I was Dora Suarez, but even before I die I am not her any more; I have just become something appalling. Looking at myself naked in the mirror I see that I have lost the right to call myself a person; what's left of me now is barely human' (*Dora Suarez* 54).

Dora's circumstances are withheld from the reader until much later in the novel. She is dying from Aids and spends her final months working in a clandestine sex club where she suffers ever more appalling abuse. However before the introduction of this startlingly topical plotline (Aids narratives were not common in British fiction at the time), the journal draws upon established Gothic devices. As the sergeant reads on the boundary between the diary and the suicide note becomes increasingly permeable, while the content recalls the finale of Stevenson's *Jekyll and Hyde* (1886), Jekyll's anguished statement which reveals how two entities have lived and fought within the same body and how Hyde has 'severed me from my own face and nature' (Stevenson 75). As argued by Kelly Hurley: 'The abhuman retains vestiges of its human identity, but has already become, or is in the process of becoming, some half-human other . . . perhaps simply "unspeakable" in its gross, changeful corporeality' (Hurley 190). The metamorphosis means that the body has 'lost its claim to a discrete and integral identity' and hence 'a fully human existence'. In short, Dora's diseased flesh has placed her in a liminal state between life and death that disrupts 'the two terms of an opposition . . . by which cultures are meaningfully able to organize experience' (Hurley 190).

Raymond's fascination with the ways that terminal disease complicates the apparent polarities of existence plays a key part in *How The Dead Live*, which is set in a small Wiltshire town suffering from the same psychic and moral malaise as the metropolis. Again the device of audio recordings allows the dead to address the living without mediation: Dr Mardy uses recordings of his wife to tell the story of her illness and death, and his doomed attempt to keep her in a state of suspended animation. The plot makes it the most obviously Gothic of the series, clearly influenced by Poe's 'The Fall of the House of Usher' and 'Ligeia' (1845). Mardy, 'a hollowed-out shadow of a man in his sixties', (*How the Dead* 61) tapes his conversations with his wife during her last hours before he carries out the operation that he hopes will allow her to return, restored, once medicine has found a cure for her cancer. 'You can't grasp the music of the dead', observes Mardy, as he shows the sergeant his wife, cryogenically preserved, in his near ruined house (*How the Dead* 155). Hearing these recordings, the sergeant sweats yet is 'icy cold', 'convinced that the woman's voice I was listening to was dead' (*How the Dead* 149). At this point, the polarized worlds of life and death become uncannily blurred.

Mardy has had built a sepulchre in which he can lie preserved beside his wife in the hope of reunion through reanimation. As in *I was Dora Suarez*, the dead speak to the living and through the transmission of their stories are projected into a half-life in which, physically dead but imaginatively and emotionally affecting, they reach out to those capable of extending sympathy to them. As the sergeant says: 'The way I am, I sense tears as well as hear them' (*Dora Suarez* 120). Again, there are parallels with James Thomson's *City of Dreadful Night*: 'Some say that phantoms haunt those shadowy streets, / 'And mingle freely there with sparse mankind'. Their voices 'tell of ancient woes and black defeats, / And murmur mysteries in the grave enshrined' (*City of Dreadful Night* 563). The sergeant's susceptibility to these voices and their suffering distances him from his superiors and many of his colleagues. For him police work is a vocation rather than a career: 'I'm always the same; I'm always on the side of the victim . . . It's my nature; it's like putting a mongoose on a snake' (*Dora Suarez* 87). Such convictions drive him to reject promotion and privilege, as higher rank would only remove him from the world where 'the ghosts go . . . where the evil is' (*Devil's Home* 24). He may be their relentless nemesis, but his successes in bringing to what passes for justice the murderers he pursues are tempered by his feelings of wider impotence and his knowledge that he is always too late, and that his skills can only punish crime, never prevent it. The last two 'Factory' novels present this realization with particular clarity: the epigraph of *I was Dora Suarez* is 'The tragedy of help is that it never arrives'.

Iain Sinclair remarks that Raymond was accustomed to speak of himself as if he were already deceased just as Suarez does (Sinclair 342). A further example of Raymond's use of the death-in-life motif is a little different, however. In *Dead Man Upright* Ann Meredith is romantically involved with Jidney, a man the sergeant is increasingly convinced is a serial killer. Ann refuses to break with her lover, is uncooperative when under surveillance – 'a mouse refusing to see the trap for the cheese' (*Dead Man* 97) – and is finally killed despite the sergeant's best efforts to protect her. She might be read as a parallel to Nicola Six, the 'murderee' of Martin Amis's *London Fields* (1989), a figure who has somehow stepped out of a Wedekind play into the bedsit lands of North London. But whereas Amis surrounded Nicola with blackly comic curlicues and postmodern trickery, Raymond emphasizes Ann's obstinacy and her inability to accept the monstrous. 'Nothing's believable till it happens', the sergeant tells her (*Dead Man* 96) in a vain attempt to stress how the 'normal' world of her pre-Jidney existence has been replaced by a Gothic one in which civilizing influences no longer operate. Ann ignores his warnings and is brutally murdered only to live again in a self-justificatory letter Jidney writes before his suicide. Whereas Staniland, Dora Suarez, and Marianne Mardy undergo a quasi-reanimation through the sergeant's treatment of them, Ann lives under sentence of death with an uncertain reprieve. Her murder uses the Gothic motif of the woman in peril to stress the 'vile psychic weather' of the 'Black Novel' and to rebut the detective story's often redemptive overtones.

The sergeant is therefore tormented if not possessed by these 'spirits'. It is not that they ask for vengeance, or that they are able to avenge themselves. Rather, their suffering compels the sergeant to act on their behalf. Although it is his job to do this, his motivations are metaphysical rather than contractual. At the conclusion of *How the Dead Live* he broods over Dr Mardy's suicide recalling once more the doctor's observations: 'if I were to live now, from now on I would always live for others' and 'passion changes us back again into what we once were, must have been' (*How the Dead* 203). 'I told him I understood,' the sergeant says, 'even though I wondered if I did' (*How the Dead* 203). The Suarez murder affects him even more powerfully: 'Dead people are very clean, too clean', he reflects. 'They have been purged, white and even as the light on snow, but why? Where's the justice in that?' (*Dora Suarez* 120). There are, of course, no answers to his question and the intuitive associations which he forges between himself and the dead leave him psychically exhausted and socially marginal. At the conclusion of *I was Dora Suarez* he has tears in his eyes 'for the rightful fury of the people', but these are the closing words of the book and his anger and pity have no outlet until he is once again tracking down criminals (*Dora Suarez* 186).

Dreaming the Dark

The nightmare has long been a key aspect of the Gothic as can be seen in works as temporally distant from each other as Henry Fuseli's painting *The Nightmare* (1781) and Wes Craven's film *A Nightmare on Elm Street* (1984). Nightmares allow for horrific episodes which the narrative cannot otherwise accommodate (such as the Bleeding Nun in Matthew Lewis' *The Monk* (1796)). In subtler hands they can offer premonitions or symbolic suggestions that foreshadow subsequent events, or grant access to the dreamer's psychological state. Wilkie Collins combines all these elements in *Armadale* (1864–1866), where 'the treachery of Sleep open[s] the gates of the grave' to the novel's hero (*Armadale* 164). 'The City is of Night, but not of Sleep' writes Thomson, and Raymond's detective is usually kept awake by the insistent horrors he has experienced (*Dreadful Night* 554).[8] On those rare nights when he does sleep, he is troubled by dreams of his past such as when his wife, Edie, who is now hospitalized, pushed their nine-year old daughter, Dahlia, under a bus following a row in the supermarket (*Devil's Home* 30). The madwoman in the attic (or the asylum) is an obvious nod to Victorian Gothic convention, but the sergeant's disastrous relationship with Edie is more significant as a means of reiterating his deep wells of pity and compassion and the incomprehensible nature of the world in which he finds himself. As Thomson asks: 'What men are they who haunt these fatal glooms? / And fill their living mouths with dust of death?' (*Dreadful Night* 568). The sergeant's sensitivity to the dead and the living dead means that, for all the bravado of his dialogue and his frequent insubordination, he feels too much rather than too little.

The sergeant's dreams add another layer of haunting to the city he polices. In one, he is troubled by 'a man the colour of death in a white suit' who 'came up to me in the West End out of a side street and offered me his love' (*Devil's Home* 56). His dead father appears to him and urges him to 'Take the rain out of the names on our graves' (*Devil's Home* 57). In another 'frightful dream', Dahlia appears bleeding in her shroud and saying 'come to me, Daddy, come quickly' (*Devil's Home* 166). In *How the Dead Live*, the sergeant dreams of a city with 'an atmosphere of terror and sadness everywhere' with corpses propped in doorways or lying under sacks of cabbages (*Dead Live* 47). These nightmares intensify the novels' claustrophobic atmosphere of despair as well as shadowing their London with the morbid menace of Thomson and Eliot. Indeed, Eliot's *The Waste Land* (1922) evokes a metropolis haunted by the dead of the Great War and the influenza epidemic that followed it.[9] Thomson's poem claims 'life is but a dream whose shapes return, / Some frequently, some seldom, some by night / And some by day, some night and day'. Those caught in the city are tormented by these visions, no longer able to distinguish between the actual, the recollected, and the imagined. 'We count things real; such is memory's might', concludes a stanza encapsulating the sergeant's predicament (*Dreadful Night* 552–53). The dead are everywhere, and, just as opposites fuse in a Coleridgean Death-in-Life, so dreaming and waking lose their discrete identities.

The haunted London of these novels is at once topographically accurate, if verbally idiosyncratic, and a psychogeographical construction of Raymond's own, akin to Grahame Greene's and Thomson's purgatorial cityscapes. Every street seems to contain the seeds of reminiscence or the recollection of tragedy and loss. 'I'm always using memory in my work, as a writer does' (*Dead Man* 24), the sergeant admits, and the result is an epistemology in which the fragmented details of previous cases crowd into his mind challenging him always to put them to new use, or to reaffirm what he knows of his environment. Only by internalizing the city even as he recognizes its alterity can the sergeant, the quintessential Londoner, begin to make sense of its narratives and solve his cases.

Moving between his joyless flat in Acacia Circus, Earlsfield, and the bleak Soho of Department A14, the sergeant stalks a London of post-industrial decline which feeds on the carcass of the Thatcherite optimism of the mid-1980s. His world is one of strip-clubs, pubs, shabby flats and abandoned warehouses, which like the demoralizing environs of Iain Sinclair's *Downriver* (1991) or the menacing backwaters photographed by Paul Barkshire for *James Herbert's Dark Places* (1993), offer perennial ironic asides on the capital's former greatness.[10] Everything is decaying, entropic. In *How the Dead Live*, the sergeant drives west out of London towards Wiltshire noting fire-blackened cinemas, and 'a heap of smashed cars frosted over on a stretch of waste ground; next to them, black with grime, its forecourt wet with dirty snow, stood a shut-down petrol station' (*How the Dead* 32). In *Dead Man Upright*, North London is smeared with 'patches of freezing damp that reminded me of our daily crime scenes' (*Dead Man* 40). The sergeant's first case, recalled in *The Devil's Home on Leave*, concerns the unsolved killing of sixty-two-year old Jonquil Mayhew. Once again, the weather mirrors the disturbances in the human psyche which led to her death: her body is found beside a flooded motorway on a rainy autumn night, and the murder receives 'four lines in the *Watford Observer*' (*Devil's Home* 15).

'I've got my territory', says the sergeant, 'and I know it the way a blind man knows each wall he taps on when he goes down his front steps into the street' (*Dora Suarez* 88). The sergeant's journey into a morally blind world begins in the London streets, but moves inexorably inwards, first into buildings and then into the human psyche itself. 'Four walls can suddenly become a heart too full for words', the sergeant notes (*How the Dead* 160), connecting Mardy's ruin with that of his property. Typically, many of the buildings in the Factory novels are physically decrepit, including the headquarters of A14 itself, which are always too hot or too cold. The old grain warehouse where the body is discovered in *The Devil's Home on Leave*, Staniland's desolate bedsitter, 'one of the most putrid I ever saw' (*Devil's Home* 60), Dora Suarez's pathetic rooms, the abandoned factory where Tony Spavento hides out in the same novel, threatening pubs and clubs, are all past their prime. It is scarcely surprising that no healthy roots can thrive in such diseased soil. The sergeant becomes a bridge between not only the living and the dead, but also between the visible landscape of London and the uncharted psychological territory which mirrors it.

Philip Larkin's 'Going, Going', written in 1972, foresaw a time when 'that will be England gone' and tradition and history are buried beneath 'concrete and tyres' (Larkin 190). Raymond's work is similarly pessimistic, at times even succumbing to nostalgia and a tendency to idealize a vanished past.[11] In *The Devil's Home on Leave*, 'dignity' has disappeared from everyday life (*Devil's Home* 49), but by *Dead Man Upright*, the situation has deteriorated dangerously. London is a 'war zone' (*Dead Man* 23), a Sadeian universe whose inhabitants pursue their desires with neither restraint nor concern for others. Even its parks are overshadowed by Dahlia's death and the novels resolutely avoid tourist locations or famous public spaces. This is a London which is heartless in every sense; a rancid, squalid city poised on the edge of a moral abyss, under-funded, uncared for and profane. As in *The Waste Land*, disembodied voices proliferate; the sergeant takes his orders from The Voice, a superior whom he never meets, while radio bulletins and newspaper reports allude to the city's growing lawlessness or else crassly misrepresent its tragedies. The formulaic 'KENSINGTON AXE HORROR' (*Dora Suarez* 110) hardly does justice to what the sergeant found in Dora Suarez's room.

'We must love one another or die', wrote W.H. Auden (246). It was part of Raymond's originality that he should have argued this so strongly in fiction of such bleakness and horror. So disturbing that they traumatized even their creator (*Hidden Files* 220, 317), the Factory novels use Gothic devices to intensify a series of urban nightmares, but the Black Novel is more than a nihilistic reflex response to the socio-political anxieties of the late-twentieth century. It insists also on the equality of human life, and on the individual's responsibility for protecting and celebrating it. Bleak though Raymond's city may be, unlike Thomson's it is not entirely hopeless.

Notes

[1] 'Through me you pass into the city of sorrow': one of the epigraphs to James Thomson's *The City of Dreadful Night* (1880).

[2] Born Robert William Arthur Cook in 1931, Raymond swiftly metamorphosed into Robin Cook, the name under which his first novel, *The Crust on its Uppers*, appeared in 1962. Educated privately and at Eton, he was never comfortable with the trappings of his class and took every opportunity to rebel against convention. He walked out of Eton and embarked on a life of scams and bad company, fronting bogus businesses for the London gangster Charles de Silva, until becoming a novelist. He published several novels as Cook but abandoned fiction after *The Tenants of Dirt Street* (1971) and left England for Italy where he worked as a vintner, and rural France, where he settled as a labourer in 1974. When he re-emerged in the 1980s, another Robin Cook, the author of medical thrillers such as *Coma* (1977), was associated with the name, and the original Cook was forced to adopt a pseudonym, although he retained his original name for European editions. To avoid confusion, I have referred to him as Raymond throughout.

[3] The 'Factory' is the Poland Street police station that houses an adjunct of the Metropolitan Police, A14, 'Unexplained Deaths'.

[4] My thanks to Dr Victoria Stewart of Leicester University for her discussion of these ideas.

[5] A 'snide young pathologist' displays 'cynicism and remote-control emotion' in *The Devil's Home on Leave* (49). Lansdown, the pathologist in *I was Dora Suarez*, is a more humane figure whom the sergeant respects, but even he is caught between struggling to 'stay calm' when he examines Dora's diseased and wounded body and referring to her as '87471', the number on her morgue file (*I was Dora Suarez* 80–1).

[6] The sergeant is far less concerned with the deaths of professional criminals such as the grass, Jack Hadrill, in *The Devil's Home on Leave* or the sex-club owner, Felix Roatta in *I was Dora Suarez*.

[7] Raymond took this to an extreme in *Nightmare in the Street* (2006, though first published in French in 1988), in which Kleber, a Parisian policeman, is visited ever more frequently by the ghost of his murdered girlfriend. Whether she is an actual ghost, a recurrent memory, a fantasy or a hallucination is ambiguous and ultimately irrelevant.

[8] Thomson suffered horribly with insomnia and wrote about it at length, as Tom Leonard shows in *Places of the Mind* (1993).

[9] Edmund Spenser's 'Sweet Thames run softly, till I end my song', quoted by Eliot in *The Waste Land*, drops unbidden into the killer's mind towards the end of *I was Dora Suarez* (168).

[10] See especially Barkshire's images on 146–47, 150–51, 154–55,156, 161.

[11] The treatment of the Second World War veteran, Colonel Newington in *How the Dead Live*, is one example of many (73–77).

Works Cited

Amis, M. (1989), *London Fields*, London: Cape

Auden, W. H. (1978), *The English Auden: Poems, Essays and Dramatic Writings 1927–1939*, (ed.) Edward Mendelson, London: Faber

Beardsley, A. (1997), 'Carmen CI', in (eds) R. K. R. Thornton and M. Thain, *Poetry of the 1890s*, London: Penguin

Beckett, S. (1959), *Krapp's Last Tape* and *Embers*, London: Faber

Collins, W. (1860), *The Woman in White*, London: Sampson Low

Collins, W. (1875), *The Law and the Lady*, London: Chatto and Windus

Collins, W. (1989), *Armadale*, Oxford: World's Classics

Crawford, R. (1987), *The Savage and the City in the Work of T.S. Eliot*, Oxford: Clarendon

Eliot, T. S. (1969), *The Complete Poems and Plays*, London: Faber

Gaylin, A. (2003), *Eavesdropping in the Novel from Austen to Proust*, Cambridge: Cambridge University Press

Hamilton, P. (1941), *Hangover Square or The Man with Two Minds. A Story of Darkest Earl's Court in the Year 1939*, London: Constable

Herbert, J. (1993), *James Herbert's Dark Places: Locations and Legends*, London: Harpercollins

Hurley, K. (1996), *The Gothic Body: Sexuality, Materialism, and Degeneration at the Fin de Siècle*, Cambridge: Cambridge University Press

Hurley, K. (2002), 'British Gothic fiction, 1885–1930', in (ed.) J. E. Hogle, *The Cambridge Companion to Gothic Fiction*, Cambridge: Cambridge University Press

Larkin, P. (1988), *Collected Poems*, (ed.) Anthony Thwaite, London: Faber

Leonard, T. (1993), *Places of the Mind: The Life and Work of James Thomson ('B. V.')*, London: Jonathan Cape

Lewis, M. (1796), *The Monk*, London: J. Bell

Miller, D. A. (1988), *The Novel and the Police*, Berkeley: University of California Press

Petit, C. (1990), 'O. E. can stand for distinctly Outré Evil', *The Times*, 13 December, 21

Raymond, D. (1984), *He Died with His Eyes Open*, London: Abacus

Raymond, D. (1985), *The Devil's Home on Leave*, London: Abacus

Raymond, D. (1986), *How the Dead Live*, London: Abacus

Raymond, D. (1990), *I was Dora Suarez*, London: Abacus

Raymond, D. (1994a), *The Hidden Files*, London: Warner

Raymond, D. (1994b), *Dead Man Upright*, London: Warner

Raymond, D. (2006), *Nightmare in the Street*, London: Serpent's Tail

Sinclair, I. (1991), *Downriver*, London: Paladin

Sinclair, I. (1997), *Lights Out for the Territory*, London: Granta

Stevenson, R. L. (1987), *The Strange Case of Doctor Jekyll and Mr Hyde and Weir of Hermiston*, Oxford: Oxford University Press

Thomson, J. (1997), *The City of Dreadful Night*, in (ed.) D. Karlin, *The Penguin Book of Victorian Verse*, London: Penguin, 550–86

Wilson, Colin. (1956), *The Outsider: A Study of a Human Type*, London: Victor Gollancz

Wolfreys, Julian (2002), *Victorian Hauntings: Spectrality, Gothic, the Uncanny and Literature*, Basingstoke: Palgrave

Chapter 9

Rats, Floods and Flowers: London's Gothicized Nature

Jenny Bavidge

In 2008, rodenticide producers Sorex launched the Deleuzean-sounding guide to rat eradication, 'Think Rat', a title which suggests that professional rat-catchers must become a little rattish themselves in order to seek and destroy their enemy. The idea of thinking or moving like a rat is an idea which filters into Gothic writing on London in all periods and registers, from the explicit horror of James Herbert to the neo-urban Gothic of China Miéville. This chapter will consider what it means to think rat in the context of ecocritical ideas about urban nature and ecophobia, and to trace the appearance of the rat in London Gothic. In so doing, I am influenced by Maud Ellman's elegant essay 'Writing like a rat' which explores modernism's rattishness, figuring the rat as an emblematic collector of scraps and fragments. Ellman's rats are those of Freud, Eliot, Beckett and Joyce, skittering over the remains of language and significa-tion. My London rats are a little more brutish and unsubtle, but to track their appropriation by Gothic literature is to notice how writers have 'thought rat' in order to uncover and explore networks, spaces and modes of being in the city.

Ecophobic and Ecogothic

The potential of a specifically 'urban ecocriticism' has been intermittently investigated by ecocritics. At various points in Michael Bennett and David W. Teague's *The Nature of Cities: Ecocriticism and Urban Environments*, contributors suggest that ecocritical readings of urban spaces and practices or urban litera-tures can reveal how cities operate as ecosystems, or how definitions of nature/culture or rural/urban are mutually implicated; they point out that urban ecocriticism could take notice of the particular properties of city parks or urban wildlife, or note the use of tropes such as the 'urban wilderness' or the technological dystopia. I would suggest that ecocriticism could also usefully incorporate a subgenre of 'urban ecogothic'. The term 'ecogothic' is currently picking up adherents, and has been used by Young Adult (YA) authors such as

Elizabeth Bear, to describe that particular genre of fiction for teenagers which addresses the fear (and desirability) of a post-eco-apocalypse world. Apart from the global terrors of climate chaos, however, the category of the ecogothic could also include aspects of the more mundane Gothic which seems suited to London stories in particular.

Tom J. Hillard's recent ecocritical article on the character of Gothic nature, suggests that ecocriticism has 'largely overlooked representations of nature inflected with fear, horror, loathing or disgust' (Hillard 687). Hillard addresses Simon Estok's earlier article in the same ecocritical journal which introduced the idea of 'ecophobia' and argued that 'contempt for the natural world is a definable and recognizable discourse' (Estok 208). Hillard imports the vocabulary and critical approach of criticism of Gothic fiction to show how ecophobia is both a mainstay of Gothic fiction itself, in that nature has so often been associated with the monstrous and ineffable, and crucially how 'Gothic's source in cultural contradictions' makes it a mode particularly suited to exploring our ambivalent and contested relationship to the natural environment (Hillard 209). These approaches and the sense of ecophobia as a real force in our past and present dealing with nature are intensified and magnified when we are dealing with urban nature. For every moment in London's literary history where the parks, gardens and residual nature of London offer a moment of respite or freedom, there is a corresponding horror story. London's green spaces, animal life and resilient physical environment are often represented as minatorial and *unnatural* in London literature. From the fog and mud of *Bleak House* to Martin Amis' Dogshit Park, the unpleasant stuff of nature has leant itself to both a mundane Gothic of everyday abjection, as well as Hollywood-scale extinction events via flood, cold or carnivorous plants. Gothic-inflected narratives respond, very obviously, to how the city's built environment buries and represses the natural environment. Nature's return in floods, extreme weather, pests, disease, or more pleasantly, the survival of wild plants and animals in odd corners of the metropolis, lends itself to Gothic narratives of irruption and destabilization. In the Gothic mode, nature, when it re-emerges in the city, has always 'come back wrong'. The appearance of non-human or extra-rational forces in London speak of unease and crisis in the city's culture and material structures. I'll suggest some of the places we can search out London's Gothic nature and focus particularly on the ubiquitous and protean figure of the London rat, sniffing out some of the stories that have been told about it and tracing its generic adaptability.

London's Gothicized Nature

The 'lost rivers' of the city have proved a popular touchstone in recent writing about London, haunting the work of Iain Sinclair and Peter Ackroyd as classic examples of the 'spectral turn' in London Gothic (Luckhurst, 2002, *passim*).

U. A. Fanthorpe's 'Rising Damp' links the lost rivers 'Effra, Graveney, Falcon, Quaggy, / Wandle, Walbrook, Tyburn, Fleet' with the rivers of the Underworld, 'Phlegethon, Acheron, Lethe, Styx'. Previously a source of life, and now 'Buried alive in earth / Forgotten like the dead', these concreted springs inevitably return with trickling, malign effects, allied to the treacherous unconscious and the pull of death (Fanthorpe 42–43). An ecocritical reading of London fiction reveals a similar, continuing tension between a faith in the restorative slivers of pastoral surviving the pressures of the city (such as the Fountain Court in *Martin Chuzzlewit*), and urban nature's manifestation as a degraded and parodic form of the lost garden, or a sinister reminder of extra-human forces.

In genre fiction, science fiction, horror and urban fantasy writing in particular, these long-standing tensions and anxieties in the representation of London's natural history take on an intense focus. We can certainly talk about a general or global sense of ecophobia which could be liberally applied to all urban places (as in the gleeful scenes of international destruction of significant global landmarks, most commonly the Eiffel Tower and the Statue of Liberty in Hollywood eco-disaster movies such as *The Day After Tomorrow* or *2012*). However, London has its own longstanding and specific ecophobia. While John Wyndham's *Day of the Triffids* (1951) follows a narrative arc from the city to the country and finally to an off-shore holding position, the most memorable scenes of both novel and the 1981 television adaptation are those which take place in London. After these scenes, Wyndham doesn't much bother with charting the destruction of other British cities; London stands for all urban centres and its disintegration is imagined with a particularly London edge. Devious cockneys conspire to capture more trusting middle-class characters and Wyndham moves his characters through a series of London tableaux: alleyways, hotels and boozers. Josella and Bill finally agree that something is definitely up when they witness the Triffids in post-comet action 'herding' a crowd of hapless, helpless Londoners. As Shelley Saguaro suggests, *Day of the Triffids* manages to be both ecophobic and ecocritical: the 'killer garden plants' are inherently malevolent but it's heavily hinted that their evolutionary step-up comes as a result of a man-made arms race (Saguaro 207). *Day of the Triffids* continues what ecocritic Lawrence Buell has termed 'toxic discourse'. Buell argues that contemporary rhetorics surrounding the 'fear of a poisoned world' resemble descriptions of polluted and degraded urban landscapes in nineteenth-century realist fiction, and further back. (Buell 30). The particular rhetoric of Gothic or sci-fi horror ties in with much older literary and cultural representations of anxieties about man and nature, industrial development and lost idylls.

The destruction of London by flood is another 'toxic discourse' and an old story which readers have been enjoying in different forms since Richard Jeffries looked down on the city from Eltham and imagined a future where it was underwater in his *After London* (1884). In *The Drowned World* (1962) J. G. Ballard submerges London in prescient visions of a globally-warmed Europe existing in 2145 as a tropical lagoon. In recent years, as climate change becomes a more pressing concern, Will Self's *Book of Dave,* Stephen Baxter's *Flooded* and Maggie Gee's *Flood* have all imagined London's death by drowning while Adam Robert's sci-fi novel *Snow* buries London under a mysterious blanket of permafrost. Gee's vision of a drowning London is an almost ecstatic conclusion to a satire which depicts a moribund city disintegrating in the steady fall of unnatural rain before the big wave hits. Tom J. Hillard's examples of Gothic nature belong to a litera-ture which deals with these kinds of 'extreme states', but even when London is facing environmental threat it tends not to be in the epic or heroic style, but a rather more workaday register. The 'city wilderness' metaphors common to cinematic representations of New York or Los Angeles for example, as identi-fied by eco-critic Andrew Light, are not the primary mode by which we sense the workings of Gothic's destabilizing forces in London literature (Light 138). Instead, London's mundane Gothic noses its way out through cracks in the pavements, grows from seeds in suburban gardens or accumulates through the steady drip of rainwater. Of all the traditional literary Gothic motifs, it is per-haps the London rat which best exemplifies this conjunction of extreme eco-phobia and a more mundane Gothic of everyday, a force which is distressingly familiar and ubiquitous, and yet disturbingly other and strange, even supernat-ural. The experience of murophobia (fear of rodents) is a less exotic form of ecophobia: rather than a swoon in the face of the sublime or a trembling at the irreducible immensity of nature, rat fear takes us into the dirtier and more shameful domestic anxieties of Freud's Rat Man.

London's Rats

The image of the rat has always featured in anti-urban discourse, whether as part of racist representations of immigration or as an expression of fear of dis-ease and poverty, while a quasi-supernatural anxiety about their indestructible and illimitable nature makes them a staple feature of post-apocalyptic land-scapes. We call them up to express our everyday frustrations (the rat run, the rat race, 'city rats', a ratfuck[1]) as well as our Room 101-level fears. Dick Whitting-ton, one of London's founding heroes, is a rat-killer and the rat remains a particular source of anxiety, fear and identification in literary and cultural rep-resentations of London. While many of the stories in which rats appear are not the most subtle of Gothic narratives, the image of the rat is protean in London fiction and doesn't only appear as a fiendish carnivore or as an instrument of torture. The rat has variously been linked to Londoners themselves or has stood as an emblem of the underground (physical and imagined) of the city. It has appeared as a symbol of the most abject poverty or been celebrated for its rebel-lious energy. Paul Cowdell points out that rats have often embodied the threat of 'immigrant populations for a settled community' (Cowdell 20) and it is this resonance which emerges in possibly the most famous moment of rat-related

London Gothic. Dracula's faithful servant Renfield recounts his encounter with a swarm of rats which form themselves into the body of his vampiric Master:

> Rats, rats, rats! Hundreds, thousands, millions of them, and every one a life. And dogs to eat them, and cats too. All lives! All red blood, with years of life in it, and not merely buzzing flies! . . . And then He moved the mist to the right and left, and I could see that there were thousands of rats with their eyes blazing red, like His only smaller. He held up his hand, and they all stopped, and I thought He seemed to be saying, 'All these lives will I give you, ay, and many more and greater, through countless ages, if you will fall down and worship me!' And then a red cloud, like the colour of blood, seemed to close over my eyes, and before I knew what I was doing, I found myself opening the sash and saying to Him, 'Come in, Lord and Master!' The rats were all gone, but He slid into the room through the sash, though it was only open an inch wide, just as the Moon herself has often come in through the tiniest crack and has stood before me in all her size and splendour. (*Dracula* 263)

Maud Ellman comments on how this scene clearly calls up a whole series of interlinked fears, phobias and prejudices, (Ellman 64) uniting anti-Semitic distrust of immigration from the east, with the fear of 'swamping' and the endless reproduction which links vampire and rat ('hundreds, thousands, millions of them'). Whether based in discourses about race, class or species, the appearance of rats always foregrounds struggles over territory and spatial boundaries. As Gargi Bhattacharyya has suggested, writing about London's pigeons, it is the animals that live most successfully among us and within our messy streets that we most fervently wish to eradicate, and about which we spin horror stories and urban myths. Her explanation itself has a Gothic edge: 'the battle with these most human of animals, those that arrange their lives around the business and rhythm of the human world reveals an extra-rational intensity' (Bhattacharyya 216). Jonathan Burt also employs Gothic rhetoric as he concludes his wonderful study of the cultural history of rats with the observation that the rat embodies a 'dark vitality, that despite all the control and killing we do not overcome' (Burt 149). Robert Sullivan in his *Rats: A Year with New York's Most Unwanted Inhabitants*, talks of the rat as a 'mirror species' to ourselves (Sullivan 42), calling up a Gothic doubling of rat/human which is a frequent element of rat narratives. As Burt also suggests, the human/rat crossover often occurs in moments and places of crisis and horror, war, urbanization, slum living, torture: 'Like evil twins with no redemptive qualities, [rats'] rapacity, appetites, breeding abilities and adaptability make them world-devouring' (Burt 13).

Rats have a more positive profile in cultures where they are connected with characteristics of charm, cleverness and fertility (as in China). An interesting feature of their London persona, however, is that while they are often connected with Londoners themselves, it is often as victims rather than aggressors.

Cowdell notes that rats 'rarely turn up as trickster figures' in Western literature and indeed, a London rat is rarely cast in the role of a loveable cockney figure. More often, if rats are personified it is as lowly, broken and desperate figures (Cowdell 2).

Gothic Statistics

Given that *Rattus rattus* is popularly held responsible for killing a third of Europe's population in the Black Death of 1347 to 1352, it's not surprising that they join the pantheon of London Dungeon-style horrorshow villains. For a modern audience, reading Daniel Defoe's *Journal of the Plague Year* is rather like the experience of watching a horror film where the hapless victims don't know that the killer is *just behind them*. As Defoe's H. F. meticulously records the mounting number of dead, we sense the presence of the disease-carriers out of sight in the narrative itself. Indeed, our fascination with counting and accounting for the numbers of rats around us can often seem like a hysterical reaction to a sense of uncontrollable and boundless increase.

All discussions of rats focus on a Gothic statistical increase, vertiginous numbers of unstoppable rattiness. Burt provides us with a calculation from 1857 which claims that a single pair of rats could produce 48,319,698,843,030,344,720 offspring in ten years (Burt 45). According to Robert Sullivan, '[i]f you are in New York while you are reading this sentence or even in any other major city then you are in proximity to two or more rats having sex.' (Sullivan 11). Male rats can mate with 20 females in a few hours; the gestations period is just three weeks and a litter can produce up to 20 pups.

The UK's National Pest Technicians Association keeps careful track of statistics which prove a 44% rise in reported 'treatments' for rat infestations from 2006–2007 to 2007–2008, due to a warm summer. Such statistics are gleefully reported, and rather than focusing on the spread of disease or rat-attack, the primary threat is of ever-increasing *proximity*. 'Last year Londoners were estimated never to be more than 18 metres (20 yards) from a rat; the new figures suggest that the distance is now closer to 14 metres', reports *The Times*. (*The Times* 7 December 2006). Whether the cause *du jour* is changes in refuse collection, the scrapping of free pest-control services by city councils, properties left empty in the economic recession, warmer summers, wetter winters or more junk food outlets, the one constant is that the rat population is in a state of hysterical increase. 'A ten year high . . . 15% rise' (*Daily Telegraph* 10 February 2009); 'Wet weather has been blamed by experts for the 1.6m infestations reported across the country in 2006' (*BBC News* 19 December 2007); 'rat population to treble to 200 million . . . the rodents will outnumber Britain's 60 million residents by three to one'. (*Daily Mail* 16 December 2008). Burt points out that after plague outbreaks at the beginning of the twentieth century, the accumulation of data on the 'plague-bearing rat' not only made plague visible but

became the means of its control. It became the central focus of the bureaucra-
tization of disease control, with the recording of addresses, the counting of
fleas, the documentation of size, gender, species, leading to the assembling
of large quantities of statistics. (Burt 129)

Any horror story or reportage featuring rats will also mention, alongside
population statistics, the prodigious size of individual rats. Henry Mayhew's
rat-catchers and sewer-hunters tell tales of the 'ferocious and formidable'
sewer rats:

> Many wondrous tales are still told among the people of men having lost their
> way in the sewers and of having wandered among the filthy passages – their
> lights extinguished by noisy vapours – till, faint and overpowered, they
> dropped down and died on the spot. Other stories are told of sewer-hunters
> beset by myriads of enormous rats, and slaying thousands of them in their
> struggle for life, till at length the swarms of the savage things overpowered
> them and in a few days afterwards their skeletons were discovered picked to
> the very bone. (Mayhew 150)

As Burt suggests, our belief, grounded or otherwise, of the dizzying number of
rats and their excessive collective and individual size, must be related to our
sense of the danger and ill health of our urban environments. Of course, the rat
and its Gothic numbers are produced by the material conditions of urban living
itself, by its architecture, waste systems, its life and its death. Rats thrive in the
busiest places (fast food strewn streets and uncared for but populated buildings) they sidle into the spaces we neglect. But they are also the focus for the
imagined dimension of our occupation of urban space, our guilt and anxiety
about the unnaturalness of our cities. As Ellman says, 'The rat is the phobic
image of our own excess; our distortion of the balance of nature' (Ellman 62).
Christopher Herbert reads Mayhew's detailed account of the many lives of rats
in London as betraying a horrified fascination with an animal that connects
with ancient taboos against dirt, sex and *mingling* of all kinds:

> Mayhew claims to discuss rats, like every other topic in strictly factual terms,
> but the evil glamour that they take on his pages identifies them as playing
> a very specific cultural and imaginative role: that of taboo animal par excel-
> lence, the superlative modern-day referent, at least for city dwellers, of the
> many biblical injunctions against contact with unclean "creeping things" that
> it is forbidden to touch . . . (Herbert 14)

Such a reading of the rat suggests why analogies between rats and London
crowds, specifically the population of the slums and the East End are so frequent, and are used to suggest a variety of degraded characteristics: cowed
hunger, hardened playfulness or cannibalistic viciousness. In Augustus Mayhew's
Paved With Gold, a pavement mob 'huddled together as closely as rats in a corner'

in a crowd which 'seemed to leak in from all sides' (*Paved With Gold* 1). However, elsewhere in the same novel, it is poverty itself that is rattish, 'pauperism . . . infected our workhouses as thickly as rats do a sewer' (*Paved With Gold* 47). William Booth's *In Darkest England* records how on one of his Salvationist journeys through slum streets, '[m]iserable little children, with sin-stamped faces, dart about like rats' (Booth 32). Ben Tillett's account of the struggles between dock workers for daily work uses the image of rats to depict unthinking desperation: 'Coats, flesh and even ears were torn off . . . [the stronger men] battled through kicking, punching, cursing crowds to the rails of the "cage" which held them like rats – mad human rats who saw food in the ticket' (Fishman 15).[2]

Even in documentary reports such as this, or in realist texts, descriptions of rats or the queasy slippage between human and rat share this Gothic undertone. In *Bleak House*, a rat appears in the most luridly Gothic scene of the book, where Jo and Lady Deadlock visit the grave vault, slinking into a hole in this 'place of abomination' (*Bleak House* 139). Mrs Rudge's deserted house in *Barnaby Rudge* is rat-infested; Oliver Twist shrinks from the resemblance of the miserable inhabitants of a desperate tenement to the rats outside, 'hideous with famine' (*Oliver Twist* 37). In his autobiographical sketches, Dickens recalls the particular horror of the rats in his childhood workplace, and how their aural invasiveness compounded the misery of his situation. He calls up the memory of the riverside warehouse, 'literally overrun with rats . . . swarming in the cellars . . . the sound of their squeaking and scuffling coming up that stairs at all times'.[3]

Supernatural Rats

Renfield's vision of Dracula as rat(s) takes its force from this discourse of ratness. This is an obvious rhetoric of swarming, infinite reproduction, abjection and uneasy slitherings between one state and another. Rats, of course, appear frequently in Gothic stories as agents or signifiers of impending doom. Their ravenous appetites do the narrator of Poe's 'The Pit and the Pendulum' an inadvertent favour as they bear down on the narrator in 'troops' and 'accumulating heaps' ('The Pit and the Pendulum' 220). Bram Stoker's Paris story 'Burial of the Rats' fictionalizes the kind of accounts Mayhew recorded from those forced to make their living in or around the territories of sewer rats. A man has lost his way in the sewers, and although he has made a 'fight for it, even when his torch had gone out. But they were too many for him! They had not been long about it! The bones were still warm but they had been picked clean' (*Dracula* 102). The 'burial' of the title refers to the efficient dispersal of dead bodies by rats, and links are made between the desperate and murderous poor who assail the hero to try and rob him and pursue him through the streets, and the rat pack itself, watching him with gleaming eyes from a pile of bones.

The pursuers at one point enter the water with a 'soft splash just as a rat will make when he enters the water' (*Dracula's Guest* 103).

In another Stoker tale, 'The Judge's House' the rats are in league with a murderous ghost, and H. P. Lovecraft's tale 'The Rats in the Walls' perhaps takes the prize for the sheer number of flesh-eating monster rats, in nineteenth-century fiction at least. Both tales are set in isolated Gothic houses and work through the motif of rats undermining and lurking in the foundations and infrastructure, remerging to reveal guilty secrets and hidden horrors. Stories that feature swarms of rats as massed agents of doom, appearing to punish a hidden crime tend to end with the protagonists driven mad by the rats, pursued by forces of unreason and implacable vengeance. In a similar vein, Dickens' tale of the unfortunate Chips in *The Uncommercial Traveller* begins with one (talking) rat which then slowly multiplies into thousands of rats that appear in every corner of Chips' life (including his trouser pockets and the scene of his marriage proposal). Chips is the cursed with ability to know what every rat in London is doing and finally flees to sea to escape them. The rats follow, eat the ship away and then eat Chips and his drowning crewmates. The story ends with 'an immense, overgrown rat' sitting laughing on the corpse of Chips 'what the rats left of Chips' (*Uncommercial Traveller* 233). Richard Marsh's rats in *The Joss* (1901) replace the insects of his earlier bestseller *The Beetle*. They are a demonic hoard, a 'hundred thousand' of them swarming all around the heroines' ankles in a derelict Lambeth house, in a 'not particularly reputable street' (*The Joss* 45). The rats of *The Joss* are, like Stoker's, harbingers of a monstrous Eastern power and act merely as part of the Gothic set-dressing for the real menace (and are entirely replaced by snakes at the end of the novel). Nevertheless, it is the particular ability of the rats to be both a mundane element of the miserable London surroundings and a sinister embodiment of the real foreign evil to come that makes the chapters in which they appear easily the most effective of the novel.

The hysterical plenitude of the Victorian rat speaks of mobs and the massed ranks of diseased and disobedient poor. The rat in the early twentieth century is a different sort of creature; in modernism, the rat is a symbol of starving and picking, textual burrowing and the production of waste. Ellman argues the rat symbolizes modernism's dissolving of boundaries:

> The rat in modernism . . . stands for waste, whether bodily, civic or semantic, But that is waste that can never be eradicated: it is the abject that returns upon the subject, dissolving the bounds between self and non-self, inside and outside, civilised and savage. . . . The rat stands for the garbage of signification, the sounds left over when the sense if gone – the gnawing, the scurrying, the little cries. (Ellman 73)

If, in nineteenth-century writing, the rat is most associated with places of depositing and mass accumulation (warehouses, slums, graveyards), while the modernist rat is a foraging networker, burrowing its way through boundaries and chewing up fragments, then London's contemporary rats are victims, most at home in disreputable literary forms and genres, in narratives of homelessness, marginalization and suffering.

King Rats: The New Rats on the Scene

James Herbert's best-selling *Rats* trilogy (*The Rats, Lair* and *Domain*) was inspired, according to the author's own account, by the Renfield scene in Todd Browning's 1931 adaptation of *Dracula*, but also his childhood experiences growing up in Whitechapel (Jones and Herbert 53). Herbert's *Rats* launched an entire sub-genre of British ecophobic horror writing featuring malevolent swarms (the prolific John Halkin following Herbert's successful format with a series of books covering killer lizards, bloodworms, beetles, caterpillars and jellyfish.) The novels trade on the Lovecraftian horror of carnivorous rat-packs, as giant flesh-eating rats (mutated by laboratory experiments) attack the vulnerable in the slums at first and then appear in tube stations and schools. The trilogy trades on established rat lore and long-standing anxieties about rats. *Lair* enjoys some scenes of the rats devouring courting couples in Epping Forest and *Domain* is set in the period after a nuclear attack and hands over the whole city to the rats, now mutating into a grotesque human/rat hybrid. In the denouement of the associated graphic novel *The City*, a mysterious Pied Piper figure known as The Traveller appears and lures the rats over London Bridge which is then detonated.

Herbert's rat stories have been praised for their implicit social critique, but their primary use of the figure of the rat is for out-and-out horror. The link between illicit sex (particularly extra-marital sex and also homosexuality) and death by rat is forcibly and graphically made throughout the trilogy. In Herbert, the mundane horridness of the London rat is exacerbated by the fear of exotic connections to even more horrifying *foreign* rats. Herbert's rats originally come from New Guinea, and are in fact black rats (*rattus rattus*) rather than the London brown rat. Likewise, the fantasies of psychosexual sadism inspired in the Rat Man emerge from stories of alleged Eastern war punishments of the sort described in Mirabeau's China-set *Torture Garden*. The toxic transformation of London's rats into instruments of torture is echoed in *Nineteen Eighty-Four*. D. J. Taylor links Winston Smith's rodent nemeses with Orwell's experiences in Burma; subsequently 'the rodent tide flows endlessly through his work', through the dosshouses of 1930s Southwark, to the trenches of Spain (Taylor 143).

After the Herbert assault, the rat has been somewhat rehabilitated in popular fiction. In the contemporary urban Gothic of Neil Gaiman and China Miéville, the complex stylistic rattinesss identified by Ellman in Joyce or Kafka is replaced by a thematic return to the idea of the closeness of rat and human, particularly rat and Londoner. Both Gaiman's *Neverwhere* and Miéville's *King Rat* tell stories of mythological power struggles in fantastic versions of the contemporary city; both tell of young male protagonists who fall out of everyday London and into its shadow side. In Gaiman, Neverwhere lies in 'London Below', a place populated by human interlocuters ('rat-speakers') who serve the super-intelligent rats.

> He had long hair, a patchy brown beard, and his ragged clothes were trimmed with fur – orange-and-white-and black fur, like the coat of a calico cat . . . he walked with a pronounced stoop, his hands held up at his chest, fingers pressed together. . . . There were now more than a dozen of the fur-trimmed people standing around them, women and men, and even a few children. They moved in scurries: moments of stillness, followed by dashes towards Richard. (*Neverwhere* 32)

Miéville's hero Saul discovers he is next in line for the position of King Rat and sets about discovering his rodent heritage and new powers. He defeats the sinister Piper figure and the novel ends with an upbeat chapter where Saul announces the dawn of a rat republic and names himself 'Citizen Rat', a development the reader cheers along with. *King Rat's* most effective scene comes in the climactic stand-off between Saul and the Piper in a drum 'n' bass club. Dancers, rats and spiders throng together in thrall to the Piper's music and are caught up in a *dance macabre*. In both texts, rats are far from the brute monsters of Herbert's imagination. Instead, they are vulnerable Londoners; easily distracted by the temptations of easy living in the city's junk, imprisoned by the city's physical architecture and in thrall to powers they barely understand. Both novels flirt with the ecophobic, but end with an assertion of the cohesion of the underground and a celebration of its dark energies. In Miéville in particular the rat world becomes the site of utopian projections.

Children and Rats

In general, rodents have a far better profile in children's literature than in adult culture. Stories about empathy and affiliation between child and rat have recently been revivified by Disney's 2007 *Ratatouille*, where the humorous inversions of children's culture allow for a story about a cute rat pursuing his dream to become a chef.[4] Gary Wesfahl suggests that in fantasy literature, rats have often been given the particular role of sidekick and helper to a child or another animal protagonist (Westfahl 650). Mice are more frequently portrayed as loveable, and perhaps the best known rat in Edwardian children's fiction, *The Wind in the Willows'* Ratty, is really a water-vole. Beatrix Potter's Samuel Whiskers is a charming psychopath, an 'enormous rat' who wants to eat up Tom Kitten in a 'roly-poly kitten dumpling'. When Samuel and his wife have to flee the scene of their kitten-rolling crime they dispatch to a farm where their many descendents cause havoc: 'There are rats, and rats and rats . . . There is no end to them!'

(*Tale of Samuel Whiskers* 77). Kenneth B. Kidd discusses the importance of the rat/child nexus to Freud's account of the Rat Man, but the pathological associations of the Rat Man have a more general application to children's and animals' marginalized status in urban culture. (Kidd 144) The affinity of stories for children with a rodenty world is obvious: both groups are identified with small spaces, with misappropriation of the materials and detritus of the adult world, and of course, the children of the poor are especially discussed in terms of unwelcome and excessive numbers. Children and rats are figured as problematic in terms of their presence in the city; they move at a different speed to the rest of the urban world and summon ideas of secret, feral worlds outside of the control of adults (an idea used with particular effect in Michael de Larrabeiti's London-set *Borribles* trilogy). They are unproductive, ill-disciplined and an inconvenient embodiment of social ills.

However, in children's literature the rat is often celebrated as smart, funny and resourceful, or is empathized with as victimized and bullied. Richmal Crompton's William generally has a rat about him somewhere, (although he also celebrates the rat-killing skills of Jumble, his dog) and in contemporary children's literature there are a number of picture books for even the youngest children featuring rats as friendly protagonists: Lauren Childs' *That Pesky Rat* (2008), James Cressey's *Fourteen Rats and A Rat-Catcher* (1979) *Cinderella's Rat* (2002) by Susan Meddaugh or Maria Sellier's retelling of a Chinese folktale *What the Rat Told Me* (2008). For older children, Philip Pullman's *I was a Rat! Or, the Scarlet Slippers* (1999), a retelling of the Cinderella story, *Mrs Frisby and the Rats of NIMH* (1971) by Robert C. O'Brien or *Emmy and the Incredible Shrinking Rat* (2007) by Lynne Jonell all use ratness to highlight themes of belonging and not-belonging, loneliness and marginalization.

Even the London rat has benefitted from the more empathetic portrayals in children's literature. Frances Hodgson Burnett's heroine Sara Crewe in *A Little Princess* makes a friend of the rat that lives in her attic, empathizing with his friendless state:

> 'I dare say it is rather hard to be a rat,' she mused. 'Nobody likes you. People jump and run away and scream out, "Oh, a horrid rat!" I shouldn't like people to scream and jump and say, "Oh, a horrid Sara!" the moment they saw me. And set traps for me, and pretend they were dinner. It's so different to be a sparrow. But nobody asked this rat if he wanted to be a rat when he was made. Nobody said, "Wouldn't you rather be a sparrow?"' (104)

The Rambles of a Rat (1864) by A. L. O. E. (Charlotte Maria Tucker) celebrates the rat's pluckiness and allies the sufferings of its rodent protagonists to the plight of the city's street children, as expressed by one of the empathetic and articulate Ratto, who narrates the tale.

> If ever I felt pity it was for those ragged little urchins. We were well-fed, but they were hungry; Nature had given us sleek warm coats, but they trembled

with cold. It was very clear that it was much harder to them to support life
than if they had been rats. I wondered if in this great city there were many
such helpless children, and if there were none to care for them!

"I say, Ratto," observed Oddity, licking his soft coat till the beautiful polish
upon it made one almost forget its ugly colour, 'tis a pity that these children
are so dirty; but may be they are not so particular about such matters as we
rats". (*Rambles of a Rat* 22)

In recent children's literature, rats have taken on more evolved roles. The
power struggles of Robin Jarvis' *The Deptford Mice* features both heroic and
villainous rats, in struggles with victimized mice, and the ultimate villain is a cat.
Larrabeiti's Borribles are children, who have left home and live on the streets,
growing pointed ears and evading capture. The Borribles distinguish themselves from their loathed enemies, the 'stinking rodent', rat-shaped Rumbles
(a thinly veiled parody of Elizabeth Beresford's Wombles) but the Borribles
themselves are energetically rattish, anti-materialist and independent:

Borribles are generally skinny and have pointed ears which give them a
slightly satanic appearance. They are pretty tough-looking and always scruffy,
with their arses hanging out of their trousers, but apart from that they look
just like normal children. (*Deptford Mice* 4)

Implicitly, these kind of stories, directed at child-readers, go some way to
engaging with the labelling of London's children as 'street-rats', a toxic discourse still very much in current tabloid use. Children's literature seems to be
interested in how 'thinking rat' suggests an empathetic connection between
marginalized groups. Such representations and those of the adult urban Gothic
of Gaiman and Miéville which revel in the outsider identity of ratness, also offer
an idea of a different kind of London space. Where the traditional Gothic rat is
a creature of rank interiors and genetic mutation, children's Gothic literature
(or literature which employs some limited use of the patterns of Gothic) 'thinks
rat' as an imaginative reaction to how its protagonists might intercede between
underground and overground and forage for small freedoms in the city.

Conclusion

In contemporary climate change narratives, ecophobia occurs on a global
scale. However, London's more mundane Ecogothic, whether it is traced in the
despised London rat, or in the backdrop of exhausted or derelict land, offers a
mode of Gothic which departs, perhaps, from a preoccupation with dematerial-
ized 'hauntological' elements which Roger Luckhurst has critiqued. The Gothic
of ecophobia dramatises and foregrounds the multiple anxieties and discom-
forts of our relationship with the natural environment and so provides a
different perspective on the city's historical fragility and uncertain future.

Thinking about or noticing nature takes us into different spatial and temporal scales and reveals new dimensions of our environment to us. Rats, as the most weirdly human of Gothic creatures come to represent all aspects of our uneasy sense of ourselves as both natural beings and parts of an urban machine. The London rat may sometimes be called on as a supernatural manifestation of mindless evil or an emblem of the waste and squalor of the city, but it is also a figure of curious affinity with the way the city can make us suffer. Rats are narrative raw material that can be manipulated into monstrous forms or pitiful victims as London keeps producing its own innumerable brood of rats, and rat stories.

Notes

[1] One of the many variations on rat-based slang offered by the Urban Dictionary. com; to ratfuck is to steal or root around for an object, leaving a mess behind.

[2] See also Hugh Cunningham, *The Children of the Poor: Representations of Childhood Since the Seventeenth Century*, who cites similar examples from Blanchard Jerrold and John Hollingshead and writes extensively on the representation of London's 'street-rats'.

[3] Dickens, C. (1875), 'An Autobiographical Fragment' in *The Life of Charles Dickens* by Forster, J. (1875), *Life of Charles Dickens*, London: James R. Osgood and Company: Volume I, Chapter II, at Project Gutenberg http://www.gutenberg.org/dirs/etext96/batlf10.txt, accessed 30 July 2009.

[4] I'm grateful for comments made on an early version of this paper during a session on London Gothic at the 2009 Literary London Conference held at Queen Mary College, University of London. Scott McCracken, Emily Horton and Minna Vuohelainen spied the rats in *A Little Princess*, *Ratatouille* and Marsh's *The Joss* respectively.

Works Cited

Bhattacharyya, G. (2003), 'Rats with Wings: London's Battle with Animals', in *London From Punk to Blair* (eds) Joe Kerr and Andrew Gibson, London: Reaktion

Booth, W. (1890), *In Darkest England and the Way Out*, http://www.gutenberg.org/dirs/etext96/detwo10.txt, accessed 30 July 2009

Buell, L. (2001), *Writing for an Endangered World: Literature, Culture and Environment in the U.S. and Beyond*, Cambridge, MA: Harvard University Press

Burnett, F. H. (1961), *A Little Princess*, London: Puffin

Burt, J. (2006), *Rat*, London: Reaktion

Cowdell, P. (2008), 'If not, shall employ "Rough on Rats": Identifying the common elements of rat charms', in Jonathan Roper, *Charms, Charmers and Charming: International Research on Verbal Magic*, London: Palgrave, 17–25

Cunningham, H. (1991), *The Children of the Poor: Representations of Childhood Since the Seventeenth Century*, Oxford: Blackwell

De Larrabeiti, M. (2003), *The Borrible Trilogy*, London: Tor Books

Dickens, C. (1843), *Oliver Twist* (1838), Leipzig: Bernard Tauchnitz

Dickens, C. (1861), *The Uncommercial Traveller*, London: Chapman and Hall

Dickens, C. (1868), *Bleak House*. London: Chapman and Hall

Dickens, C. (1875), 'An Autobiographical Fragment' in Forster, J., *Life of Charles Dickens*, London: James R. Osgood and Company

Edgecombe, R. S. (1994), 'The Urban Idyll in Martin Chuzzlewit', The Review of English Studies, 45(179), 370–83

Ellman, M. (2004), 'Writing Like a Rat', *Critical Quarterly*, 46(4), 59–76

Estok, S. (2009), 'Theorizing in a Space of Ambivalent Openness: Ecocriticism and Ecophobia', *Interdisciplinary Studies in Literature and Environment* 16(2), 203–25

Fanthorpe, U. A. (1986), 'Rising Damp', *Selected Poems*, London: Penguin

Fishman, W. J. (1988), *East End 1888: A Year in a London Borough Among the Labouring Poor*, London: Duckworth

Forster, J. (1875), *Life of Charles Dickens*, London: James R. Osgood and Company

Gaiman, N. (2005), *Neverwhere*, London: Headline

Heise, U. K. (2008), *Sense of Place and Sense of Planet: The Environmental Imagination of the Global*, Oxford: Oxford University Press

Herbert, C. (1998), 'Rat Worship and Taboo in Mayhew's London', *Representations*, 23 (Summer, 1988), 1–24

Herbert, J. (1974), *The Rats*, London: The New English Library

Herbert, J. and Jones, S. (1992), *James Herbert: By Horror Haunted*, London: New English Library

Hillard, T. (2009), ' "Deep Into That Darkness Peering": An Essay on Gothic Nature', *Interdisciplinary Studies in Literature and Environment*, 16(4), 685–95

James, M. R. (2006), 'The Rats' in *The Haunted Doll's House and Other Stories*, London: Penguin, 172–77

Kidd, K. (2004), *Making of American Boys: Boolog and the Feral Tale*, Minneapolis: University of Minnesota Press

Light, A. (1999), 'Boyz in the Woods: Urban Wilderness in American Cinema' in *The Nature of Cities: Ecocriticism and Urban Environments*, (eds) M. Bennett and D. Teague, Tuscon: University of Arizona Press, 137–56

Luckhurst, Roger (2002), 'The Contemporary London Gothic and the Limits of the "Spectral Turn" ' *Textual Practice* 16(3), 530

Marsh, R. (2007), *The Joss: A Reversion*, Chicago: Valancourt Books

Mayhew, A. (1858), *Paved with Gold, or the Romance and Reality of the London Streets*, London: Chapman and Hall

Mayhew H. (1861), *London Labour and the London Poor*, London: Griffin, Bone and Company

Poe, E. A. (2003), 'The Pit and the Pendulum' in *The Fall of the House of Usher and Other Writings*, London: Penguin

Potter, B. (2002), *The Tale of Samuel Whiskers or the Roly-Poly Pudding* (1907), London: F. Warne and Co

Saguaro, S. (2006), *Garden Plots: The Politics and Poetics of Gardens*, Aldershot: Ashgate

Stoker, B. (1998), *Dracula*, Oxford: Oxford World's Classics

Stoker, B. (2007), 'The Burial of the Rats' in *Dracula's Guest and Other Weird Tales* London: Penguin. 93–118

Sullivan, R. (2006), *Rats: A Year with New York's Most Unwanted Inhabitants*, London: Granta

Taylor, D. J. (2003), *Orwell: The Life*, London: Chatto and Windus

Tucker, C. M. ('A. L .O. E.') (1864), *The Rambles of a Rat*, London: T. Nelson and Son

Westfahl, G. (2005), *Greenwood Encyclopaedia of Science Fiction and Fantasy: Themes, Works and Wonders*, volume 2, Westport, CT: Greenwoood Press, The National Pest Technicians Association website: http://www.npta.org.uk/, accessed 10 September 2009

Part Three

Sites, Performance and Film

Chapter 10

Gog and Magog: Guardians of the City

J. S. Mackley

In *Master Humphrey's Clock* by Charles Dickens there is a scene where two giant statues in the London Guildhall, Gog and Magog, animate during the night. The giants are initially presented as terrifying; however, they seem content to settle with a cask of wine and recount stories until dawn.

The Gog and Magog section in *Master Humphrey's Clock* epitomizes some aspects of Gothic fiction. The story alludes to events in a constructed pre-Renaissance time, an era that writers of Gothic fiction may have considered as something existing outside the civilized order of their own society, something medieval and barbaric; a time filled with superstition and fear. Even Magog refers to them as 'the old simple times'. The monstrous presence of the giants, associated with the Apocalypse, suggests that they originated from distant lands, yet they have infiltrated the heart of London: they are in positions of power; they 'guard this ancient city' (Dickens 275).

This essay will consider Gog and Magog in literature and London pageantry: the first part will consider three medieval legends that refer to the origins of the giants who would eventually become protectors of the city. It is ironic that even in the era that writers of Gothic fiction generally considered to be unrefined, the Middle Ages, there was still a focus on an earlier culture considered crude and uncivilized. This society existed before the Roman invasion of Britain in the first century AD; yet, it was also something that had broken away from Classical civilization. Medieval writers such as Geoffrey of Monmouth heard, and then embellished, legends of the first settlers on the shores of a land called Samothea, later called Albion and then Britain. Resonances of these legends have echoed through the centuries, and are still present in London.

The legends incorporated some non-canonical themes that bubbled beneath the surface of Biblical texts. These references were not explained, possibly because the oral tradition meant the apocryphal legends were so well-known it was unnecessary to write them down. The ambiguous characters of Gog and Magog, who are mentioned in, amongst others, the books of Genesis and Revelation are transformed into one (and sometimes two) giants in the medieval versions of the story. The legend of the giants was adapted by later writers, bringing their story into London. Effigies of these giants, which have recently been paraded at the Lord Mayor's Show, have been part of London's heritage for many centuries, possibly since the reign of Henry V (1413–1422). The second part of this article will consider the representations of these effigies in pageants that celebrated significant royal events, in particular between 1415 and 1588. In addition, statues of the giants have been displayed in the Guildhall for the last five centuries. Thus, this article will consider the giants' place in 'London Gothic' as well as the more sinister undertones attached to these pageants, and the repercussions of inviting the Pagan 'Other' into the city.

Origin Mythology

There are three separate, but not wholly independent, strands of British mythology concerning the first settlers of the island that came to be known as Britain. These include the origin of the giants who became sentinels in the London Guildhall. The legends present a textual conundrum in that the earliest stories concerning the first settlers of the island were not the first to be written: Geoffrey of Monmouth composed the *Historia regum Britanniae* (History of the Kings of Britain) in Latin around 1135–1138 (Wright xvi). He claimed that his work was a direct translation into Latin of a book in the 'British Language'; such a book is yet to be identified, but clearly he has based some of his pseudo-histories on the writings of Nennius (Rowley 14–15).

Geoffrey's *Historia* was considered (by most) to be a reliable history for many centuries (Morris 427). The legends were composed to give a mythological status to the earliest British settlers and to give the country a greater presence on the world stage. The first settlers included Brutus, the great-grandson of Æneas of Troy, who put ashore on the south coast of Albion and gave his name to the land. Brutus's crewmembers included Corineus. Together they cleared the land of the aboriginal giants, in particular Gogmagog, who lived there. (Gogmagog, or Goemagog, the leader of the giants, is an amalgamation of the Biblical names Gog and Magog; the significance of this name will be discussed later). Brutus then founded the city of *Troy-Novant* (New Troy), later called London.

Although Geoffrey (and others) discussed the noble heritage of the founders of Britain through the arrival of Brutus, there was a gap in the legend about how the indigenous giants arrived in Albion in the first place. Subsequently, around a century and a half after Geoffrey produced his version of the Trojan settlers, writers included further embellishments to explain the origins of the giants. In an Anglo-Norman version, *Des Grantz Geanz*, Corineus spares Gogmagog so that the latter can explain his origins (Brereton ll. 521ff.). The legend was also translated into Middle English in a short Metrical Chronicle in London around 1340. It is this legend that I wish to address first.

1. Albina

The Short Metrical Chronicle describes a King of Greece (called Diocletian) who had twenty beautiful daughters. Despite all being 'maride wel' to men of 'gret honour' (ll. 29, 31), as daughters of a king themselves, their pride forbids them to submit to their husbands' wishes. The devil tempts the eldest to lead her sisters in a revolt and to plot the husbands' murder (ll. 39–40). They plan to hide knives under their pillows and to murder the men while they sleep (ll. 90–93). However, the youngest daughter reveals the plot to her husband and her father.

The source for all these stories of mass husband-killing is found in the Greek legend of the Danaids, the daughters of Danus, King of Argos, who kill their husbands at their father's command (Apollodorus II.I.15). Holinshed notices the parallels between the story of Diocletian and Danus in his *Historie of England* (1577); however, he gives little credence to the legend, listing Danus's fifty daughters by name and observing 'none of them hight [was called] Albina' (5.8).

As a consequence for their intended murder, the conspirators are exiled, 'set adrift in a boat without sails, oars or a rudder' (ll. 287, 294). The sisters land on an island, to which Albina gives her name: 'I take this land as my own. After my own name, Albion, you shall all call it' (ll. 314–16).

The first task that the sisters undertake is to hunt for venison (l. 329), and, after feasting to excess, they are overwhelmed with lechery: 'They fared well [on that island] although among them, they had begun to long for lechery, and they all said amongst themselves that they desired nothing, except the company of men', ll. 337–40). The irony is that the women intended to slaughter their husbands and then realized they missed the intimacy of their company.

The story could have ended with the women contemplating their actions in a state of enforced celibacy; however, as before, the devil offers a solution to Albina's problem and 'engendered them with giants' (ll. 343–44). The Anglo-Norman *Des Grantz Geanz* takes the unpalatable nature of this scene further: first, the women are visited by incubi, male sexual demons believed to possess mortal women while they slept (l. 407), and then there are acts of incest between mothers and offspring, and between brother and sister: 'Children, by great outrage, engendered in their mothers, boys and girls who were big. Sisters were impregnated by their brothers' (ll. 434–37). The union between humans and demons that produces giants as their offspring has resonances from an apocryphal Old Testament legend of the Nephilim, or Watcher Angels. This legend describes how the Watcher Angels desired the human women and came down to impregnate them. Their offspring were giants, the Grigori. Between them, the Nephilim and the Grigori taught mankind forbidden sciences – weapon making, astrology and witchcraft – and practised sexual perversions. Because of this secret knowledge, God sent the Great Deluge to erase all traces of the Nephilim and their teachings (1 Enoch 7; Sinistrari 83).

The inhabitants of Albion accumulate a list of transgressions that pervert the natural order, including the murder (or planned murder) of their husbands, mating with demonic entities and then acts of incest. This continues for eight centuries. There are no *human* inhabitants left by this time and nothing is said of the death of Albina and her sisters. The Classical order of a daughter of a Greek King and her sisters descends into the chaos of the Pagan 'Other' which ultimately must be suppressed.

This descent into inhumanity is a trope that would be well positioned in eighteenth- and nineteenth-century Gothic literature. Writers in the era of Horace Walpole regarded the medieval period as something unrefined and barbaric, but the composers of the Albina myth did the same four hundred years earlier. They reflected upon a time when they considered that society had broken away from the natural order, and elements needed to be cultivated or eradicated. In the light of the parallels with the myth of the Watcher Angels, as described in the *Short Metrical Chronicle*, Brutus's violent conquest of Albion and the slaughter of its inhabitants become more palatable. The 'ethnic cleansing' serves the same purpose as the Great Deluge: to wipe those who commit obscene acts from the Earth.

2. Brutus

The legend of Brutus as founder (or more accurately *re*-founder) of Albion was popularized through the circulation of Geoffrey of Monmouth's *Historia*. Geoffrey chronicles that, after Æneas flees and settles in Italy, his great-grandson, Brutus, accidentally kills his father whilst out hunting and is banished (Brutus's mother had died when Brutus was born). On his travels, Brutus finds an abandoned temple to Diana; she directs him in a dream towards Albion. (Diana promised that the land would be empty for his compatriots to settle; however, Brutus later finds that this is incorrect). Discovering a group of other Trojan descendants led by Corineus, together they travel to Albion. Just as Albina named the land after herself, so Brutus gives his name to the land as well (Wright 13).

The idea of naming a location after oneself is an important medieval trope. The founding of nations or cities can be seen in, amongst others, *Gawain and the Green Knight*, which speaks of the descendants of Troy's survivors founding cities, for example, Romulus founds Rome and Langaberde founds Lombardy. In this instance, Brutus is the only character credited with naming an entire nation after himself. The repetition of legends, such as the descendants of the survivors of Troy founding cities, serves to promote the idea that the nation's ancestry dates back to Æneas and therefore places it in context back to ancient, Classical gods. As Seznec points out, 'civilisation is a treasure which has been handed down through the centuries; and as no further distinction is made between the sacred and profane precursors of Christianity who first forged that treasure, it is at last possible for medieval man unreservedly and even with pride to claim the heritage of antiquity' (Seznec 18).

These mythological characters ceased to become representations of humanity; they became patrons of a nation or a city (Seznec 19). Heroes of Classical mythology were often of divine provenance and 'endowed with gigantic frames', and this same exaggerated belief was indulged by the Gothic nations (Fairholt 2). The Franks claimed to be descended from the Trojan Francus, a legend first seen in the *Chronique de Frédégaire* (composed around 660 AD). Seznec observes that, although this legend was the invention of Merovingian scholars, it was taken seriously as genealogy (Seznec 19). Æneas held a mythical status and yet was close enough to be a plausible ancestor. Furthermore, while there are two generations separating Æneas and Brutus, there are *fourteen* generations separating Æneas and Romulus. Indeed, Stow recognizes Geoffrey's intention to equal or surpass the heritage of the city of London with that of Rome, and cites FitzStephen's *Description of the Most Noble City of London*, who declared 'this citie is auncienter then Rome' (Stow I 80). The Roman claim on Æneas is further diluted as Romulus is descended through the line of Lavinia, Æneas's second wife. Therefore, Britain had a tie closer to Æneas than most cities, consequently it was well-established long before Rome.

The land of Albion proves to be fertile; however, despite Diana's promise, Brutus and Corineus discover it is inhabited by giants. Here, as Withington observes, Pagan giants are not ugly or deformed; 'they seem to be merely giant men' (Withington I 52). The descriptions of 'Britain' as a bounteous land, and the presence of the giants, draw parallels with the Biblical description of Canaan (Numbers 13:27–29). Here, the explorers anxiously explain that they 'saw the Nephilim there' (13:33), thus linking this description with the legend of the Watcher Angels. Brutus and his compatriots settle and then repulse the indigenous giants, led by Gogmagog (Wright 14). The giants are repelled from the majority of Albion by the Trojans, and forced into mountainous caverns.

The names of Gog and Magog are found in the Bible; in Revelation 20:8, they are supporters of Antichrist and symbolic of all future enemies of the Kingdoms of God. Medieval Biblical commentators sometimes ran two names together, creating a supreme evil entity: Corineus fought a battle on a Biblical scale.

Although in Geoffrey's *Historia* the giants have no voice after they are routed, they are able to regroup, and twenty giants return when Brutus is celebrating a day dedicated to the gods: they slay many Britons. In this instance, the giants are horrific and abnormal because they act as a disturbance against the structure of the natural order (Carroll 16). Brutus and Corineus then lead a slaughter of the giants, killing them all save Gogmagog, who is 'spared' for a wrestling match against Corineus. The wrestling is nothing more than a demonstration of the strength of the invading Trojans over the indigenous giants. Corineus is injured, but he still carries Gogmagog on his shoulders to the 'nearby coast' and launches him out to sea where the giant falls on to rocks and is smashed into a thousand pieces, staining the waters with his blood (Wright 14).

This imagery parallels Revelation, where Satan is hurled into a lake of burning sulphur. Only once the old order has been destroyed can the new civilization flourish, being either the New Troy or the New Jerusalem.

When Geoffrey included these legends in his *Historia*, he clearly had neither any concept of the distances of the south coast, nor indeed the disproportionate sizes of the two adversaries. He describes the place from which Gogmagog was thrown as 'Saltus Goemagog' – Gogmagog's leap. A record dating from 1494 describes the figures being recut in the turf at Plymouth Hoe. In the *View of Devonshire* (*c.* 1630), Westcote describes them as 'two men with clubbes in their hands cut in the turf, the one bigger, the other lesser, whom they term Gogmagog and Corineus, imitating the wrestling to have been between these two champions and the steep rocky cliff affording aptitude for such a cast' (Westcote 383). The hill figures, perhaps similar to the Cerne Abbas Giant in Dorset, were destroyed in 1671 with the building of the citadel on Plymouth Hoe.

Geoffrey's description of the battle between Corineus and Gogmagog leaves open the question of how the giants first arrived on Britain's shores. The inclusion of the Albina episode suggests the importance that later writers attached to their foundation mythology as well as needing to streamline the narrative to explain both the origins of the names 'Britain' and 'Albion' and where the giants came from. Accordingly, the explanation at the end of the Anglo-Norman version *Des Grantz Geanz* is more satisfying: Corineus spares Gogmagog's life, and the latter, articulate, despite his demonic origins, tells his story so that future generations will remember it (l. 546). Henry of Huntingdon argues that the knowledge of history 'distinguishes rational creatures from brutes, for brutes, whether men or beasts do not know . . . about their origins, their races, and the events and happenings in their native land' (Henry of Huntingdon 4). As Johnson observes, 'Gogmagog's ability to produce a coherent narrative of his own origins works against the projection of the giant community as one of non-civilized aliens' (Johnson 30–31). Speech carries presence; therefore, Gogmagog becomes a rational being, rather than a marginalized brute, and as we shall see later, one who plays an important role in the protection of the capital city.

3. Samothes and Albion

There is another, significantly later, version of the origins of the giants and the name of Albion. John Bale, writing in 1548 in *Illustrium majoris Britanniae scriptorum* ('Of Great Britain's Illustrious Writers'), includes the story of Samothes, an apocryphal son of Japheth, son of Noah. According to Bale, after the Great Deluge the sons of Japheth (whose sons, according to Genesis 10:2, also included Magog) populated the countries of Europe, and the name *Samothea* was given to the island that we now call Britain (Bale 1). Just over three centuries after Samothes, the island was invaded by a giant named Albion, the son of Neptune and Amphitrita. Holinghead's *Historie of England* (5.3) perpetuated the story of Samothea and describes how Albion enjoyed a long reign before helping his brother in a fight against Hercules, where he, Albion, was killed.

Details from this version of the legend were used by Sarah Bates in her *New History of the Trojan Wars*: she ascribes leadership to a giant *named* Albion, who Brutus slays, while Gog and Magog, two giant brothers, were taken to *Troy-Novant* as prisoners where they were chained to the Guildhall (Bates 142–44). The legend describes how Brutus built a palace where the Guildhall now stands. He also established a Temple to Diana where St Paul's Cathedral now stands, as was prophesied on his journey. During the reign of Edward I, thousands of oxen heads were excavated from a place near St Paul's formerly called *Diana's Chamber*. It is suggested that these were sacrifices at Diana's temple (Fuller 2–3). Legend speaks of a part of the remains of this temple, which was once called the Brutus stone, now called the London Stone, the mythological heart of the city. The London Stone on Cannon Street was most likely to have represented the *milliarium*, marking the centre of the city from which Romans measured the distances in Britannia (Bell 1966 82–88). A legend promises *So long as the stone of Brutus is safe, so long shall London flourish*; consequently, the city's fortune is linked to that of the stone itself. It is ironic that, like the nation's Pagan heritage, the safety of the city appears to be linked to the remains of a Pagan temple. Indeed, in view of Brutus establishing a temple to Diana, it has been suggested that the name is *Luandun* – the City of the Moon, or even *Llan Dian* – the Temple of Diana (Crossley 505).

The Giants in London

So far, we have considered three origin legends which offer conflicting explanations as to how the giants came to Britain. Giants were the savages of Romance stories, and Geoffrey of Monmouth's *Historia regum Britanniae* speaks of the bloody end of Gogmagog at the hands of Corineus. By contrast, the Anglo-Norman *Des Grantz Geanz* speaks of Corineus sparing Gogmagog, and Johnson argues that in this version, Gogmagog is not an uncivilized brute, but one who has the ability to communicate his origins.

The legends that include the subjection of the last two giants brought in chains to London are an eighteenth-century embellishment popularized by compilers of legend such as Sarah Bates and Thomas Boreman. They describe how Gog and Magog were taken to Brutus's palace – a building that later became the Guildhall – where they were chained to the gates to serve as porters (Bates 144; Kent 45). In the *Gigantick History of the Two Famous Giants*, Boreman posits that the effigies were placed there to commemorate the giants' service:

> two brave giants . . . richly valued their honour, and exerted their strength and force in defence of their liberty and country; so the city of London, by placing these their representatives in their Guildhall, emblematically declare,

that they will, like mighty giants, defend the honour of their country, and liberties of this their city. (Boreman 53)

The Guildhall is situated just off Gresham Street and Basinghall Street. Although parts of the hall (as it currently stands) date from 1411, excavations by the Museum of London Archaeology service (MoLAS) found that the thirteenth-century gatehouse appears to have been built directly over the southern entrance to the Roman amphitheatre (C. Thomas 7). There is also documentary evidence of a London Guildhall dating from 1128, as it is mentioned in the survey of the lands of St Paul's (A.H. Thomas xxxv).

The audiences of the pseudo-histories circulated by Bates and Boreman may well have been aware that the giants have been a part of London's pageantry, at least since the early fifteenth century. However, like the audience that questioned the giants' origins when they encountered them in Geoffrey's *Historia*, later audiences wondered how the giants were brought to London. There are resonances of the earliest records of their participation in the pageants: in 1415, a male and female giant greeted Henry V on his return from Agincourt at the Southwark entrance to London Bridge. The male carried an axe in his right hand; his left hand held a staff upon which the keys to the city were hanging as if he was a porter to the city (Cole 125–28; Fairholt 27–28). The giantess was of scarcely less stature, 'as if they were man and wife' (Cole 62). Kingsford argues of these giants that there is 'no doubt they are the mediæval ancestors of the modern Gog and Magog' (Kingsford 156). Withington suggests that the effigies were only used on single occasions and 'were apparently not kept' before 1554; consequently, they 'acquired no individuality' (Withington I 202).

However, the giants remained popular in the pageants: Thomas Eltham chronicles that in 1421 when, returning from France with his bride, Henry V saw 'Giants of immense stature, of wondrous craftsmanship' (Cole 76). It is chronicled that in 1432, Henry VI was met by a single giant champion, rather than two giants and it is unlikely that this was the same giant used in the 1415 pageant (Withington I 142).This giant carried a sword and an inscription corresponding with Psalm 109:29, 'Let mine adversaries be clothed with shame, and let them cover themselves with their own confusion, as with a mantle'.

Although giants have been a part of the city pageants since the fifteenth century, only in the sixteenth century are they given names. In 1522, a pageant to celebrate the visit of the Holy Roman Emperor Charles V names the giants as Samson and Hercules, a curious marrying of Classical and Biblical characters. A contemporary account of the pageantry describes how:

Att the drawe bryge off London the entering off the gate off the cytee dyd stande ij greate Gyauntys one presenting the parson of Sampson and the other hercules standing in ryche apparel holding between a grete cheyn of yron and a table hangyng in the myddys off the chayne wheryn was wryttyn in goldyn lettyrs sett in byce [from Fr. meaning light grey, tawny] the namys of all the landys and domynyons where the emperor is Kyng and Lorde in token-nyng thatt the emperor is able to holde all those domynyons by pour and strength as the seyd gyauntes holde the same cheyne by pouer and strengyth. (Withington I 56, 175–79)

Traditionally, Samson represents strength and Hercules embodies virtue. However, as Wofford argues, the giants are also symbolic of the king's power: Samson demonstrates the king drawing on the strength of the body politic, whereas Hercules defeats nations by eloquence rather than combat (Wofford 336–37). The connection of Samson and Hercules is not unique: there is a Samson and Hercules House in Tombland, Norwich, dating from 1657. Two white statues of giants wielding weapons stand as doorway pillars. Lethbridge suggests that the Cerne Abbas giant is actually a representation of Hercules; soil testing has shown that once there was something – possibly a representation of a lion skin – hanging from the extended left arm. Lethbridge suggests it is possible that the Gogmagog in Plymouth and the Cerne Abbas Giant, both of whom carried clubs, were both representations of a similar legend which even-tually streamlined into the legend of Gog and Magog (Lethbridge 77). As shall be discussed later, there are further connections between the legends of the Guildhall giants and Samson and Hercules.

In a procession to celebrate the marriage of Mary and Philip of Spain in 1554, the figures that performed the pageant at the drawbridge are called *Corineus Britannus*, and *Gogmagog Albionus* (Withington I 190). Furthermore, in 1558 on the accession of Queen Elizabeth, the final pageant on her journey was at Temple Bar, which was 'finely dressed with two giants, Gotmagot the Albion and Corinæus the Briton, who held between them a poetical recapitulation of the Pageantries, both in Latin and English' (Tottill 38–58). The various pageants along Elizabeth's route were to remind the future Queen of her responsibilities, including the unity of the Houses of Lancaster and York, the virtues of worthy governance, and her responsibilities of being a morally strong leader. The inclusion of the giants was to remind her of principal landmarks in the coun-try's history. Kent suggests that the same effigies were paraded before Queen Mary and Queen Elizabeth and that it was these figures that were destroyed in the Great Fire of London in 1666 (Kent 46); however, not all sources agree on their identities: a pamphlet in 1661 reportedly describes them as 'Big-bon'd Colbrant and great Brandamore,/ The giants in Guildhall' (Carlyle 714).

A pamphlet of the 1672 Lord Mayor's Show describes replacement figures fifteen feet tall, possibly manufactured from wicker and plasterboard:

they are to be set up in Guildhall, where they may be daily seen all the year, and I hope never to be demolished by such dismal violence as happened to their predecessors. (Withington I 60; Bell 1921 12)

When Ned Ward discussed the statues in *London Spy* around 1700, he suggested that 'they were set up to fright Stubborn Apprentices into obedience . . . for some of them are as much frightened at the names of *Gog* and *Magog* as little Children are at the terrible Sound of *Raw-Head* and *Bloody-Bones*' (Withington I 61). Ward was describing how the giants were positioned over two cupboard-like cells (called 'Little Ease', named after the dungeon in the White Tower) where the apprentices were confined (Ward-Jackson 184). However, as well as sardonically observing what he considered the absurdity of Britain's Trojan ancestry ('I am wholly Ignorant of what they intended by 'em, unless they were set up to show the City what huge Loobies their Fore-fathers were'), Ward could have been recounting how the once-proud statues now appeared frightening only because they had succumbed to decay through damp and rats and had become irreparably damaged.

Figure 10.1   Gog *c.* 1920. Courtesy of the London Metropolitan Archives

In 1706, the renovation of the giants described in the 1672 Lord Mayor's Show pamphlet was first proposed by the Committee for Guildhall Repairs (Ward-Jackson 184). Captain Richard Saunders constructed new hollow figures in a neo-Classical style in 1708. These wooden effigies stood some fourteen and a half feet high, for which Saunders was paid £70. By this time, the characters were called Gog and Magog: Gog was mostly naked, his body decorated as if with woad, a blue dye associated with the Picts; his hair was worn long in the manner believed associated with druids and ancient Britons. He carried a morning star, that is, a long pole to which a spiked ball is attached by a chain, a weapon associated with the ancient Britons. Conversely, Magog is depicted in a manner reminiscent of Corineus, younger and more muscular than his counterpart. He wears Roman armour, carrying a halberd, and a shield adorned with a spreadeagle, which suggests, to some, the character's Teutonic origins (Ward-Jackson 184). Magog has either replaced Corineus, or Corineus has

FIGURE 10.2 Magog. Courtesy of the London Metropolitan Archives

managed to transform himself into one of the giants. Either way, the name of one of Britain's earliest inhabitants has passed into disuse. The two characters are represented as one being of ancient origin (such as Gogmagog in the earlier legends), the other being of Classical heritage (Corineus). As guardians of the City, both characters were wreathed in laurel as a symbol of victory, as were Roman military and government officials in parades.

The two figures flanked the door to the Council Chamber on the North side of the Guildhall until 1815 when they were moved to the West End. Given the weight of the effigies, it was unlikely that they were ever paraded for the Lord Mayor's Shows; however, in 1827, lighter representations of the figures (although of a similar size to those displayed in the Guildhall) appeared at the parade (Kent 47).

On 29 December 1940, parts of the Guildhall were damaged by a fire in the Blitz; the statues of Gog and Magog were among the casualties. The pair of giants that now stand in the Guildhall were carved by David Evans as a gift to the City by Alderman Sir George Wilkinson who had been Lord Mayor during the Blitz. Wilkinson offered to pay for a replacement only a year after the giants' destruction (Ward-Jackson 184). The giants were inaugurated, along with a new clock, on 8 June 1953. The statues are lime wood with gold leaf decoration. Both wear Roman armour and are adorned with laurel crowns; Gog carries a staff with a morning star, as well as a sword and a quiver of arrows. Magog has a halberd and a shield with a phoenix relief (Ward-Jackson 183). Like the phoenix, the Guildhall Giants have risen from the ashes of the City.

Through the disjointure of the past with the present – that is, a Classical heritage that already exists in a medieval past and the presence of both of these heritages in today's present – we see the creation of a spectral realm of the Guildhall giants. This realm does not belong to one past, but to many. Having been through so many incarnations, the Guildhall giants have become spectres, witnesses to events over the past five centuries. Yet they are also a manifestation; they are what Derrida would describe as 'visibility of the invisible' (Derrida 1994 100). The statues at the Guildhall may evoke memories – at least in some people – whether they are memories of the Lord Mayor's Show, the unveiling of the statues in 1953, the blitz-torn streets of London in 1940, or before. Memories are hauntings; hauntings are the association with names and dates and the memories that they carry. Such hauntings are invoked by the uncanny anticipation of the Pagan 'Other'.

The Pagan 'Other'

The Guildhall giants represent a construction of cultural differences; if the Trojans are the ancestors of Britain, then we may consider them as binary opposite with the giants: Classical and Pagan; civilized and unrefined; diaspora and aboriginal; godly and diabolical; self and other. When Geoffrey's *Historia* described the conquest of the indigenous population, he was effectively trying to subdue the monstrous elements of his narrative with humanity. However, he was unable to silence the later embellishments to his work which included explanations as to how the giants first arrived. The initial suppression, and then public display of the giants at the Guildhall and in pageants, represents the crucial definition of the uncanny that Freud takes from von Schelling: something that 'ought to have remained secret and hidden but has come to light' (Freud 345). At the same time, the repetition of original elements combined with the additional material represents what Derrida would call *hauntology*, the impossibility of repeating something happening, and yet of it happening for the first time (Derrida 1994 10). By their very nature, the giants are supernatural entities, existing outside of the laws of nature as we understand them. However, in these legends they are also the unnatural product of demonality and incest.

The spectre begins by coming back: the giants are Pagan *revenants* that exist in both the Bible and contemporary medieval literature and who must be either Christianized or suppressed. The suppressed spirit of Paganism becomes incarnate, assumes a form, and becomes a re-apparition of the departed. Derrida observes that the spectre does not exist in 'a date in the chain of events' (Derrida 1994 4). These spectres are not restricted by temporality or locus. The Guildhall is haunted by a foreign guest; however, it is a guest that may have always been there: before Corineus cornered the giants into Cornwall, they had the free-run of the country, which would have included the forests and marshland that eventually became London.

In the Guildhall, the giants exist in this time, yet, paradoxically, out of it. References to them in the Bible occur in Genesis and Revelation: they are associated with beginnings and endings. Their futures are linked with an apocalyptic purpose. When Dickens recounts the Guildhall giants' discussion, the giants are aware of what is to come: Magog announces that they shall entertain each other with 'tales of the past, the present, and the future' (Dickens 274). Consequently, it is unsurprising that Gog and Magog are also associated with *time*. They appear as quarter-jacks – figures that strike a clock's bell – in places such as the Royal Arcade in Melbourne, Australia and Herald Square, New York; in England they are found in York Minster and in St Dunstan in the West, London. Likewise, the statues unveiled at the Guildhall in 1953 were inaugurated with a new clock. According to legend, the Guildhall statues animate at the stroke of midnight, and this legend is echoed by Samson and Hercules House in Tombland, Norwich who also reportedly come to life at midnight. As we have seen before, Samson and Hercules were precursors to Gogmagog and Corineus in the 1522 pageant. This animation blurs the boundaries between life and death. Their association with clocks suggests that they are charged with waiting for something. A correspondent to the *New Monthly Magazine* in 1828 describes a dream of Gog and Magog, listing 'dire calamites' associated with an 'era of luxury, corruption and desertion [of responsibility] had now manifestly arrived':

> Then Gog shall start, and Magog shall
> Tremble upon his pedestal. (Campbell 37)

The giants are connected to something that has been repressed, something that is no longer familiar. They belong to a mythology that has been all but forgotten; they represent something ancient that still echoes through the streets of London. Even to those who are familiar with the legends, there is slippage as the sources do not agree or finalize a single version of events. Each aspect of the story is embellished and enhanced; details are changed so that the pieces fit together. Geoffrey of Monmouth claims that Gogmagog was hurled from Plymouth Hoe; Bates argues that Gog and Magog (or Gogmagog) were led, chained, into London. Were they already *revenants* by this time? Or perhaps it was later – in 1554 – that Gogmagog and Corineus were resurrected to replace the other Classical and Biblical heroes, Samson and Hercules. There is constant slippage: they cannot be identified by their names, as they have repeatedly changed through history. Their identity has become a duality, both co-existing as Gogmagog and Corineus, or in their inherited names of Gog and Magog, or even their assumed names of Colbrant and Brandamore. Derrida observes that 'only the name can inherit' (Derrida 1988 7). A name implies familiarity. The power of naming is also the power of invocation; invocation implies that the named individual will perform a named task. If there is no certainty concerning the names, there can be no certainty that they will perform a particular function.

As porters to the City, the Guildhall giants are given positions of responsibility. However, their duty places them in liminal positions on the borders of the City; after all, the prophecy in Revelation suggests that they are the enemy at the gate. The erection of statues in their memory implies that the giants have been localized, although being cognizant of their location does not necessarily imply knowledge of their function, or even their identity. Are Gog and Magog sentinels, protecting the City? Historically, the effigies are not both giants, but a giant and a hero, so does Corineus stand guard over Gogmagog, ensuring that his demonic influence extends no further? Or are neither of them giants, but representations of Gog and Magog, two virtuous twins who, according to a different legend, rescued the Princess Londona from Humbug the Giant (Goodfellow 11, 72).

Despite the giants' heritage, perhaps as offspring of exiled murderesses and incubi, or as the representatives of a race that was untamed and uncivilized that needed to be suppressed, the fact that Gog and Magog currently stand guarding the City from the Guildhall suggests that the City has welcomed the Pagan 'Other' and given it a position of prominence. However, the giants potentially represent more sinister resonances that have – like their heritage – largely been forgotten. Even now, the giants are paraded as part of the Lord Mayor's Show: the ones used at present were manufactured out of wicker in 2006 by the Worshipful Company of Basketmakers. In 2006, the Basketmaker's Company had its first lady Prime Warden, Olivia Elton Barratt. Aware of the inclusion of the giants in earlier pageants, she considered it appropriate to make new ones to be carried at the Lord Mayor's Show. Roger de Pilkyngton, the current Clerk of the Worshipful Company of Basketmakers, suggests that 'it is possible that in the seventeenth century the wicker figures were burnt at the end of the show' [Pers. Comm.]. Fraser argues that the sacrificial rites of the Celts, particularly those that include the fire festivals, can be traced in the popular festivals of modern Europe (Frazer 859–60). These observations recall Julius Caesar's *Commentarii de Bello Gallico*, where he describes the druids' practice of human sacrifice: 'colossal images made of wickerwork; the limbs of which [the Celtic druids] fill with living men; they are then set on fire, and the victims burnt to death' (Julius Caesar 141). Indeed, Arnold suggests that hill giants represented a sacrificial site where wicker effigies were burned in the manner that Julius Caesar described, and sometimes named as a 'wicker Gogmagog' (Arnold 559; Kingsley 807).

Conclusion

When Geoffrey of Monmouth composed his 'history' of Britain, he embellished details from a tradition that had been established by earlier writers such as Nennius. The tradition of claiming mythological ancestry followed a pattern that was recognized across Europe. In effect, Geoffrey attempted to create a cohesive force for his audiences. He tied the country's heritage to the survivors of Troy in the same way that medieval knights tied their genealogy to characters from the Bible and ultimately ascended to Adam. The mythology that Britain has inherited has mutated out of recognition and also has largely been forgotten. Later legends that explain the ignoble heritage of the giants – incestuous demonic offspring of murderesses – make the violence of Brutus's foundation more acceptable. Yet Brutus himself is not without sin because, albeit unintentionally, he is flawed with parricide.

The identity of the two giants remains veiled in uncertainty; throughout history, the characters are subject to etymological migration. The names, Gog and Magog, appear in the Bible as separate entities (Genesis 10:2; 1 Chronicles 1:5; Ezekiel 38, 39; Revelation 20:8). In the legends contained in Geoffrey's *Historia* and in the later legends of Albina, the two Biblical entities are spliced into a conglomerate of evil – Gogmagog. In the pageants, after 1554, the giants are named as Gogmagog and Corineus (even though it is reported that the latter was never a giant, both in the descriptions by Geoffrey of Monmouth and by the depictions on Plymouth Hoe). Before then, the same characters had been male and female, then the two merged into one, then split again, eradicating the female gender. Indeed, like the violence of twins fighting for domination, when the effigies were reconstructed in 1708, the name of Corineus was eradicated. The presumed unity between the two characters has blurred and shifted. This could have been to match the changing socio-cultural beliefs over the centuries as to what denoted 'acceptable' histories. The names have now settled, but only through a lack of interest in the present day in the giants' history and mythology.

The symbolism of the giants has also been lost. Gog and Magog could represent the genocide that was inflicted upon Albion by Brutus of Troy: the giant represents the civilized descendant of Troy who has overcome the savage 'Other' that must be either Christianized, or hurled from Plymouth Hoe. Alternatively, the giants represent a re-enactment of the parading of two prisoners of war in front of the jeering crowds – indeed, centuries later, the effigies are still paraded in front of the Lord Mayor. In this instance, however, the identities of the giants shift from Classical and Biblical names (Hercules and Samson, and we might pause to observe the irony that, in one legend, Hercules kills Albion), to pseudo-Classical and adapted Biblical names (Corineus and Gogmagog), only to split one of the characters once more into two entities: Gog and Magog, the original form favoured in the Apocalypse. The duality of the 'Other' has perhaps created a split within itself. Finally, the statues may represent the Guardians of the City, silent in their service because the majority of the City's inhabitants do not know their purpose. All we really know about these characters is the etymology of their names: Gog, from the land of Magog, or Gog and Magog appear in the Bible in the books of Genesis and Revelation. They are associated with beginnings and ends.

The giants – in whatever guise – have been part of the City pageantry for nearly five centuries. The statues had a troubled time in the years between the Great Fire in 1666 and the reconstruction of the hollow wooden figures in 1708. Effigies were in place within six years after the Great Fire, and although those figures succumbed to damp, decay and rodents, Withington suggests that the figures carved in 1708 were 'to take the place' of those mentioned in the 1672 pamphlet about the Lord Mayor's Show (Withington I 61). Likewise, when the statues were destroyed in the Blitz in 1940, new statues were planned only a year later. Thus, these 'Guardians of the City' have been present for the majority of the last five centuries. They also punctuate principal horrors in the City's history: when they have been subjected to violence on a seemingly apocalyptic scale (fire, pestilence and war), they are swiftly replaced. This suggests a superstition like the Ravens in the Tower of London – without them, the City would fall. Yet, the statues endure: with a Dunkirk spirit, they are built again, bigger and stronger.

Although 'the Gothic' was initially considered to represent an eighteenth- and nineteenth-century construction of an uncultivated period, the issues that were discussed were not restricted to 'The Middle Ages': even medieval societies looked back at something that was pre-Roman. This Pagan world is a forgotten construction: the descriptions are filled with a longing for the prime-val, and the distance presents an important discursive space in which the writers could explore new ideas. In particular, it represented an epoch containing incontestable events which allowed the medieval Britons an opportunity to establish themselves on the world stage because of their proud lineage. It also allowed them to define themselves by what they were not: their Brutus / Trojan heritage established that the Britons were not Frankish, Norman or Saxon. By placing the statues of the giants in London then, the capital is linked with the earliest settlement legends that demonstrate it *is* possible to incorporate the Pagan 'Other' into our culture. As Gogmagog's narrative about his origins in *Dez Grantz Geanz* shows, what is presented as monstrous is not necessarily brut-ish or horrific.

The secrets of Gog and Magog, their precise origins and functions, have been silenced. Many modern Britons may have forgotten the legends of the found-ing of Britain, but their echoes still whisper to us across time. The giants are still with us: a representation of this Gothic legend is constantly on display in the Guildhall, and annually paraded through the streets of London.

Works Cited

Apollodorus (1921), *The Library*, trans. J. G. Frazer, Loeb Classical Library Volumes 121 and 122, Cambridge, MA: Harvard University Press; London: William Heinemann

Arnold, E. L. (1927), 'Giants and White Horses', *The North American Review*, 224, 554–59

Bale, J. (1548), *Illustrium majoris Britanniae scriptorium*, Wesel: Printed for Ioannem Ouerton

Bates, S. (1735), *The New History of the Trojan Wars and Troy's Destruction in Four Books*, London: Printed for Sarah Bates at the Sun and Bible in Giltspur Street; and James Hodges at the Looking Glass on London Bridge

Bell, W. G. (1921), *More About Unknown London*. London: John Lane

Bell, W. G. (1966), *Unknown London*, London: Spring Books

Brereton, G. E. (1937), (ed.), *Des Grantz Geanz*, Medium Ævum Monographs II, Oxford, Basil Blackwell

Boreman, T. (1741), *The Gigantick History of the Two Famous Giants, and other Curiosi-ties in Guildhall, London*, third edn, London: Printed for Thomas Boreman

Campbell, T. (1828), '*Vindiciæ Magogianæ*, or a Modest Defence of Gog and Magog', *The New Monthly Magazine and Literary Journal*, 23, part II, London: Henry Colburn, 33–37

Carlyle, T. (1846), 'The Lord Mayor and Lord Mayor's Day', *Fraser's Magazine*, volume 43, December, London: G. W. Nickisson

Cole, C. A. (1858), *Memorials of Henry the Fifth, King of England*, London: Longman, Brown, Green, Longmans and Roberts

Crossley, F. (1851), *Notes and Queries*, 27 December

Derrida, J. (1988), 'Otobiographies: The Teaching of Nietzsche and the Politics of the Proper Name', *The Ear of the Other: Otobiography, Transference, Translation,* (ed.), Christie V. McDonald, trans. Peggy Kamuf, Lincoln: University of Nebraska Press, 1–38

Derrida, J. (1994), *Specters of Marx,* trans. Peggy Kamuf, London: Routledge

Dickens, C. (1907), 'Master Humphrey's Clock', *The Mystery of Edwin Drood and Master Humphrey's Clock,* London: Chapman and Hall, 257–370

Fairholt, F. W. (1859), *Gog and Magog, The Giants in Guildhall: their Real and Legendary History,* London: John Camden Hotten

Frazer, J. G. (1957), *The Golden Bough,* London: Macmillan

Freud, S. (1985), 'The "Uncanny"', *Art and Literature,* trans. James Strachley, volume 14, Pelican Freud Library, Harmondsworth: Penguin, 339–76

Fuller, T. (1655), *The Church History of Britain; From the Birth of Jesus Christ until the Year 1648,* London: Printed for Iohn Williams at the Signe of the Crown in St Paul's Church-yard

Goodfellow, R. (1819), The History of Gog and Magog, the Champions of London. London: J. and C. Adlard

Henry of Huntingdon (2002), *The History of the English People 1000–1154,* trans. Diana Greenway, Oxford: Oxford University Press

Johnson, L. (1995), 'Return to Albion', *Arthurian Literature* XIII, 19–40

Julius Caesar (1982), *The Conquest of Gaul,* London: Penguin

Kent, W. (1952), *London Mystery and Mythology,* London: Staples Press

Kingsford, C. L. (1901), *Henry V: The Typical Mediaeval Hero,* London: Putnam's Sons

Kingsley, C. (1850), 'Sketches of Life. By a Radical', *Harper's Magazine,* November, 803–07

Lethbridge, T. C. (1957), *Gogmagog: The Buried Gods,* London: Routledge and Kegan Paul

Morris, J. (1973), *The Age of Arthur: A History of the British Isle from 350 to 650,* London: Weidenfeld and Nicholson

Rowley, R. (2005), *Historia Britonum (The History of the Britons) attributed to Nennius,* trans. Richard Rowley, Lampeter: Llanerch Press

Seznec, J. (1972), *The Survival of the Pagan Gods,* trans. Barbara F. Sessions, Princeton: Princeton University Press

Sinistrari, L. M. (1927), *Demoniality,* London: The Fortune Press

Stow, J. (1908), *A Survey of London,* 2 volumes Oxford: Clarendon Press

Thomas, A. H. (1943), *Calendar of Plea and Memoranda Rolls.* Cambridge: Cambridge University Press

Thomas, C. (2002), *The Archaeology of Medieval London,* Stroud: Sutton Publishing

Tottill, R. (1558), *The Passage of our most drad Soveraigne Ladye Queene Elyzbeth through the Citie of London to Westminster, the day before her coronation, Anno 1558,* London: Richard Tottill

Ward-Jackson, P. (2003), *Public Sculpture in the City of London,* Liverpool: Liverpool University Press

Westcote, T. (1845), *View of Devonshire in MDCXXX with a Pedigree of Most of its Gentry,* Exeter: William Roberts

Wofford, S. L. (1992), *The Choice of Achilles,* Stanford: Stanford University Press

Wright, N. (1984), *The Historia regum Britannie of Geoffrey of Monmouth I: Bern Burgerbibliothek MS 568*, Cambridge: D. S. Brewer

Online resources

Holinshed's Chronicle http://www.cems.ox.ac.uk/holinshed/
The *Short Metrical Chronicle* in the Auchinleck manuscript http://www.nls.uk/auchinleck/mss/smc.html.

Chapter 11

'West End Ghosts and Southwark Horrors': London's Gothic Tourism

Emma McEvoy

In recent years London has acquired a range of Gothic tourist attractions: The Clink in Bankside (which announces itself as the London prison museum); the London Dungeon; its neighbour, the London Bridge Experience; the Ghost Bus Tours (the Necrobus); Dennis Severs' house in Folgate, Spitalfields; Simon Drake's House of Magic ('hidden away at a secret Central London location'[1]). They are a new breed of tourist attraction, generic hybrids, all performance-based, sitting uneasily on the boundaries between fiction and history, amusement and edification, mock-up and historical site. They may be seen as part of a wider trend of Gothic performance-based modes which includes Gothic theatre, Gothic circuses, Gothic clubs, pubs and restaurants with their literalization of Gothic tropes of consumption. As Catherine Spooner points out in *Contemporary Gothic*: 'Gothic narratives have . . . spread across disciplinary boundaries to infect all kinds of media, from fashion and advertising to the way contemporary events are constructed in mass culture' (Spooner 8). This chapter will be considering some of these examples of London's Gothic tourism, asking what they tell us about London, its relation to its past, and to its material remains. It will discuss the locations of London's Gothic tourism, asking whether the nature of the tourist attractions differs in different parts of London and discussing how the attractions relate to the known history and heritage of different areas.

The vexed relation between history and heritage in London, between its past and its material remains (or lack of them) and its relationship to this past, has particular significance for this chapter. The areas it will discuss are those of the West End (home of London's theatre land) and Southwark, an area to the South of the river, and, like the West End, an area associated with theatre in that it was home to the majority of the great Elizabethan and Jacobean public playhouses. Unlike the more glamorous West End though, Southwark is an area which until recently seemed to possess little in the way of attractive historical

I'd like to thank Herbie Treehead, Catherine Spooner and Robert Lee for their comments on this chapter at various stages of its construction and, in the case of Herbie, for being an invaluable source of information about Gothic performance.

tourist sights. Its predominant architectural character bears witness to its industrial heritage and history of poverty. The chapter will look at these instances of
contemporary London tourism in terms of the rich history of Gothic itself, asking what Gothic exemplars they draw upon and how they remediate them? The
answers, of course, relate to the type of clientele that the attractions wish to
draw, but they also relate suggestively to the areas in which they are situated. In
answering these questions the chapter will cross the river. What follows is divided
into two sections, the first focusing on West End Gothic in terms of the ghost
industry, and the second looking at Southwark Gothic and its feast of horrors.

West End Ghosts

The Theatre Royal, Drury Lane runs an interactive theatre tour entitled
'Through the Stage Door'. Twice daily on most days punters, advised to don
'sensible footwear',[2] are met in front of the box office and conducted on a
guided walk of the theatre, from front of house to underneath the stage. In the
course of the walk they encounter 'three professional actors' and 'the history of
The Theatre Royal Drury Lane is brought to vivid life as key characters, writers
and actors from the theatre's three hundred year old past take you back through
time as you look around this famous theatre'.[3] The tour, though it doesn't
announce itself as such, is constructed as a Gothic experience; it is peripatetic
Gothic, offering a proliferation of hauntings from a variety of time zones. The
theatre itself, for the duration of the tour, is constructed as Gothic building, a
mise-en-scène of a series of Gothic narratives. The beginning of the tour presents
a story of warring royals and an acrimonious father/son relationship (that of
George III and the Prince of Wales) which the very architecture of the theatre
bears witness to (there are separate King's and Prince's entrances). The erotic,
subterranean strands of Gothic are touched on in stories of Charles II visiting
Nell Gwynne by secret underground passages. The split character of the theatre
is stressed as the tour moves from the sumptuous public spaces to the relatively
depauperate backstage areas.

The *Alice in Wonderland*-sounding title of the tour, 'Through the Stage Door',
with its contorted, mock-historic subtitle ('A tragical comical-magical Historie
of The Oldest Operating Playhouse in the World') suggests gleeful generic
trespass. 'Through the Stage Door' is a strange mixture of guided tour, promenade performance, and site-specific work performed not only by 'three professional actors' but by invisible ghosts. The Drury Lane tour is both displacement
and reinvention of the theatre experience, experimenting with audience
trespass onto the areas associated with actors and theatre staff. In the tour many
of the actors are dead, but the audience is placed in the narrative, the Gothic
victim in the haunted house.

The tour actualizes the space of Gothic narratives and mobilizes the narratives themselves. The 'Through the Stage Door' experience stresses the palimpsestic nature of the theatre, its rebuildings, the resitings of the stage; the plenitude

of different time zones and significant spaces that co-exist and co-haunt. Tourists are informed that the tunnel they follow is part of the seventeenth-century theatre, which itself was constructed on the site of a nuns' burial ground and is currently said to be haunted by a nineteenth-century ghost (that of Dan Leno). As the tourists pass through an arch, they are told that this is where a corpse was found bricked up in a wall in the nineteenth century – and that the ghost of this man in grey has walked here ever since that discovery. They are told of another ghost who walks to where there was once a stage, attempting to complete a performance cut short by his death. The very spaces of the theatre are shown to be liminal. Ghosts walk spaces that because of the many resitings of the stage are no longer in existence. In this palimpsestic theatre, space has become haunted not just by ghosts of humans but by traces of former spaces.

Drury Lane's self-construction as Gothic in 'Through the Stage Door' resembles many other examples of London's Gothic tourism, which are also characterized by their employment of different modes of performance enacted on a semi-fictionalized space. In the case of the Drury Lane tour and, I would venture to argue, in the case of the other examples of Gothic tourism discussed in this chapter, the Gothic construction is suggested by the problematics of a history/heritage dichotomy. The theatre's website conveys the point somewhat elliptically. It stresses the long history of the theatre dating it back to the early seventeenth century, it mentions its design by Wren, its occupation by Garrick, but has to point out: 'The present Theatre Royal in Drury Lane, designed by Benjamin Wyatt, opened on October 10, 1812 . . . The interior has been substantially redesigned and overhauled many times since then'.[4] In other words, Drury Lane's impressive history is not visible in its architectural remains. The theatre which stands is not the one built by Wren or commanded by Garrick. It is not even, strictly speaking, the one which opened in 1812.

The Theatre Royal, Drury Lane, is a prime example of an institution, a site even, possessed of a celebrated history which it cannot display. It exemplifies what can be seen as a phenomenon relevant to much of the West End – relentlessly built-over, updated and expanded in the late nineteenth century – 'history without the heritage'. It is a phenomenon which proves common in many districts of London and leaves the tourism market with some pressing problems. However, where material heritage is absent Gothicization may take its place and this is what happens in many areas of London in a variety of ways which, suggestively, mirror not so much the various pasts which have been (or are perceived to be) razed, but the various presents which have survived, and their relation to those pasts. Where marketable heritage proves elusive, Gothic tourism supplements the heritage industry, creating, in some of the more extreme cases like the London Dungeon, false histories where development has blotted out the more picturesque aspects of the past, and pencilling in as ghosts historical detail which has left no trace. The ghosts of London's ghost tours and those haunting the theatres are testimony to London's lack of heritage at certain points in its fabric.

The elusiveness of London's heritage is brilliantly capitalized on in some of its ghost tours. On Thursdays, at 7.30pm, a guide named Russell from the London Walks company leads the 'Apparitions, Alleyways and Ale' walk from Embankment underground station. The very process of walking is constructed as a method of summoning up the past in a London where many of the material remains have vanished, but many of the street patterns persist. Walking becomes the means of summoning up the invisible past; the process of tracing a journey is that which will resurrect the traces of the old city, or, if you're lucky, a ghost. The London Walks website makes the most of the conflation of time and place brought about by the act of walking, in typically jaunty fashion:

> Funny thing that. Because when we turned into this alley it was June 26, 2008. That's creepy old London for you. You're not careful where you're going – you turn certain corners – and time bends. What's this? It's a gas lamp. . . . And there's the famous actor, William Terriss. William Terriss, who's just been murdered tonight, right here, December 16, 1897.[5]

The cleverly-planned walk makes a virtue of the irrepressible modernity, or relentless Victorian development, of much of the route. The relative lack of pre-Victorian material, of heritage of the kind that characterizes a city such as York, for example, becomes the structuring principle of the walk. For Robert Mighall, Gothic fiction 'depicts the anachronistic survival of *vestigial* customs into the enlightened present' (Mighall 21), likewise Russell's walk is planned around the vestigial survival of barbaric traces of the past in an otherwise modern city. Russell takes his walkers from the busy Strand, through to what the website calls 'crepuscular, crooked little alleyways'.[6] The relative scarcity of these places, their uncharacteristic nature, the sense that they are in some ways a backwater, is the premiss of the tour. In one claustrophobic lane of late seventeenth-century houses, Russell recounts a brilliantly-framed murder story, drawing on the motifs of theatrical costume and Gothic contamination.

'Apparitions, Alleyways and Ale' takes the predominant Victorian-ness of its surroundings as its template at another level by drawing upon the structures and tropes of the Victorian ghost story. The devices of third-hand evidence, of the relayed witness of the most sceptical of observers are built into the narrative of the tour, and the moment of proof is set up as narrative climax. Figures representative of the tour's readers/consumers are incorporated into its telling and observers from the New World (so often associated in Victorian fiction with modernity) are used to give credence to tales of haunting. This habit is perhaps most pronounced when we are told that a group of novices to the Old World visiting Britain for the first time from the United States (appropriately enough Virgin Atlantic executives!), witness the ghost of a monk in St James's Park. Another anecdote tells of pints of beer pulled by ghosts at five in the morning and registered by the pub's computer system. This detail is reminiscent of the alignment of the ghost with technological modernity which also characterizes the Victorian ghost story (see, for example, Barry Pain's 'The Case of Victor Pyrwhit' (1901) where the ghost communicates by telephone).

At one point, as mentioned above, the tour guide leads the group down a passage where there is a blocked-up doorway and a gas lamp, and it is here that he recounts the murder of the actor, William Terris, in 1897. The story is wonderfully framed, for the passageway is also said to be the place where the ghost of Terriss's killer (with top hat, cape and dagger) was captured on photograph on a previous ghost tour by, appropriately enough, an American. Both the blocked door and the figure of the actor are common and fertile motifs. The image of the blocked door suggests, on the ghost tour, not only our relation to the past, but also London's relation to its own pasts. The ghost tour presents the past as blocked, impassable, impracticable – the doorway that was, but can no longer be entered (though it can, it seems, still be exited from). The figure of the actor is a similarly fertile motif and actors feature heavily in the West End's Gothic tourism, as with case of Drury Lane theatre where the tourist is told of the jealous actor Macklin stabbing his rival in the eye in a quarrel over a wig. The focus on actors ties in with the current culture of the West End, reflecting back on theatre land and giving guides a chance to illuminate the past with the reflected glory of current celebrities who encounter obdurate material remains – stray books for example – that project themselves from the past into the present. Yet it also reflects back on the nature of the tour itself – Russell, the guide, we are told, is himself 'the best kind of English actor'.[7] More than this, the focus on theatre, actors, and performance is part and parcel of the theatrical origins and preoccupations of Gothic more generally.

Southwark Horrors

Scholars in tourism studies have found a variety of ways to refer to the phenomenon of 'Gothic tourism'. The term 'dark tourism', coined by Lennon and Foley primarily to refer to tourism of death and disaster sites, has been adapted by others to encompass a range of other destinations. Philip R. Stone examines a spectrum that he considers to range from 'Dark Fun Factories' at one end to 'Dark Camps of Genocide' at the other (Stone 152, 157). Stone argues that 'dark tourism' has a long history – his range of examples includes nineteenth-century visits to see floggings at houses of correction and tours to the site of the Battle of Waterloo (Stone147). However, the practices of what Stone terms 'Dark Fun Factories' also need to be viewed in terms of the history and of Gothic more generally and its relation to space, place and performance.

Since its inception in the mid-eighteenth century, Gothic has notably been a discourse characterized by its drive towards hybridity, reflected in its precarious generic positioning and its cross-contamination of literary, architectural, and performance modes. The rise of Gothic is intimately associated with new modes of experiencing space which arose in the mid to late eighteenth century and which included the experiencing of public and private spaces as theatre. Indeed, it is a period in which we see specific modes of architecture being understood as theatre. Walpole's and Beckford's Gothic fantasy architectures Strawberry Hill and Fonthill Abbey may be seen as architecture theatricalized, or, made into masquerade; they are houses that are made to be performed and require a degree of performance from both their hosts and their visitors. Even more striking an ancestor (though one that skips several generations) is the example of the Phantasmagoria as played in post-Revolutionary Paris which was a theatricalized experience of the kind we would now describe as promenade. Robertson's Phantasmagoria, as Mervyn Heard informs us, had its visitors led around a building,[8] which had previously been a convent but more recently seen service as a revolutionary headquarters (indeed it was where the impresario Robertson himself had suffered interrogation). It was an immersive experience featuring live actors, disembodied voices, blackouts, reversible portraits, fantasti-cal paintings, machines, and magic lantern technology.

As in the late eighteenth century we are once more sculpting places into the spaces of communal fantasy. However, there are many significant differences between these early examples of Gothic performed architecture and contem-porary Gothic tourism. Perhaps the most striking difference between the French Phantasmagoria and the examples of Gothic tourism as practised in contempo-rary Southwark is the fact that the Gothic is not being played out in a building associated with real and recent horror.[9] Furthermore, in contrast to Walpole's and Beckford's performed architectures, Southwark's Gothic tourism does not pretend to the status of 'Art'. The contemporary experiences are the product of a consumer-saturated culture and the type and level of consumption as well as the available technologies have changed. As the final page of *A Short History of The Clink Prison* tells us: 'The facilities of the Clink Prison can be made avail-able for all your Corporate Entertainment and Private Parties' (Burford 15) and the same is true for the London Dungeon, though its language of partying is even further from that of Walpole and Beckford – 'birthday party packages are available for all of your little horrors!'[10] The London Dungeon is a multina-tional corporate entity with counterparts in Amsterdam, Hamburg, Edinburgh and York. Visitors include British and foreign tourists. Many of the visitors are parents with children which, as I listened to babes in arms screaming in the darkened rooms, gave me an interesting new take on the question of parent/children relations in the Gothic.[11]

Southwark Gothic, which will be discussed here with reference to The Clink and the London Dungeon, sets out from a variety of different premises and premisses to those of West End Gothic. To begin with, these are in-situ attrac-tions whose main purpose (unlike Drury Lane theatre, for example) is to act as Gothic tourism and, unlike the more glamorous West End, the material worked on is that of urban squalor – or rather urban squalor enfranchised. (The con-struction of Gothic tourist sites in this part of central London was no doubt originally driven by the relatively low cost of the sites involved.)

Southwark Gothic is considerably more low-brow than its West End counter-parts, but is refracted through an even greater variety of Gothic allusions and texts while its range of generic hybrids is more mixed and inventive. These Southwark 'experiences' are generic mixtures that are part-theatre, part-theme park, and part-installation. The Clink is its own accompanying booklet – *A Short History of the Clink Prison* – made manifest. It is museum, radio play, theatre, and installation drama that relies for much of its effect on its precarious generic positioning and importation of other texts. The London Dungeon is Gothic pantomime crossed with the fairground and promenade theatre. In terms of generic allegiances we have moved from the predominance of the Victorian ghost story to a whole range of other sources, not the least of which are 'cheap horror movie clichés' (Spooner 34).[12]

However, as in the West End examples, the patterns of theatrical practice are dominant in the retelling of London as Gothic narrative. The experiences marry Gothic narrative with the determinate nature of space and the passivity of the audience spectator. The Clink is the museum as Gothic theatre with all the apparatus of set, lighting, sound effects and (inanimate) actors salaciously performing the past. To enter the Prison museum is like entering onto a stage set – it is a world of artexed ceilings and walls, false flames, coloured lights of yellow, red, white, and green. In the opening room visitors are positioned as spectators facing talking spot-lit waxworks as they listen to a looped recording of a scripted encounter between a blacksmith and the prisoner he is fettering. What is presented, however, has already been many times remediated – through film, literature, theatre, and Madame Tussauds – for The Clink is presenting not only its subject matter but its use of technologies – waxworks, old-fashioned recording techniques – as antiquated, even Gothic.

Like the Clink, the London Dungeon features disembodied voices (though they tend to be more Hammer Horror than Radio Four) flickering lights and waxworks, yet is more self-avowedly theatrical than the Clink. It uses a variety of theatrical forms – monologues, shadow theatre, promenade, and pantomime – and the understanding of theatre as archaic mode in an age of electronic media means that theatre itself, associated with the body, real space, captive audiences, acts to underpin the Dungeon's Gothic. Within this site-specific promenade theatre visitors are not just bemused spectators, but become partici-pants. In a court scene they are incorporated into a Kafka-esque parody of the eighteenth-century judicial system as a bewigged judge condemns to the gallows a non-English-speaking tourist, unable to defend him or herself. The Dungeon first commissioned waxworks with sophisticated mechanisms to deliver its thrills, but quickly discovered that the use of actors was far more effective. The actors at the Dungeon are mostly young and enthusiastically throw themselves into their parts, hamming up their performances, trilling their 'r's, raising corpses to life, throwing mad fits, using a vernacular that much of the audience will not understand.

The emphasis in these examples of Southwark Gothic is not on haunting, as in West End Gothic, but on the tyranny of place and bodies themselves understood as antiquated concepts. These attractions construct a sense of a Gothic past based on their situatedness and an understanding of the sense of place as limit, as prison. Yet the understanding of the specificity of place as an antiquated concept is, by the same token, a mark of the specific modernity of these practices. Ultimately, however, the London Dungeon and the Clink have less to say about the nature of space and more about the nature of the body. They insistently mark their separation from the Gothic past through their proclamation of attitudes towards the body. There is an emphasis on physicality not just the actualizing of the space of Gothic narratives, but the physicality of the consumer him- or herself. The visitor to the Clink enters the site and proceeds through a series of rooms that are supposedly reconstructions of the prison at different stages in its past, where various exhibits from Victorian whipping posts to Tudor torture equipment are on display. This is a construction of the past as the site of Gothic pain; the past as the suffering Gothic body. The world of the Clink is populated by whore-mongering clerics, tyrannical kings, and the suffering poor; it is 'Old England' as tarts and bishops. The modern body proves both the continuation and differentiation from the Gothic past in that the horrors of the past are enacted as titillation for the present. During my visit I turned a corner and found myself in a room where one young woman was photographing another who had positioned herself on the Victorian whipping bench, trousers pulled down to expose her thong.

The London Dungeon has a similar focus on the body in its vision of the Gothic past and, as with the Clink, attitudes towards the body become the means of distinguishing between past and present. In a characteristic show of bravura the Dungeon sees its own opening as part of a paradigm shift in a timeline of pain and torture – '1969 Capital punishment is abolished 1975 The London Dungeon opens'.[13] The point at which certain histories can become offered up for consumption is the point of our discontinuity with the past. The pattern is similar to that which E. J. Clery discusses in *The Rise of Supernatural Fiction* where she sees the consumption of ghosts as entertainment, dating from the moment when belief in ghosts becomes outmoded. The Dungeon provides a take on the past which constructs the historic body as the site of abuse / terror / injustice while engaging in the business of moving and assaulting the contemporary body for fun. Visitors are positioned as passive victims of an ordeal of gruesome surprise as they are assaulted by ghastly sights, sudden noises, and noisome smells. They become lost in the maze, go on the journey to traitors' gate, are treated as one of the plague-infected, and experience Gothic contagion as they are splattered by the droplets of a plague-victim's sneeze. Audience seats suddenly tip back in Sweeney Todd's darkened barber's shop. At the beginning of the experience visitors process through suffocatingly close medieval houses peering in at the figures of tortured and disembowelled corpses, and gazing at a gruesome waxwork representation of a figure being boiled alive. The Dungeon is designed as a journey, which commences by positioning visitors as spectators of the horrors done to other bodies, and finishes by treating them to the fun that can be experienced by our own. The London Dungeon transforms the horrors of the past to the delights of the funfair – a maze of mirrors (the Labyrinth of the Lost), a rollercoaster (the 'boat ride to hell' through the sewers on the way to execution in the Tower of London), and seems to have been conceived as an extended ghost train ride.

From Histories to History

One of the most interesting differences between West End and Southwark Gothic tourism is the move from Gothic as haunting (or, to be more specific, as the stories of individual ghosts) to Gothic as 'History'. Both the Clink and the London Dungeon purport to recount History with a capital H, not just histories of theatres or unfortunate individuals, but of England or London despite the Dungeon's international formula. The Clink presents itself in a way that nicely illustrates Robert Mighall's theory of Gothic as Whig and progressivist,[14] as a Gothic monument to Enlightenment detailing the history of imprisonment through centuries.[15] They both establish a narrative of feudal oppression. A sign in the Dungeon reads: 'Behind the bloodshed of the Medieval battlefield lay a darker force. The Church and Royalty in the name of God and the King murdered, hanged and burned their way through history'. The turn to History, rather than histories, I would argue is again symptomatic of an absence, for nowhere is the vexed relation between history and heritage more apparent than in Southwark. Southwark is possessed of an exceptionally rich history. It has been the site of the southern end of London Bridge since Roman times and thus the gateway to London from the South of what is now England. Pilgrims (including Chaucer's) took this route out from London to Canterbury. In Elizabethan times, Bankside was the location for the extra-mural activities of public theatre, gaming and prostitution. And yet its material remains, at least those above ground, are lacking, with the notable exceptions of the National Trust-owned George Inn and a few walls of the Bishop of Winchester's Palace.[16] Not only has London Bridge been rebuilt more than once, but its very position has changed; it was relocated 100 yards upriver in the 1820s. Even the more recent memorable past has gone: of the infamous Marshalsea prison all that remains is a portion of one of the walls.

Southwark's Gothic tourist attractions illustrate the point well. Despite protestations of authenticity on the part of Clink's marketing information which claims that it is on 'the site of the original "Clink" prison', only a fraction of the space is actually positioned on the former site. Whereas the Clink possesses a bare claim to authenticity, the London Dungeon is jubilantly inauthentic in its relation to the past not only borrowing the histories of other places, but, more curiously, ignoring its own local history (the Marshalsea, for example). Careless of any claim to historical accuracy, little attempt is made to conceal the security cameras or even the Stena stairlift. It is convolutedly inauthentic, masquerading as a variety of places in a variety of different times. Newgate Prison, the Tower of London, the 'East End', Fleet Street, and an avowed fantasy inspired by a supposed wooden sign in a supposed Saxon ruin under a supposed All Hallows Church.[17]

At one level, Southwark's Gothic tourist attractions can be read as a substitution for the absence of 'heritage'. Yet there is also a sense in which The Clink and the London Dungeon, though spurious and inauthentic, do actually accomplish some interesting cultural work as regards the history of the area. Though the Dungeon and the Clink possess little in the way of mediaeval remains they are undeniably in the midst of the remains of an urban past which, through the work of nineteenth-century novelists – Dickens in particular – has come to be understood as a Gothic phenomenon. These attractions could not have been constructed in any anonymous, or, in particular, more recent, part of the city. There has been an attempt to make the grim remnants of the industrial past stand in for other pasts. The construction of the Dungeon and the Clink tells us much about London's own relation to its Victorian heritage re-embodied as the medieval past; the evocation of the mediaeval past as a site of terrible pain could even be said to act as a kind of displacement of the perceived horrors of a Victorian industrial past.

There is also a bizarre way in which the very inauthenticity of Southwark's Gothic tourist attractions becomes a form of authenticity. The well-known tropes – waxworks, Hammer horror theatricality, ghost-train rides – and the hallowed locales of specific instantiations of Gothic constitute a kind of heritage in themselves. Furthermore, the determined history-making that characterizes the London Dungeon has itself a long history in the area. In the absence of impressive material remains (which in a few cases have been bizarrely relocated – an alcove of old London Bridge may be found in Victoria Park, East London), a perceived need to reinvent Southwark has characterized the area for a long time. Since the Victorian period there have been attempts to figure its varied past through reconstructions. Even Southwark Cathedral, splendid though it is, is testimony to the Victorian habit of reconstruction/restoration and its preoccupation with Gothic and actors.[18] The Gothic tourist attractions are of a piece with other sites in an area which has, for a long time, been conspicuously and impressively reinventing itself. A sign-posted tourist walk in the area takes visitors from London Bridge station past the Victorian-restored Southwark Cathedral, past the replica of the Golden Hind, the remaining walls of the Bishop of Winchester's palace, the Clink and, eventually, past the biggest reconstruction of them all: Shakespeare's Globe. The Clink and the Dungeon may be said to sit comfortably beside the more respectable reconstructions of the Globe and the Golden Hind which are also replicated in other places and even other countries.

Southwark's Gothic attractions continue in the traditions of not only of Victorian habits of reinvention, but of a long history of theatre in the area. Not only was Bankside home to the playhouses of the early modern period, but in more recent times Southwark has hosted a variety of different kinds of theatrical, non-West End, experiences. The home of the collective Shunt, who pioneer performance events, is only a few yards away from the Dungeon in a 'sprawling labyrinth of railway arches under London Bridge Station'.[19] Two well-considered fringe venues, Southwark theatre and the Union theatre, both of which also occupy railway arches, are also in the vicinity. The site-specific promenade theatre played in the London Dungeon is mirrored by the more high-brow theatrical experiences played out in similar spaces nearby.

Gothic tourism in London, or in any city, town or village, can tell us much about the place it is located in, particularly about the self-image of that place and its relation to its own history/histories. This relation, however, is often expressed obliquely. As I have shown in this chapter, Gothic tourism at times supplements history; sometimes it creates a focal point where the absence of heritage is problematic, and often it supplants certain histories in favour of others. Such acts of deflection inevitably reveal interesting attitudes. Thus both Southwark's feast of medieval horrors and the tales of haunting that characterize the Gothicization of the West End, tell us about the relation of these areas to their Victorian fabric.

In looking at Gothic tourism more generally, there is a range of useful questions that may be asked. What, in terms of the fabric of the city, is and isn't Gothicized? How are attractions Gothicized? What significant structures and tropes are employed? Do the attractions have specific generic allegiances or allude to specific texts? And, if so, what historical periods do they derive from? The most satisfying Gothic tourism, I would suggest, employs forms and tropes that relate, in some fashion, back to the history of the area, recasting it, or its loss, playfully and inventively.

Notes

[1] http://www.houseofmagic.co.uk/home.html accessed 30th November 2009.
[2] Theatre Royal, Drury Lane's promotional leaflet for 'Through the Stage Door'.
[3] http://www.londontheatre.co.uk/lashmars/backstagetour/index.html accessed 4 August 2009.
[4] http://www.theatreroyaldrurylane.co.uk/theatre-history.htm accessed 4 August 2009.
[5] http://www.walks.com/Homepage/Thursdays_Walks/default.aspx#12882 accessed 5 August 2009.
[6] http://www.walks.com/Homepage/Thursdays_Walks/default.aspx#12882 accessed 5 August 2009.
[7] http://www.walks.com/Homepage/Thursdays_Walks/default.aspx#12882 accessed 5August 2009.

[8] The building no longer exists but it was located near the Place Vendôme. For further details of the Phantasmagoria, see Heard, 2006.

[9] As is the case, as Fred Botting points out, with Romania's Castel Hotel Dracula, built originally for Nicolae Ceausescu. (Botting 3).

[10] From the back cover of the London Dungeon's Guidebook (Anon, undated, unpaginated).

[11] Waiting in line for the tickets in a space which contained 'Gothic' graves, spurting gargoyles triggered by a movement detector, and wreathes of ragged drapery, a child reluctant to partake of the experience, asked of his father, 'Do you think it's good for me?' His father only laughed. The boy countered with 'OK, I'll go in if you think it's necessary'. His father evidently did, so in they went.

[12] Spooner uses the phrase in relation to the Eerie pub chain though the comment is also highly relevant to the set pieces of the London Dungeon. Consider, for example, at the opening of the tour, the use of the recording of a guide with an evil/camp German-accented voice.

[13] From the Time Line inside the front cover of the London Dungeon's Guidebook (Anon, undated, unpaginated).

[14] See the introductory chapter to Mighall, 1999.

[15] Although it isn't as anti-Catholic as many other Gothic texts, in that Henry VIII, with his introduction of the punishment of boiling in oil for husband-murderers and others, and of the death sentence for sodomy, features as the foremost tyrant, and it gives details of the persecution of Catholic recusants. A curious parallel can be made between the ideological import of the Clink and of the Bastille (whose inhabitants at the moment of its "liberation" numbered only seven) for we are told that the census of 1732 revealed the inmates of the Clink to number only two.

[16] As the English Heritage website puts it: 'A few walls are all that remain of the palace of the powerful Bishops of Winchester, one of the largest and most important buildings in medieval London.í http://www.english-heritage.org.uk/server/show/nav.20292 accessed on 30th November 2009.

[17] For an interesting discussion about Gothic inauthenticity see Hogle 2000, *ibid*.

[18] Southwark Cathedral is known as the actors' cathedral.

[19] http://www.shunt.co.uk/shunt2.php accessed 4 January 2010.

Works Cited

Anon. (undated), *The London Dungeon* (guide book), Poole: Merlin Entertainments

Burford, E. J. (1989), *A short history of The Clink Prison* (no publisher or place of publication)

Botting, F. (2008), *Limits of Horror: Technology, Bodies, Gothic*, Manchester: Manchester University Press

Clery, E. J. (1995), *The Rise of Supernatural Fiction, 1762–1800*, Cambridge: Cambridge University Press

Heard, M. (2006), *Phantasmagoria: The Secret History of the Magic Lantern*, Hastings: The Projection Box

Hogle, J. (2000), 'The Gothic Ghost of the Counterfeit and the Progress of Abjection' in (ed.) Punter, D., *A Companion to the Gothic*, Oxford: Blackwell, 293–305

Lennon, J. and Foley, M. (2007), *Dark Tourism: The Attraction of Death and Disaster*, London: Continuum

Mighall, R. (1999), *A Geography of Victorian Gothic Fiction: Mapping History's Nightmares*, Oxford: Oxford University Press

Spooner, C. (2006), *Contemporary Gothic*, London: Reaktion Books

Stone, P. R. (2006), 'A dark tourism spectrum: towards a typology of death and macabre related tourist sites, attractions and exhibitions', *Tourism: An Interdisciplinary International Journal*, 54(2), 145–60

http://www.londontheatre.co.uk/lashmars/backstagetour/index.html accessed 4 August 2009

http://www.theatreroyaldrurylane.co.uk/theatre-history.htm, accessed 4 August 2009

http://www.walks.com/Homepage/Thursdays_Walks/default.aspx#12882 accessed 5 August 2009

Chapter 12

Zombie London: Unexceptionalities of the New World Order

Fred Botting

Not Anything to Show More Fair

A patient awakes, naked, in an empty hospital twenty-eight days after a deadly virus has been released from a medical test facility. The city outside is also deserted. An old newspaper headline in close-up tells of the city's evacuation. He wanders, a solitary figure amid familiar London sights: the Houses of Parliament, and Whitehall; Horseguards, Horseguards Parade, and the Guards Memorial; Pall Mall and the Mall; Mansion House, the City and Piccadilly with its statue of Eros; St Paul's and the London Eye. The journey offers a tour of historical and heritage locations, places of tourism and entertainment, centres of government and commercial power, and sites of regal and martial tradition.

The opening scenes of *28 Days Later* (Danny Boyle, 2002) replay fictional (literary-cinematic) apocalyptic scenarios of modern urban devastation. Daniel Defoe, Mary Shelley, Richard Jeffries laid out a pattern of modern urban apocalypse subsequently developed in genre fictions and further elaborated on film. *The Last Man on Earth* (Ubaldo Ragona, 1964), with its 'vampires' (that move like zombies), is set in an evacuated modern Rome. The same story (Richard Matheson's *I Am Legend*) becomes *The Omega Man* (Boris Sagal, 1971), with a lonely survivor bunkered in a Los Angeles house and harassed by radioactive mutants and, ultimately, *I Am Legend* (Francis Lawrence, 2007) where New York hosts a fast-moving swarm of zombie-vamps. *28 Days Later* and *28 Weeks Later* (Juan Carlos Fresnadillo, 2007) acknowledge their trash zombie horror apocalyptic forebears: *Night of the Living Dead* (George A. Romero, 1968), with its besieged farmhouse; *Dawn of the Dead* (1978), with its consumerism; *Day of the Dead* (1985), with its military presence; *Land of the Dead* (2005) with its corporate tower. The virus theme, too, comes from the TV series *Survivors* (BBC, 1975–1977), and *Resident Evil*'s (Paul Anderson, 2002) genetic experimentation and fast-moving zombie-mutants. The reflexive awareness of *28 Days Later*'s citations of its zombie horror apocalypse precursors are given a wider frame of reference in its very striking and recognisably unfamiliar opening scenes.

Prominent amongst the shots of London is a sequence in which the wandering survivor crosses a rubbish-strewn Westminster Bridge. The camera pans across the river to Big Ben and the Houses of Parliament warmly illuminated against a gentle sky as the city sun sets. More than a provision of a distinctive location scene for a global cinema audience, crossing the bridge in an empty city recalls Wordsworth's sonnet, 'Upon Westminster Bridge', in which London is majestic and beautiful in the morning sun, sublimely touching the Romantic (urban) wanderer's soul with its stillness, its absence of crowds, smoke and noise. At this moment the city becomes admissible to nature, rather than at odds with its rhythms. As a singular 'mighty heart' lying still, the urban body is unusually peaceful and unified, thereby containable in a single imaginative vision. The mighty heart, however, suggests another London, a sleeping giant ready to awake and beat faster. The other city is more apparent in Wordsworth's poetry. In *The Prelude*, London is reduced to the chaos of Bartholomew Fair, a 'city with a City' that exceeds and threatens Romantic visionary unity, as a messy multiplicity of disorganized sights, sounds, sensations, not properly humane or natural, a 'parliament of monsters' (Hertz 77–80). Overwhelming individual consciousness with an excess of spectacle, the city is seen as a place of subjective and physical otherness in which sense and self-assurance loses itself to the pressures of other egos: 'the sublime renewal of our consciousness and desire for self-presence' both 'frees us' and returns us to a 'world of circumstances beyond our control' (Ferguson 7). The price, it seems, paid by Romantic consciousness to overcome the sublime threat of the monstrous urban spectacle is utter devastation, a destruction and evacuation of all other bodies, signs, and symbols pressing upon and competing with a singular poetic vision. It is an apocalyptic tendency played out in various Romantic guises, Byron's 'Darkness' notably. For Percy Shelley, in 'Peter Bell III', 'hell is a city like London', a 'crepuscular demi-world' of commerce and politics in which ruination forms the prelude for nature to reclaim urban space (Wolfreys 77–79). For Mary Shelley in *The Last Man*, the scale of devastation is global and destructive: a worldwide plague – a monstrous force of nature – wipes out humanity and its centres of civilization (London, Paris, Rome) until 'everything was desert' (*Last Man* 242).

28 Days Later's opening prepares the film's Romantic trajectory, skipping over the more prevalent features of the darkly modern city as charted by Edgar Allan Poe, Charles Baudelaire and Walter Benjamin. Poe's story, 'The Man of the Crowd', provides one of the key aesthetic figures of modernity, and outlines another London, frightening, dark and ruined, and associated with crime and debauchery: the other side of prosperous Victorian modernity. Poe's crowd is multiple, but its effects draw out a sense of a danger and contagion, a place of poverty and crime in which the city itself 'becomes almost a drunken mob' (Highmore 30). Unlike Paris, it engenders a 'paranoid wandering subject' whose experience is one of terror: 'the outer environment has returned like a wave, threatening to engulf him, and instead of consuming, he is consumed in a neatly twisted version of cannibalism' (Warwick 82). Benjamin, working through Baudelaire and Poe, charts urban experience in a context in which subjectivity, vision and visual culture move to the rhythms of industrial and urban organization; the crowd's heterogeneous singularity repeats the relation of worker and mechanical labour (Benjamin 178). Shock – both shattering tradition and breaking into everyday experience – becomes the dominant mode of work, life, and leisure (Benjamin 178; 17). Technology, Benjamin notes, 'has subjected the human sensorium to a new kind of training' (Benjamin 176); it decentres Romantic humanity and aesthetics, based on the 'aura' of artistic experience.

The legacy of modernity's technological shocks, in particular of its mass visual media, is laid out in the pre-credit sequence of *28 Days Later*. Providing the back-story to the release of infection, it begins in a research laboratory with its experimental subject watching an array of screens depicting scenes of urban violence from around the world, visual images of rage correlated to the production or cure of the virus. Media, it seems, mime or (re)produce urban violence. Television news, indeed, has been analysed as both creating and curing shocks (Mellencamp; Doane). It suggests a process of production and evacuation of sensation which subjects all viewers (all experimental animals) to the shocks and stimulation of multiple screened events. A cycle of exciting and deadening spectatorial responses is manifested, on the screens within the screen and in the camerawork and the editing as soon as the RAGE virus is released. The slow, suspenseful close-ups and pans across a darkened lab are quickly replaced by closed-circuit TV shots of balaclava-wearing activists breaking in. As the animals are freed, so, too, is the highly contagious virus; slow, blurry motion, rapid and jerky camera movements, sudden close-ups of bloodshot eyes and bloody vomit, angry chimps battering their own cages and violently attacking their rescuers. These scenes present a media form that has accelerated modernity's modes of mechanical reproduction, producing sensation and stimulation to enraged excess, movements too rapid for consciousness to process or screen off. The cinematic tradition in which the film locates itself, however, is very much bound up with modernity. Zombies, despite their colonial origins (Williams 1983), are figures of industrial production and mechanical reproduction. Fritz Lang's *Metropolis* (1927) provides a stark and Gothicized vision of urban life and labour in its shots of the city, of the slow-moving and homogeneous mass of workers marched to and from their dark, subterranean habitations, reduced to a state of automation, 'depersonalized, faceless, dressed identically' (Tulloch 41). The 'Gothic modernism' of *Metropolis* stresses the darkness of factory labour and urban society, and links it to monstrous and oppressive technological innovations (the scientist Rotwang and the robot double, Maria) which turn workers into a mass of 'dehumanized mechanical actions' (Gunning 55). From the emergence of film, zombies connote the mass of modernity as subjects of both production and reproduction: before the camera, the moving images of shambling, shocked and submissive workforce present repetitive industrial dehumanization; before the screen, the desensitized and shocked mass of workers turned spectators are shocked again. The pattern continues: 1950s B-movie monsters and alien invaders are 'zombie-like' figures of Fordist and bureaucratic society, manifestations of the 'depersonalising conditions of modern urban life' (Sontag 435).

28 Days Later's allusions acknowledge and transform the cinematic history of zombification and urban modernity. From the start, and the evacuation of the city, the film plots a Romantic arc to the Lake District. The emptying of London and of the institutions of urban modernity (government, banking, family), serves as the basis for imagining the reconstitution of human, even humane, social relations based on assured individuality in the context of an imaginary family unity and a post-Blairite masculinity (Blake). In the city distinctions between a private, domesticated realm and the pressures of urban public spaces remain difficult to sustain, the latter endlessly and insistently encroaching upon the other (Kaika). The modern city is double, a dupli-city, both legible and illegible and, textual and more than readable like the modern Romantic apocalypse, calling for and confounding the limits of representation (de Certeau; Wolfreys; Warwick; Goldsmith). It exists on several intersecting planes simultaneously, ordered vertically in maps, towers, lines, and grids and reshaped incessantly by cultural, subjective, and aesthetic movements – horizontal, plural – of inhabitants, pedestrians, wanderers, migrants. Lived space, traversed horizontally, metaphorically, textually, recreates the city, drawing out its 'disquieting familiarity', its deportations, relations, interdependences creating an 'urban fabric', a dense network, like the multiple weaves of Barthes' text (de Certeau 96; 103).

Though rewritten (Williams 2007), the film's ending, with its imaginary family and idyllic rural retreat, appears to remain within a persistently Romantic cultural fantasy. However, it and structures of modernity – public / private; home / abroad; country / city – are adjusted. Just as the tension between domestic and urban space and between individual and crowd were placed in tension from the start, one interpenetrated, if not overwhelmed, by the other, the fantastic distinction between city and country (urban hell versus rural idyll) appears less secure. The vision of the city as a 'dystopian nightmare' is part of a 'long-cultivated habit' of those with power and privilege able to move as far as possible from the city: 'the upshot has been not only to create endless suburbanization, so-called "edge-cities", and sprawling megalopolis, but also to make every village and every rural retreat in the advanced capitalist world part of a complex web of urbanization that defies any categorization of populations into "urban" and "rural" ' (Harvey 404). City and village are relocated in wider global political-economic networks. These appear clearly in *28 Weeks Later* where the fantasies of apocalyptic evacuation, familial reconstitution, and rural ideal are unpicked in a reversal of *28 Days Later*'s Romantic trajectory. *28 Weeks Later* begins in a farmhouse. A husband and wife prepare dinner, talking of their absent children. She looks at a photograph, an archaic reminder of the family that used to live there. A still image of a frozen, dead past, anachronistic in the rapidly moving currents of infected times. The refuge is soon invaded, and this remainder of family life is forcibly broken up, a rent exacerbated by the husband's act of cowardice, leaving his wife to a fate worse than death. His flight returns him to a London no longer recognizable in modern terms, but subjected to the forces and protocols of a new global order. In this context, the family is no longer viable; not only has the husband betrayed his wife, he lies to his children about her 'death'. Paternal figures, it seems, in the tradition of horror films (*Amityville, The Shining*), are not to be relied on (Williams 1996). The family itself, like old photographs, seems to be redundant, no longer a bulwark against the pressures of social change and global shifts (Appadurai 44); or a locus of resistance (Virilio 1991 63); or little points of cohesion, 'social solidarities', in an unstable and highly-charged urban context (Harvey 425).

Speed

'Rapidity is always a sign of precocious death for the fast species' (Virilio 1995 87). Speed reconfigures bodies and urban environments; it registers a movement beyond life. The 'infected', too, take the idea of zombies beyond their modern parameters, notably due to their distinctively rapid movement. The world of *28 Weeks Later* only retains traces of modernity, like the still images of family life; these 'zombie categories' hint at the persistence of lost ideals and institutions in times that have superseded them (Beck). Modernity's (zombie) subjects have changed – and more than in the way they move. Not really undead, multiple genre references notwithstanding, these 'zombies' – as a sequence of captions early in *28 Weeks Later* indicates – can starve after five weeks. They are as much figures of global anxieties about migrations of bodies, capital and infection (AIDS, SARS, influenza epidemics). In terms of their medium, their movement suggests a speedier, saturated, and sensational environment of stimuli, one in which shocks and counter shocks are relayed globally and daily in a more intense fashion. Mutants in the strict zombie tradition, no longer figures of mass modernity and mechanical cinematic reproduction, their mutation, nonetheless, is calibrated to the shifts of a post-industrial, mediatized global sphere. In a review of the TV zombie series, *Dead Set*, Simon Pegg (director/star/writer of *Shaun of the Dead*) complains at the failure of that series to adhere to a 'key detail': 'ZOMBIES DON'T RUN!' Acknowledging the absurdity of debating 'the rules of a reality that doesn't exist', he offers a convincing case for the slow, relentless and inevitable potency of zombies: they manifest 'our deepest fear', 'our destiny writ large' – death. For him, rapid movement reduces their power to 'a quick thrill at the expense of a more profound sense of dread'. Hence *28 Days Later* is 'misconstrued by the media as a zombie flick', Boyle and Garland drawing on *Day of the Triffids* as much as Mathieson and Romero to develop 'a new strain of survival horror'. Pegg, however, acknowledges the context for the change, and criticizes Zack Snyder's 'pointless' remake

of *Dawn of the Dead*: the 'upgraded zombie 2.0' appears 'at the behest of some
cigar-chomping, focus-group happy movie exec desperate to satisfy the MTV
generation's demand for quicker everything – quicker food, quicker down-
loads, quicker dead people'. 'Quicker everything' – the injunction to go faster
dominates all activities, the demand for speed in media, information, consumption accelerates away from the modernity which produced zombies lumbering
to the pace set by the manufacturing industry. Zombies, slow, lumbering, relentless and modern, are replaced by 'zoombies', fast-moving figures of a fast-food
culture and fast camera cinema.

Speeding up not only heightens the repetitions and shocks of industrial,
urban modernity, it marks an acceleration beyond its rhythms, disturbing its
borders, frames and categorizations. Paul Virilio, one of the cultural critics
developing Benjamin's insights in a contemporary context, traces the effects of
new optical and military technologies on urban spaces and bodies, identifying
an acceleration beyond, and eclipse of, modern logic and structures. Speed
changes the relationships between subjects, objects, screens, and their environments; retrains senses, bodies, selves; inaugurates new and shifting alignments
between physical space and media, a development of the historical interaction
between war and vision in which urban space passes from fortress city to open,
planned commercial flows regulated by military planning (Hausmann's Paris),
and on to cities that are as much virtual as they are physical, 'overexposed' cities
shaped by media, signs, image and spectacle, encountered, not by crossing a
gated threshold, but through an 'electronic audience system' (Virilio 1991 1).
Pressed by new media laws of real time and instantaneous communication, con-
forming to the 'terrorist aesthetic of optical impact', monitor screens transform
the viewer 'into an agent or potential victim, as in war' (Virilio 1995 73). The
subject that emerges, shocked beyond the quality and characteristics of its
modern human forebear, is barely a subject at all, given that a shocked subject
already teeters on the brink of oxymoronism (Foster 131); numbed, automatic,
zombie-like, it is a victim of sense and sensation and also a hypermodern
organism stimulated, hyperactivated and reactive, an effect of an incessant
'bombardment' of images and signs. With speeds being set by computer and
relayed instantly on monitor screens, mind and body become equally penetrable and more rapidly hardened so that the process of blocking and protection
demands a countervailing pressure towards increased excitement: 'superstimu-
lants are the logical extension of metropolitan sedentariness' (Virilio 1995 102).
Science is able ' "to attack" ', Virilio suggests, 'what is alive, "natural", vitality
finally being eliminated in the quasi-messsianic coming of the wholly hyperactivated man' (Virilio 1995 120). Accelerated beyond nature, the movement
exceeds life and death, to the point that bodies, in entertainments, thrill rides,
say, are not even alive until excited to the maximum. To the point of crashing,
or death (SHaH 2003). The bombardments of media and telecommunications
are aligned with new economic formations in which imperatives of 'hyper-
productivity' lead to new work-related illnesses for mind and body – stress and

RSI (Virilio 1995 134), for example – winding them up beyond natural toler-
ance thresholds, numbed and enervated in a hyperdialectic of shock. On a wider
scale, the 'structural unemployment' caused by technological and economic
innovation transforms the working mass of industrial society into redundancy,
cast-offs individuated by post-industrial practices, reduced to the 'passivity of
individuals made useless' yet remaining a 'social menace'. Romero's zombies –
Pittsburgh's fading industrial environment in the background – appear in this
form: without work, aspiration, useless, they are the meat thrown out by corporate post-industrial change (Beard; Shaviro).

   In contrast, and opposed, to the neo-lumpenproletariat cast off by post-industrial practices, 'hyperactivated man', the revved-up, flexible, fragmented, plural
bodies defined by multiple gazes and microsystems of control, comply with
contemporary corporate imperatives: 'in the context of the flexibility demanded
by contemporary capitalism, there has been a great compression of time and
space, and the body comes to be seen as a chaotic, hyperflexible site, ridden
with contradictions and warfare' (Appadurai 44). Early in *28 Weeks Later*
(following the retreat from country to city), a very specific site is shown from a
range of angles; high aerial shots from aircraft and buildings dominate the *mise
en scène*. All are mediated, showing that the movie camera is no longer alone:
telescopic rifle sights, surveillance helicopters, security cameras, CCTV, command centre monitors, and optical scanners. The impression of this city, other
than its familiar views, is of a space entirely captured by visual technologies
(and the accompanying buzz of audio telecommunications), real time surveillance and control fully wired into military command.

Docklands-Baghdad

The central location of *28 Weeks Later* situates London within a new alignment
of Gothic, local and global forces. The location is distinct from the previous
film and its allusion to an older romantic and modern tradition of Gothic
London, not so historical, nor dark, nor criminal, nor the touristic landmarks
of a heritage past (despite shots of Tower Bridge), nor the shadowy spaces
of labyrinthine alleys nor netherworlds (a brief journey through the tunnels of
the Underground aside). A new London is framed in a sequence of aerial establishing shots, transformed, rebuilt, and relocated in the economic and political
upheavals of the 1980s. Shots of Docklands, Canary Wharf, and the Millennium
Dome offer recognizable architectural emblems of Thatcherite economic and
social transformation and Blairite 'Cool Britannia'. Views of shiny corporate
towers and plazas, city airport lounges, metro stations and walkways are light,
shiny, open, and open, too, to very evident controlling gazes; these sites are
seemingly anathema to an older Gothic darkness. Canary Wharf stands as the
'most public and visual expression of 1980s aggressive monetarism' (Bird 123),
a 'city within a City populated by a migrant army of executive, managerial and

office staff serving the productive signifiers of postmodernity – microelectronics, telecommunications and international capital' (Bird 126). Docklands draws out the tensions transforming urban space: 'the urban wasteland has been repositioned within the circuits of international finance capital and recoded as a site of consumption and pursuit of leisure' (Bird 125).

The very literal de- and reterritorialization of urban space occurs as an effect of the more abstract deterritorializations associated with a global shift in flows of capital. As Fredric Jameson argues, finance capital evinces capitalism's general ability to feed on and exploit economic crises and turn away from older – and failing – economic and industrial practices and processes. It pursues a destructive almost cannibalistic logic as it moves from the first stage of capitalization associated with the realism and secularization of the Enlightenment. Moving away from industrial competition and national division, capital's abstraction, through an imperialistic stage, leaves behind the materiality of production to find profits in financial transactions themselves: capital becomes 'free-floating', separated 'from the concrete context of its productive geography' (Jameson 2000 259). Its dematerialization is akin to the virtual and informational flights associated with posthumanism (Hayles). As materiality and the globe are superseded, new ghosts appear to redefine financial exchanges: 'specters of value . . . vying against each other in a vast, worldwide, disembodied phantasmagoria' (Jameson 2000 273). Ghostly, capital moves out of reach of what once might have been called a real world. The 'Thatcherite dream of remaking Britain through private development and corporate finance under the combined ideologies of enterprise, regeneration and heritage' (Bird 135) has a darker dimension, 'the nightmare of deregulated planning and massive redevelopment' evinced in the tearing down of nineteenth-century living spaces and social infrastructures and discarding of less visible – or rich – urban populations and their histories (Coupland 161). For Roger Luckhurst, diverse Gothic and occult Londons tell different stories and engage different histories and politics. On the one hand, ghosts are part of a process that seeks 'to revivify the pasts continually swept away in the ceaseless churning of London development and redevelopment' (Luckhurst 2003 3), revenants of other lost histories, figures holding onto, or warding off, the forgetting of pressed and enforced change. In the face of progress, however, Gothic fragments operate 'as the emblems of resistance to the tyranny of planned space' (Luckhurst 2002 532). The 'deliberate evisceration of London's democratic public sphere' (Luckhurst 2002 539) is paralleled by the evacuation, reconstruction and repopulation of Docklands, a transformation that is given Gothic form in Iain Sinclair's *Downriver* which 'transposes the tyranny of one era onto another', the LDDC refracted through the eighteenth-century Gothic (Luckhurst 2003 340). Gothic, in this instance, provides a language to register political concerns, a figure of tyranny which arises as one of the 'symptoms of stalled representative government' (Luckhurst 2003 340). The spectrality of capital comes to fore, as a shadowy and powerful tyrant operating outside law, regulation or restraint.

Losing Control

In employing Docklands as the point of entry for London's (and Britain's) repopulation after viral infection has apparently subsided, *28 Weeks Later* signals its geopolitical importance, not so much as a national capital city, but in its role as a commercial zone of deregulated financial flows, a nodal point in the network of international finance capitalism. As a 'security zone', and renamed as 'District 1', the Isle of Dogs is an enclave protected by barbed wire fences, snipers and cameras. All flows of bodies are directed, surveyed, managed. The connection between finance capital and military control was already implied in the development of Docklands. The Big Bang and Canary Wharf disclose a military subtext insofar as neoliberal economic theory and digital technology adapt netrocentric military strategy. Furnished with hi-tech telecommunications equipment, with open trading floors, the post-Big Bang financial business takes the form of a 'command centre' directing operations 'at a distance', working through digital networks in a militarized model of the control society (Gere 120). *28 Weeks Later* offers starker and more direct images of the link between global financial capital and the militarization of social control; its attention to surveillance technologies and telecommunications, all operated by military personnel, is emphasized further by the shots from the point-of-view of snipers on top of buildings. Camera is equated with rifle as numerous shots track crowd movements below, individuals in their apartments, all seen through telescopic sights strategically placed high on the buildings above. Space is controlled and observed, a city newly closed off and closed in, like Jameson's (1991) Bonaventura hotel or the special zones, the 'closed off' areas of corporate plazas, shopping malls, freeways, gated communities and out-of-town business 'campuses' (Hardt and Negri 2000 188).

For Virilio, war and the city constitute each other, from a period of walled fortifications through to a nuclear era in which the city – as polis – met its end in a sprawl beyond central urban boundaries (Virilio 2002 5). The 'third era', that of the 'post-industrial meta-city', appears in a different relationship: the 'progressive militarization of science and the economy of nations' aims at 'total peace' counterpoised with a 'state of siege' no longer centred on the metropolis but threatening the entire world (Virilio 2002 11–13). National security cedes to 'global security' in the post-Cold War period, the call for total peace calibrated against 'a global and total civil war' in which cities are rife with internal conflicts and antagonisms, a 'Lebanonization' of urban zones (Virilio 2002 34). Docklands, separate from the old financial City of London, closed off to the masses, but remaining electronically open to world finance, is itself a place of migration, a fortress and a kind of ghetto, a militarized, defended zone built in the wasteland of modern urban decay. The supposed borderlessness of its successor throws up a diversity of new barriers and divisions, boundaries that remain proximate, penetrable, and in flux even as they try and close themselves off. Where the city begins and ends, in virtual, physical and psychological terms, given global openness and increasing internal division, remains a question for Virilio: in a situation of 'generalized desertion' a sense of generalized anxiety arises, an uncertainty as to where the city gates are, of how to live without borders (Virilio 1991 29).

Globalization 'involves new movements and new instabilities, from "transmigration" of capital and people to new urban forms that are "fragile" in being centred on an economy of high productivity, advanced technologies and intensified exchanges' (Sassen 1999 102); it is 'multiscalar', occupying places and non-places, and denationalizing state institutions (Sassen 2004 176). Boundaries become unclear, identities shift. Even the increased power of corporate formations remains subject to 'whole networks of urbanization that move to rapid shifts and flows of manufacturing capital' and create a dispersed global proletariat (Harvey 422–23). As the frontiers of the city blur to form internal boundaries and virtual nonspaces, so distinctions between global and local interpenetrate and transform each other in a fluid and dynamic relation (Virilio 1991 9). While global forces and media (capital, advertizing) are absorbed into the local (Appadurai 42), a new interior is hollowed out, 'a global delocalization, which affects the very nature not merely of "natural", but of "social" identity, throwing into question not so much the nation-state, but the city, the geopolitics of nature' (Virilio 2000 10). The turning inside out of global and local relations is evident in another of the major features of globalization: the migration of populations (Harvey 415). Globalization is not a homogenizing force, as Appadurai notes, but a 'cannibalizing' one in which sameness and difference, East and West, begin to consume each other in a 'cultural flux' (Appadurai 43–44). A splitting of traditional expectations and identifications occurs. Appadurai discusses the sense of 'rage' and 'betrayal' that arises in translocal ethnic contexts as a result of misunderstandings and the disclosure that one's neighbours are not necessarily identified with the same communal, ethnic or political values:

> a perceived violation of the sense of knowing who the Other was and of rage about who they really turn out to be. This sense of treachery, of betrayal, and thus of violated trust, rage, and hatred has everything to do with a world in which large-scale identities forcibly enter the local imagination and become dominant voice-over in the traffic of ordinary life. (Appadurai 43–44)

Rage defines one of the cultural responses to shifting urban constitutions. It is also an identifiable social effect of shifting economic priorities: 'the only available response on the part of those left marginalized is urban rage' (Harvey 404).

RAGE

The virus released from the laboratory showing images of urban violence is called 'RAGE'. The global context in which *28 Weeks Later* locates itself takes issues further; occupied and under reconstruction, Britain, it seems, is no different from any country in the world, no more privileged or secure than, say, Iraq or Afghanistan. Its returning population is being 'repatriated' under the protection of an external force; they are housed in a 'Green zone', like Baghdad, and under constant surveillance (Clover 6). Turning an erstwhile global financial centre into a refugee camp stages a striking reversal which forcibly underlines the ease with which national fortune can be transformed in the precarious flux of global change. Third and First World, like rich and poor in cities, are never too far apart. In globalization, the city undergoes reversals of assumptions in which the 'Third World' reappears in the 'First', in the shape of migrants, unemployment and homeless figures (Serres; Zizek). As Virilio argues: 'Our post-industrial world is already the spitting image of the old colonial world' (Virilio 2000 55), while Hardt and Negri note the 'Third World does not really disappear in the process of unification of the World market but enters into the First, establishes itself at the heart as ghetto, shantytown, favela' (Hardt and Negri 2000 253–54).

While visually and verbally US forces are the main occupiers, early captions announce that a 'US-led NATO force' is in control. Legitimated by transpolitical sanction and identifying the context as post- or hypermodern, the occupation is enforced by international authority. Other visual and verbal markers underline this difference: public announcements declare that 'the US army is responsible for your safety', warning civilians not to leave the 'security zone'. Travelling shots from the Docklands railway show soldiers in biological protection suits disposing of bodies in biohazard bags. Security – the lives of the returning population – is the main stake of this militarily-supervized repatriation. Soldiers do not wage war, but act as police to protect lives by maintaining security against civil disorder (the return of the infected) and disease (viral contagion); snipers train their sights on people within the perimeter, looking down on crowds moving in plazas below, or on individuals relaxing in their quarters. Their task is one of management and control, a task supported by advanced technological systems. New arrivals are processed by medical teams: eye scans in close-up indicate that control operates in genetic as well as corporeal terms: the boy's eyes are shown to be of different colours, a hereditary trait he, significantly, shares with his mother. The new order is biopolitical rather than political: 'biopolitics is the nexus of biology, code, and war, in which the distinction between disease and disorder is made indistinct' (Thacker). It spreads a highly flexible and extensive net over all aspects of life, materializing the shift identified by Foucault from disciplinary mechanisms to biopolitics (Foucault 1981 136–37; 2003 249).

Biopolitics has become one of the cornerstones of the new world order. For Hardt and Negri, this order takes the form of a new 'Empire' and functions with an intensely biopolitical version of life. Rather than employing disciplinary modes, rules and norms sustained in diffuse discursive formations and aimed at individuals – their bodies, resistances, subjectivities, it involves protocols of command and control whose network appears even more democratic, diffuse and immanent, intensifying and generalizing discipline 'through machines that directly organize brains . . . and bodies . . . toward a state of autonomous alienation from the sense of life and desire for creativity', into a biopolitics targeting the 'whole social body comprised by power's machine' as it penetrates 'the ganglia of the social structure', now a 'single body' (Hardt and Negri 2000 23–24). This body's nervous system, as much as its behaviour and organs, is placed under 'a network of powers and counterpowers structured in a boundless and inclusive architecture' (Hardt and Negri 2000 166) that accelerate beyond 'a liberal notion of the public, the place outside where we act in the presence of others', to a space 'universalized' – and transformed – by a gaze 'monitored by safety cameras and sublimated or de-actualized in the virtual spaces of the spectacle' (Hardt and Negri 2000 188–89).Thus, biopower 'simply *produces* the obedient subjects it needs', a combination of postmodern warfare and postfordist production 'based on both mobility and flexibility; it integrates intelligence, information, and immaterial labour' (Hardt and Negri 2006 53). Empire is monstrous in its totality, vampiric in its operations, feeding off the multitude that is a new monster of life, creativity, and nomadic affinities. (Hardt and Negri 2000 62). The multitude is a singular and multiple entity (distinct from notions of the masses, the mob, the crowd, the populace), a mode of 'life in common' (Hardt and Negri 2006 vv), that provides the basis for Empire's sovereignty and power, as well as hinting at the possibility of an affirmative excess. Multitude is found in relations among the poor and in the resistance and mobility of migrancy; with the destitute, the excluded, the repressed and the exploited lies the potential to transform relations of power in a more creative and affirmative manner. Biotechnical transformations based on the energy of the multitude suggest an outside or limit to an Empire that is conceived as boundless, immanent and total. Yet Empire, while constituting multitude, also feeds off its life and creativity, a life and creativity not its own, but which it consumes and on which it depends. Divisions, antitheses, and ambivalences remain, despite the claims to the totalizing homo-heterogeneity of Empire's immanent and global network. On the one hand Empire denotes a global condition beyond the borders, frameworks and categories of modernity but, without outside, the possibility of differentiation and delineation becomes difficult. With all exceptions, even multitude itself, included as part of its operations, Empire works through a state of permanent crisis an 'omni-crisis' (Hardt and Negri 2000 189). In this state of omni-crisis, war is transformed into a permanent and civil condition. Generalized as a constant call to vigilance and action, war is a permanent activity: the 'war on' (drugs, terror, poverty) is a matter for everyone. As a result, the enemy is no longer a specific nation or threat, but 'banalized (reduced to an object of continued police repression) and absolutized (as the Enemy, an absolute threat to the ethical order)' (Hardt and Negri 2006 13). Like the RAGE virus, the threat is everywhere and nowhere, to everyone and no one – outside the secure zone, or amongst the population within, disease and disorder form abstract and routine threats to the management of life.

Fuck the Chain of Command

Requiring constant policing at every level, the virus sustains the operations of biopolitical control and further enhances the stakes as an uncertain object of fear and anxiety. As the film develops, it is shown to be both inside and beyond networks of command and control, a point of excess to the totalizing reach of Empire. As a form of 'the Enemy' its effects are double: it crosses and restores intangible or impossible boundaries, fuelling Empire's boundlessness (its invisibility legitimating any security measures whatsoever) and, in the process, it implies a limit to the enveloping expanse of Empire and the inclusivity and immanence of power's ability to absorb and feed off any resistance at all. Furthermore, this banal and absolute threat, this particular and general Enemy, serves well as a means of introducing 'new segmentations' within network control; it offers an empty figure for projection, recoil, fear, thus enabling the redrawing of new boundaries. 'Fear of violence, poverty and unemployment', note Hardt and Negri, 'is in the end the primary and immediate force that creates these new segmentations' (Hardt and Negri 2000 335). The ambivalence extends to the relation between Empire and multitude, the latter the necessary living and creative force constituted by and feeding the former. As a site of fear and new segmentations, however, it also retains something in excess – of life, perhaps, disclosing a negativity lying within and outside Empire at the same time. Negativity, as Ernesto Laclau observes, remains a serious theoretical problem in the general affirmations of *Empire* (Laclau 21–23). Life's excess discloses Empire to be double also: its 'corruption' is evident in the manner its command 'is directed toward the destruction of the singularity of the multitude through its coercive unification and / or cruel segmentation' (Hardt and Negri 2000 391). Divide and rule and / or unify and rule. Either way, unifying or segmenting, Empire consumes the living creativity of the multitude, the negativity of fear and the destructiveness of power part of its consumptive armoury. In part, excess precisely serves in the 'function of exception' through which Empire takes and maintains control of the ever-fluid situations of heterogeneous, chaotic global milieux (Hardt and Negri 2000 16).

For Virilio, the move beyond nation to a transpolitical and militarized state in which 'peace' and 'security' are elevated over 'defence' means that the 'enemy' disappears, 'making way for the indeterminacy of constantly redefined threats' to life and ways of life: the citizen, now 'a danger to the *constitution of internal pacification*', becomes 'a subject who is a "living-dead" [*mort-vivant*], no longer akin to the Spartan Helot or the Roman slave, but a kind of "zombie" inhabiting the limits of a devalued public life' (Virilio 2008 160–61). Placing everyone under the absolute injunction of peace, however, means that all are also potential threats. In this state of transpolitical life, death becomes a vanishing horizon, incorporated (undeath) and evanescent. The new (non)subject of this of life is un-living and un-dead and, significantly in Virilio's account, a zombie situated at the borders of this regime – its enemy and threat, and its internal horizon of control. Civil peace remains – imminently – in danger of losing itself. Zombies – zoombies rather – thus manifest the (internal) excess that biopolitics produces and needs; ambivalent, un-civil, un-living, un-dead, destructive figures of fear situated along the crossing of the categories out of which the new world order emerges and on which it legitimates itself. The spectre of negativity disturbs the affirmations of Empire and Multitude alike and returns in zombie fears and zombie consumption, destruction and death. Rapid, violent, corporeally excessive, destructive; the embodiment of disorder and disease, zombies manifest a 'necrology' of the body politic and disclose the limitations of sovereignty in the new world order. Distinct from the redundant, slow, unproductive dejecta of modern industrial organization, zoombies are the speedy, hyperactivated non-subjects of a media-saturated post-industrial high-performance economy, the other face of Empire's multitude, wired up (like chimpanzee and patient in *28 Days Later*) to screens, machines, drips and monitors. While they might look like the 'People' of modern democracy – and their negatives, the masses or violent urban mob – they are not mechanized automatons, but the singular body of the multitude hooked up to the digital networks of hypermodernity, its power flowing 'through machines that directly organize brains' and producing 'a state of autonomous alienation from any sense of life or desire for creativity' (Hardt and Negri 2000 25). The multitudes retain a positive, affirmative political potential. In contrast, zombies are alienated from life and creativity to the extent that they destroy and are eliminated by forces of Empire. Neither do they hold out any promise of manifesting the 'singular power of a *new city*' (Hardt and Negri 2000 395).

28 Weeks Later's setting and elaboration of a zombie plague points towards excess. Not only is 'life' policed, managed, secured and manipulated by a technological, military and medical network, it is also, in the form of the RAGE virus itself (a living organism and agent of violent death), the point at which control exerts its most extreme and dramatic pressure. Responding to the army doctor's concern about the virus returning, the local commander asserts that it will be subjected to 'code red': it will be 'killed'. At the limits of pacification lies extermination. When the virus does return, spreading rapidly through the civilian population of District 1, security measures prove useless and panic ensures. At first, security forces are urged to 'watch out for friendlies' and 'only target infected', but the hysterical crowd makes it difficult to distinguish enraged infected from panicking civilians, all unruly bodies demanding pacification. The command is given to 'shoot everything', targeting all at ground level with the explicit instruction of making 'no exceptions'. As snipers shoot indiscriminately into the zombie-human melee, power's last-ditch attempt to secure itself fails: 'we've lost control'. Its last resort is more extreme still: the order is given for the aerial firebombing of District 1, pacification and purification at once. 'No exceptions' evinces the absolutization of Empire's enemy and the way that death and destruction mark the limit and outside of its power; it belies the securing of life on the basis of an always-imminent threat: not any life, not individual life, but life in general, the life of Empire's population, must be protected, the life of abstracted and abstractable biotechnological power, that is, life under control. When life goes too far – as virus, as rage, as exuberant, unruly excess (the condition also of creativity) – then an unbearable negativity comes to the fore. Though 'completely incapable of submitting to command', zombies do not express any desire to creative life anew, only to perpetuate death / undeath. Hence they come into closer proximity with, replicating even, the operations of Empire itself, consuming, feeding off, destroying life and creativity. Empire is the 'ou-topia', the nowhere (and everywhere), the 'non-place' where global production occurs, a non-place that 'has a brain, heart, torso and limbs, globally' (Hardt and Negri 2000 190). Empire's non-place is positioned against the multitude and 'defined here in the final instance as the "non-place" of life, or, in other words, as the absolute capacity for destruction. Empire is the ultimate form of biopower as it is the absolute inversion of the power of life' (Hardt and Negri 2000 345). Just as Empire is the non-place of life, so, too, the zombie, reconfiguring its body in hideous terms, assumes the shape of the 'ou-body', the 'no-body', its impossible embodiment and excess – its life-death. Zombies offer themselves as the barely inverted image of Empire, the virus which creates them comes to figure as the mirror of global capitalism's capacity to mutate, undermine, and destroy its precedents. With each crisis, capital mutates, spreading its reach, penetrating further and more devastatingly: 'the system is better seen as a kind of virus – its development is something like an epidemic (better still, a rash of epidemics, an epidemic of epidemics)' (Jameson 2000 258). As virus, capitalism is a kind of life, less and more than life, a barer life which escapes the controls which produce it.

In biopolitical discourse, the establishment of the new world order's legitimacy requires a sovereignty predicated on exceptionality, on life stripped down to its most basic level and located in a 'zone of indistinction' that allows for 'the circulation of "life" as an exception'. 'At once excluding bare life from and capturing it within the political order, the state of exception actually constituted, in its very separateness, the hidden foundation on which the political system rested.' When borders blur, Agamben argues, bare life 'frees itself in the city' as 'place for both the organization of State power and emancipation from it' (Agamben 9). For Thacker, zombies serve as an image of bare life's exceptionality. He cites the figure of the leper, from the twelfth century, as an example of 'living death', and goes on to assert, with reference to movie monsters, their continuity with 'the living dead, the mass of living corpses that are *only bodies*, that are *only bare life*' (Thacker). While the equation of zombie and bare life works, it only does so up to a point, the point where exceptionality is eclipsed by unexceptionality, by 'no exceptions'. In *28 Weeks Later*, zombies pose and exceed bare life and exceptionality (to have no exceptions is to equate everything and, at the same time, to make exceptionality general, a norm to be removed); bare life becomes absorbed, like zombies/civilians, onto and into the reflexive plane of Empire's operations and exposes a barer life beyond it.

For Hardt and Negri, 'there is nothing, no "naked life", no external standpoint, that can be posed outside the field permeated by money; nothing escapes money' (Hardt and Negri 2000 31). Only, perhaps the spectre of zombie capital, ruinously toxic, or the total collapse of the banking system, which, in *28 Days Later*'s apocalyptic scenario is depicted as Jim bends down near a cash machine to pick up piles of notes, just more litter blowing through the street. The exception that produces sovereignty and is to be exterminated is no exception at all when absorbed into the abstracted circulation of money and capital's own living death.

'No exceptions': the phrase is uttered – again under 'code red' – once before the command to start shooting indiscriminately. The military doctor argues with a soldier that the children, the boy especially, should remain in her care. The boy, with his mother's genetic make-up, may be immune to the virus (and also have the capacity to be a carrier). Hence he has immense value (and danger) in the search for a cure. His value is as an exception, but it is measured by the doctor, it appears, in medically humane terms, and not, like the soldier, through biopolitical protocols: 'no exception' dictates the need for pacification – in the interests of life and population – over the need to cure, in the same interests. Life, again, finds itself divided within the imperatives of Empire. As a life that has the potential to save many lives, his existence legitimates her disobedience in refusing military authority, an act of negativity performed in the interests of a higher value which, ultimately leads her to sacrifice her own life, bodily and material being given up for a human ideal. She is not alone. The friendly and jokey sniper Sergeant, Doyle, also responds negatively to the 'no exceptions' command; he leaves his post and descends to ground level to help the remaining humans flee District 1. His disobedience and refusal of authority is performed with a defiantly negative series of statements: 'it's all fucked'; 'fuck the code red'; 'fuck the chain of command'. His act of insubordination positions him outside Empire's chain of command and against its zombie mirror; its negativity, moreover, is associated with a sense of human compassion and commonality. Refusing Empire's coupling of life and undeath, Doyle takes responsibility for the survival of doctor and children; they escape District 1 with the help of a helicopter pilot and flee into the deserted city – pursued by escaping zombies. Doyle's negativity implies some humanity is still alive as the film reaches its climax; it enables him to discover a cause and meaning to his own life (and death), locating value outside the parameters of biopolitical control in a reassertion of human values. Between the excess of control manifested by the US army (and dramatized in its explosive violence) and the excess of the zombies rampaging through streets and parks, another excess emerges from the act of negativity, one that seems to permit human survival, almost sentimentally, in its focus on the lives of two young siblings. The film, however, refuses a return to human and humane values. All acts of negativity seeming to constitute a basis for or belief in something sacred are shown to be well-intentioned (like the protestors freeing animal torture victims – and the virus – in the first film), but at best misguided and futile.

The negativity that ends the film (and prepares the way for *28 Months Later*) is not a prelude to a (dialectical) restoration of human values. Though the children survive, flown by a reluctant pilot across the Channel, the boy (having been infected by his father) is now a carrier of RAGE. Humane acts, acts of compassion and kindness, are just preludes to disaster, spreading rather than containing the virus. The last two scenes underline the devastating effect of such misidentification: a crashed helicopter is filled only with the crackling of defunct communication signals; a dark Eiffel Tower announces the next urban location to be infected with silhouettes of rampaging zombies appearing against the evening skyline. Barer life spreads fast and violently. Only RAGE persists, not life or death: 'It's all fucked'.

Works Cited

Agamben, G. (1998), *Homo Sacer*, Stanford: Stanford University Press

Appadurai, A. (1996), *Modernity at Large*, Minneapolis and London: University of Minnesota Press

Beard, S. (1993), 'No Particular Place to Go', *Sight and Sound*, April, 30–31

Beck, U. and Beck-Gernstein, Elisabeth (2002), *Individualization*, London: Sage

Benjamin, Walter (1973), *Illuminations*, trans. Harry Zohn, London, Fontana

Bird, J. (1993), 'Dystopia on the Thames', in (ed.) Jon Bird, *Mapping the Futures*, London and New York: Routledge

Blake, L. (2008), *The Wounds of Nations*, Manchester, Manchester University Press

Clover, J. (2008), 'All that is solid melts into War', *Film Quarterly*, 61(1), 6–7

Coupland, A. (1992), 'Docklands: Dream or Disaster', in (ed.) Andy Thornley, *The Crisis of London*, London and New York, Routledge, 149–62

De Certeau, M. (1984), *The Practice of Everyday Life*, trans. Steven F. Rendall, Berkeley: University of California Press

Doane, M. A. (1990), 'Information, crisis, catastrophe', in (ed.) Patricia Mellencamp, *Logics of Television: Essays in Cultural Criticism*, London, Bloomington and Indianapolis: BFI and Indiana University Press, 222–39

Ferguson, F. (1984), 'The Nuclear Sublime', *Diacritics*, 14, 4–10

Foster, H. (1996), *The Return of the Real*, Ann Arbor: MIT Press

Foucault, M. (1981), *The History of Sexuality: Vol. I An Introduction*, trans. Robert Hurley, Harmondsworth: Penguin

Foucault, M. (2003), *Society Must Be Defended*, trans. David Macey, London: Penguin

Gere, C. (2003), 'Armagideon Time', in (eds) Joe Kerr and Andrew Gibson, *London: From Punk to Blair*, London: Reaktion, 117–22

Goldsmith, S. (1993), *Unbuilding Jerusalem: Apocalypse and Romantic Representation*, Ithaca, New York, Cornell University Press

Gunning, T. (2000), *The Films of Fritz Lang*, London: BFI Publishing

Hardt, M. and Negri, Antonio (2000), *Empire*, Cambridge, MA and London: Harvard University Press

Hardt, M. and Negri, Antonio (2006), *Multitude*, London: Penguin

Hayles, N. K. (1999), *How We Became Posthuman*, Chicago and London: University of Chicago Press

Hertz, N. (1978), 'The Notion of Blockage in the Literature of the Sublime', in (ed.) G. Hartman, *Psychoanalysis and the Question of the Text*, Baltimore and London, Johns Hopkins University Press, 62–85

Highmore, B. (2005), *Cityscapes*, Basingstoke: Macmillan

Jameson, F. (1991), *Postmodernism, or, the Logic of Late Capitalism*, London and New York: Verso

Jameson, F. (2000), 'Culture and Finance Capital', in (eds) Michael Hardt and Kathi Weeks, *The Jameson Reader*, Oxford: Blackwell, 255–74

Kaika, M. (2005), *City of Flows*, London and New York: Routledge

Laclau, E. (2004), 'Can Immanence Explain Social Struggles?' in (eds) Paul A. Passavant and Jodi Dean, *Reading Hardt and Negri*, London and New York, Routledge, 21–30

Luckhurst, R. (2002), 'The Contemporary London Gothic and the Limits of the Spectral Turn', *Textual Practice*,16(3), 527–46

Luckhurst, R. (2003), 'Occult London', in (eds) Joe Kerr and Andrew Gibson, *London: From Punk to Blair*, London: Reaktion, 335–40

Mellencamp, P. (1990), 'TV Time and Catastrophe, or Beyond the Pleasure Principle of Television', in (ed.) Patricia Mellencamp, *Logics of Television: Essays in Cultural Criticism*, London, Bloomington and Indianapolis: BFI Publishing, Indiana University Press, 240–66

Pegg, S. (2008), 'The Dead and the Quick', *The Guardian*, 4 November http://www.guardian.co.uk/media/2008/nov/04/television-simon-pegg-dead-set/

Poe, E. A. (1986), *The Fall of the House of Usher and Other Writings*, Harmondsworth: Penguin

Sassen, S. (1999), 'Globalization and the Formation of Claims' in (eds) Joan Copjec and Michael Sorkin, *Giving Ground*, London and New York: Verso, 86–105

Sassen, S. (2004), 'The Repositioning of Citizenship', in (eds) Paul A. Passavant and Jodi Dean, *Reading Hardt and Negri*, London and New York: Routledge, 175–98

Serres, M.(1993), *Angels: a Modern Myth*, trans. F. Cowper, Paris: Flammarion

SHaH (2003), 'How It Feels', in (eds) Jane Arthurs and Iain Grant *Crash Cultures*, Bristol and Portland: Intellect, 23–34

Shaviro, S. (2002), 'Capitalist Monsters', *Historical Materialism*, 10(4), 281–90

Shelley, M. (1994), *The Last Man*, Oxford and New York, Oxford University Press

Sontag, S. (1974), 'The Imagination of Disaster', in (eds) Gerald Mast and Marshall Cohen, *Film Theory and Criticism*, New York and London: Oxford University Press, 422–37

Thacker, Eugene (2005), '*Nomos, Nosos,* and *Bios*', *Culture Machine* 7 http://www.culturemachine.net/index.php/cm/article/viewArticle/25/32

Tulloch, J. (1977), 'Mimesis or Marginality? Collective Belief and German Expressionism', in (ed.) John Tulloch, *Conflict and Control in the Cinema*, Melbourne: Macmillan, 37–68

Virilio, P. (1991), *Lost Dimension*, trans. Daniel Moshenberg, New York: Semiotexte

Virilio, P. (1995), *The Art of the Motor*, trans. Julie Rose, Minneapolis: University of Minnesota Press

Virilio, P. (1997), *Open Sky*, trans. Julie Rose, London: Verso

Virilio, P. (2000), *The Information Bomb*, trans. Chris Turner, London and New York: Verso

Virilio, P. (2002), *Desert Screen*, trans. Michael Degener, London and New York: Continuum

Virilio, P. (2008), *Negative Horizon*, trans. Michael Degener, London and New York

Warwick, A. (1999), 'Lost Cities: London's Apocalypse', in (eds) Glennis Byron and David Punter, *Spectral Readings*, Basingstoke, Macmillan, 73–88

Williams, G. C. (2007), 'Birthing an Undead Family', *Gothic Studies*, 9(2), 3–44

Williams, T. (1983), '*White Zombie*: Haitian Horror', *Jump Cut*, 28, 18–20

Williams, T. (1996), 'Trying to Survive on the Darker Side: 1980s Family Horror', in (ed.) Barry Keith Grant, *The Dread of Difference*, Austin: University of Texas Press, 164–80

Wolfreys, J. (1998), *Writing London*, Basingstoke, Macmillan

Wordsworth, W. (1920), *The Poetical Works*, London: Oxford University Press

Zizek, S. (1993), *Tarrying with the Negative*, Durham, Duke University Press

Chapter 13

What Lies Beneath: The London Underground and Contemporary Gothic Film Horror

Lawrence Phillips

'Our world, like a charnel-house, is strewn with the detritus of dead epochs.'

Le Corbusier

The London Underground system is both a potent symbol of modernity and a projection onto the mythic and material rejectamenta of that which lies buried, abject, and forgotten. From the mid-nineteenth century the urban underground was progressively invaded to provide sanitation via sewers and water, as well as energy via the gas main. This is the birth of the modern city where the urban environment is a less defensive fortress contained behind crumbling Roman or medieval walls, but the location of a dwelling that plugs into a subterranean grid of public conveniences that have come to symbolize the basic necessities of modern urban life in the developed world. In London in 1863 it also became the locale of the epitome of modern transportation with the opening of the world's first underground railway – the Metropolitan Railway. While the new form of transportation was an immediate success – on the first day, 10th January 1863, some 30,000 journeyed on the line (Wolmar 41) – providing an escape from the paralysis of horse-drawn congestion on the roads above, initial reactions were alarmist, appalled, if not downright hysterical. *The Times* in 1862 anticipating the opening of the line observed: 'A subterranean railway under London was awfully suggestive of dark, noisome tunnels, buried many fathoms deep beyond the reach of light or life; passages inhabited by rats, soaked with sewer drippings, and poisoned by the escape of gas mains . . . to be driven amid the palpable darkness through the foul subsoil of London'.[1]

The potential horrors of this technological labyrinth include disgust at the risk of disturbing the residuum and seepages of overground London, a foul subsoil that included one of the great sanitary fears of mid-nineteenth-century London during a period of major redevelopment, the uncovered plague pit.

Moreover the journey itself resembled for some descent into Hades amid suffocating 'sulphuric fumes, and of blended smells from coke and steam' (Pinks 10). It would not be until the 1900s that the first electric trains came into use and eliminated the foul suffocating atmosphere of what by then had sprawled out into an extensive underground railway system. It was a view of the underground railway that would persist as can be seen from the terror experienced by the journalist Fred Jane writing with some rhetorical licence for the *English Illustrated Magazine* in 1893 when his train plunges

> Into a black wall ahead with the shrieking of ten thousand demons rising above the thunder of the wheels . . . a fierce wind took away my breath and innumerable blacks filled my eyes. I crouched low and held on like grim death to a little rail near me. Driver, stoker, inspector and engine – all had vanished. Before and behind me on wither side was blackness, heavy, dense and impenetrable.[2]

Victorian commentators were not blind to the engineering marvel that the underground railway represented, so much so that a new London institution quickly found a place in the contemporary consciousness. As Henry Mayhew observed in 1865: 'It was so novel a means of transport, so peculiar and distinctive a feature of the great English capital, that to omit this underground mode of intercommunication from a publication professing to be descriptive of the foremost institutions and establishments of the British metropolis would be the same as playing the tragedy of Hamlet with the principal character left out' (Mayhew 144). However, the duality evident here – an engineering marvel quickly adopted into the every day life of the capital's growing commuting hoards, versus a disturbing penetration of that very same everyday life into the foul depths of London's subsoil – held up a mirror to events in the Victorian city. As more lines were built initially using the highly disruptive and destructive cut and cover construction method (the deep tube lines would not begin to be tunnelled until towards the end of the century), the expanding railway was no modest contributor to the social engineering that saw vast public work projects driven into working-class areas of the city displacing thousands into even worse overcrowding and misery. These rookeries, as the worst areas were known, had taken on an underground characteristic of their own in the popular imagination earlier in the century. As Robert Mighall argues, working class slums were recast as uncanny impenetrable criminal labyrinths existing cheek by jowl with the most respectable streets as was still evident from influential Booth's poverty map at the end of the century: 'These darker places of the city were increasingly and almost exclusively associated with its poorer districts' (Mighall 32). The point is developed by Richard Maxwell:

> *Labyrinths* have long been a subject of allegorical works such as *The Faerie Queene*. The widespread tendency to see cities as mazes is a related but more

recent phenomenon, a product, I would guess, of historical memory. Once
Paris and London begin to be modernized – once streets are widened and
straightened to facilitate the circulation of traffic – the older, usually poorer
neighbourhoods exert a new fascination. Here there are many narrow, winding alleys, here traffic easily gets itself into knots; here the visitor who is not a
native may well feel mystified. (Maxwell 15)

Mystification if not downright fear, such a vision of urban hell is a dominant
image of the Victorian city in the twentieth-century imagination not least among
modernist urban planners. Indeed an unintentionally ironic repetition of the
Victorian ideology of slum clearances can be seen in Le Corbusier's discussion
of the redevelopment of the centre of Paris: 'In our walks through this maze
of streets we are enraptured by their picturesqueness, so redolent of the past.
But tuberculosis, demoralization, misery and shame are doing the devil's
work among them' (Le Corbusier 284). While the labyrinth of the slum and the
actual labyrinth of the underground railway rarely seem to be connected in
the nineteenth-century imagination – a notable exception to this is Doré's
huddled and homogenous working class horde in his illustration *The Workmen's
Train* from *London: A Pilgrimage* (1868) – they certainly came to be so in the
twentieth century in British popular literature, film and television.

While emerging briefly as a locus of actual or potential technological nightmare in the work of H. G. Wells and the less well-known disaster fiction of
Frederick White – in his 1903 short story, London of the near future is almost
destroyed undermined by an extensive network of deep tube tunnels – Gothic
horror and the underground railway were brought powerfully together in the
post-war era in *Quatermass and the Pit* (TV 1958–1959; film 1967) which fuses
both technological and occult horror as an alien relic once used to control
humanity's distant ancestors is discovered during the construction of a deep
Tube extension. More recently, Gothic themes in relation to the underground
railway have emerged with increased frequency. In Neil Gaiman's *Neverwhere*
(TV Series and novel, 1996) an entire alternative London is reimagined through
the lens of the arcane London history favoured by Iain Sinclair and Peter
Ackroyd. A journey down into the bowels of London finds an actual Earl's Court
in circulation on an underground train and a fallen angel imprisoned deep
underground at the Angel, Islington. Tobias Hill's 1999 novel *Underground*
charts a Tube worker's fascination for a homeless woman while he hunts the
perpetrator of a series of murders that initially appear to be suicides. This
underground is a Gothic space but grounded in the everyday underground
network explicitly linking the city above with its spectral negative below; a
ruined idealization of the metropolis it has grown under:

The Underground starts out perfect. At first it isn't like the city above it
because it is conceived all at once. Everything must be created, heat and
the passage of air. For the engineers and architects it begins as a perfect

technical form. Then years go by – decades. Cross-tunnels are found to be unnecessary, so they are bricked up. Deeper tunnels are added by the government, then closed down. Limestone comes through the concrete as if it were muslin. Up above communities die out. Stations are abandoned. (*Underground* 135–36)

In each of these post-war examples, the underground railway is a constituent part, if not the gateway, to a distortion of the world above. In *Quatermass and the Pit* human civilization is shown to be a vast alien experiment of mutated psyche and genetic manipulation; in *Neverwhere* the fantasy realm below London comes to represent the violence of the city long repressed into the psychological distortions of myth – a twilight urban subconscious half noticed and cowered from, like the homeless people that populate it. In *Underground* the anomie of the city crowd descends onto the train platform that disguises murder, but ultimately reveals the Gothic labyrinth of the daylight world above in its twisted and deformed image below ground. Conrad Williams' novel *London Revenant* (2004) underlines the psychological, political and material decay implicit in each of these texts of the city and world above. His London also divides into two – topside and underside – and fantastically exploits the psychological division this implies to point to the decay and moral bankruptcy of the city. Ultimately, the underground railway that emerges in these texts is a kind of tropic subconsciousness of the city, which this essay will further explore through two films, *Death Line* (Dir. Gary Sherman, 1972) and *Creep* (Dir. Christopher Smith, 2005).

Despite release dates some 30 years apart, both films share a similar central plot conceit and themes. In each people are disappearing from a London Underground station; *Death Line* is based around Russell Square while *Creep* is based around Charing Cross although they both stray further afield for some of their underground settings. In the earlier film travellers are explicitly being snatched to be eaten which is left to implication in the later film. In *Death Line* the perpetrator is a descendant of navvies trapped underground in the 1890s following a tunnel collapse, while in *Creep* it is the last survivor of a genetic research laboratory that had been hidden underground who has found his way into both the sewer and underground railway systems explicitly linking these two great Victorian subterranean innovations. Both films therefore create a Victorian context for their sense of underground terror though the first film does so directly in the person of the murderer who is markedly late Victorian in his appearance as is his lair, the unfinished station in which his forebears had been trapped. Indeed, 'The Man', played by Hugh Armstrong, bears a marked resemblance to Fagin as realized by Ron Moody in Lional Bart's musical *Oliver!*, the film version of which was released in 1968 a few years before *Death Line* and so very much of the same cultural moment. Dickens's original novel, Bart's musical, and *Death Line* trace a narrative continuum arguably established by Dickens of an urban Gothic very much based on the proximity of a dangerous, labyrinthine, alternative London barely a street, or a tunnel, away. As Mighall observes: 'Here perhaps for the first time, is found the situation of an innocent entrapped in the labyrinthine coils of a criminalized district brought up to date and placed in a recognizable part of the modern metropolis' (Mighall 39). The Victorian atmosphere is further emphasized in how the abandoned tunnels are lit by Victorian oil lamps and one extended scene shows 'The Man' refilling a lamp from a carefully husbanded supply of oil.

Craig, the deformed – or rather mutilated – stalker of *Creep*, remains unnamed for much of the film and while he creates the breach between the sewer and underground railway systems, his person suggests a rather disjunctive time frame. Indeed, the setting of the film appears to be contemporary judged by settings and peripheral props such as motor cars and clothes, and yet the opening scenes build a pervasive sense of the 1980s with the first appearance of the protagonist Kate at a lavish yuppie party. Likewise her contempt for the homeless man begging by the cash machine she uses, having departed in pursuit of George Clooney at another party, reinforces this impression. Her sarcastic quip in response to the ubiquitous 'Can you spare some change, please' that the machine dispenses notes increases the viewers' initial dislike of the character. Yet this latent time frame would make more sense of Craig's origins. Despite his deformity he appears to be in his twenties which with a contemporary setting would take the research laboratory where he originates back to the 1980s, yet this location has strong physical echoes of the early Cold War suggesting the 1950s or 1960s of the Quatermass era. What is clear from both films is that the monsters who provide the actual threat underground transgress historical boundaries representing in their persons anachronistic and highly disturbing embodiments of the past in the present. By crossing over from abandoned tunnels into contemporary commuter stations in search of fresh meat, a buried and forgotten past suggestively begins to consume the present bringing to mind the underground-dwelling Morlocks of H. G. Wells' *The Time Machine* emerging to consume the decadent Eloi.

The historical frame of both films is an important element of their Gothic quality. While the essentials of a Gothic narrative structure are in place both in terms of atmosphere – excess, dark labyrinthine tunnels, cannibalism, decay, deformity and monstrosity, the return of the repressed, the abject – and in situation – a vulnerable female protagonist stalked by threatening male pursuers – the peculiarly *urban* Gothic quality of the Underground is important. Robert Mighall argues that the emergence of an explicitly urban Gothic is an aesthetic development of the nineteenth century:

Therefore, although various aspects of 'modernity' (including industrial developments and demographic upheavals) may encourage writers to focus on the city and its problems, within the Gothic mode the emphasis is still on locating the source of disorder in the past. The Urban Gothic mode does not dispense with the 'displacements' of the earlier tradition, nor is it a 'primitivistic' rejection of modernity or industrialisation. Rather, it adapts the 'historical' perspective found in the early [Gothic] novels when it implies that the terrors of criminality are anachronistic anomalies, vestigial stains on the city's modernity. This defines its status as Gothic. (Mighall 51)

Mighall is of course discussing Victorian fiction, but his comments provide an interesting counterpoint from which to discuss the Gothic elements of these two films and their depiction of the city and the Underground. As already noted, the two monstrous figures from the two films embody very clearly 'disorders of the past'. 'The Man' from *Death Line* is the modern product of forebears who were abandoned in a collapsed tunnel system when the construction company entered bankruptcy and there being insufficient funds to launch a rescue attempt. This is something of a popular cliché about the Victorian era; while it was most certainly a harsh period to be working class or poor (although whether such status would be considered 'pleasant' in any era is open to question), it is hard to imagine that there would be no public outcry over such a well-publicized callous abandonment. Leaving aside the plausibility of the conceit, the film is clearly positing how the callousness of historical capitalism returns to haunt – or in this case actually consume – the present that it has brought into being. The contemporary users of the underground railway – rich or poor – are benefitting from the blood of the workers exploited to build it. Moreover, it is no accident that the first victim shown in the film is a senior upper-middle class civil servant – James Manfred, OBE – who had been cruising the strip joints of 1970s Soho. The name itself of course echoes Byron's Gothic drama *Manfred*; a tale of mysterious sins and grandiloquent defiance of religious redemption, which finds a rather tawdry 1970s counterpart here in a frequenter of strip clubs and the suggestion of sexual perversion in his home. When the film cuts to the investigating police inspector's office it is the status of the missing person that prompts an investigation despite the working-class origins of the Inspector. It is only at this point recalled that there have been a series of missing persons reports from Russell Square station involving people of rather more modest status. Clearly in terms of class hierarchy nothing much has changed in the intervening hundred years between the two events. The implication seems to be that while physical conditions have improved, stark social disparities remain. Indeed, it is the two middle-class students who initially find Manfred collapsed on the steps leading from the station platform who forcibly energize the investigation. The implication is that it is less the criminality in the present that is the source of Gothic disorder, but a callous disregard for the lives of those of the lowest social status which disturbingly persists in the modern city, if with more bureaucratic subtly.

In *Creep* there are similar class overtones. While Kate is not English (she is played by the German actress Franke Potente), as already noted the 'yuppie' quality of the party she attends and attitude towards the homeless man at the cash machine quickly, and unpleasantly, signify distinct class boundaries.

However, it is the two homeless drug addicts Jimmy and Mandy she later turns to for help who are most intriguing. On one level they signify an alternative London that by association Kate has to cross over into; an urban environment barely recognizable to the inhabitants of the 'normal' city. In both the film resembles both Gaiman's *Neverwhere* and Williams's *London Revenant*. In these novels the distinction between the near invisible homeless and 'normal' worlds is given a fantastic turn by signifying quite literally other cities that overground London characters cross over into. *Creep* comes closest to the representation of the homeless in Hill's *Underground*. In both novel and film the fantastic is kept at bay, but Jimmy and Mandy only truly come into focus when Kate's need is desperate. Intriguingly, though, while friendlier than the threat she is running from they are far from idealized and in some respects mirror aspects of the economic world on which they exist at the margins. Mandy is first encountered offering to sell a used Travelcard when Kate is frustrated by the ticket machine which, true to the 'yuppie' elements of her character, she purchases for twenty pounds. Later, trying to persuade Jimmy to help her find her attacker from the party, Guy, who has in turn been attacked, she has to offer him fifty pounds and again he has to be bribed to help her get him onto the platform once found fatally wounded. Ultimately when Kate finally emerges back onto the station at the end of the film, she is joined by Jimmy's dog Strapper and early morning commuters just gathering on the platform mistake her as a homeless woman and drop money by her. Kate has made a full transition from hard-nosed, insensitive, middle-class socialite into the semblance of homeless beggar. The experience of being chased through subterranean London has stripped her of her class identity and pretentions and breaks her down to a basic humanity she disregarded at the outset of the narrative. Clearly the Underground in this instance is a narrative mechanism dedicated to class levelling, forcing alliances between Kate and Jimmy, and latterly Kate and the sewer worker George who is captured by Craig in the opening scene of the film. He is a small-time drug dealer on community service.

This grim parody of a classless society challenging the stratified world overhead recalls the quotation from *Underground* above – an initially ideal conceptualization of the city above gradually distorted by the city it rationalizes. David L. Pike has argued that an idealized conceptualization of the subterranean city emerged from the nineteenth century to influence modernist notions of urbanism (a term first used in 1912):

The modernist dream of the vertical city analogous to the conception of Beck's subway map emerged out of several decades of fervid literary speculation on the nature of this new underground. From a time-honoured way of dividing up the actual city both physically and metaphorically, subterranean space became a means of conceptualizing the ideal city. The nineteenth-century obsession with the subterranean was appropriated to envision the city of the next century; the results of such a combination were, not surprisingly, both eccentric and informative. (Pike 75)

In terms of both *Death Line* and *Creep* a progressive, technological, idealized vision is shown to be badly misconceived. Amid the Victorian Gothic clichés evoking the iniquities of class struggle and the greed of rampant capitalism, it is as well to remember that the construction of the deep tube tunnels at the turn of the nineteenth century contributed to a future vision of the city as technological utopia. 'The Man' is both atavistic throwback and the descendant of pioneers, literary digging their way into that future. As Doré's illustration of the Workman's Train demonstrates, the spread of cheap transport throughout London would ultimately directly benefit the working classes. Likewise, Craig in *Creep* signifies another vision of the future as the nuclear-age experimentation with genetics suggests a sly allusion to contemporary debates over genetic manipulation. Once more the consequence is an atavistic throwback. This recalls themes that preoccupied J. G. Ballard for many years, particularly in relation to the planning and manipulation of modern urban environments. This is most readily evident in Ballard's 1975 novel *High Rise* published only a few years after *Death Line*. In Ballard's narrative the tower block of the title creates a rigidly stratified society based on spatial disposition; those on the lower floors feel themselves dominated by those on the floors above and likewise, those on the upper floors feel themselves superior to those below despite all the inhabitants of the block belonging to a similar narrow strata of the middle class. This is the modernist vertical city in moral and actual decay as the inhabitants of the block turn inwards as a markedly violent atavistic struggle begins. Pike further suggests in a reading of H. G. Wells' *The Time Machine* that 'it is the physical division of space rather than any comprehensible chain of events that leads to the new social division; time has changed everything except the essentially vertical division of space' (Pike 80).

The debilitating effects of Ballard's interpretation of the vertical division of space challenges this presumption since the 'progressive' thrust into the sky of the high rise produces anything but a viable vision of the future. While the comparison of this novel set so ostentatiously above ground with the underground setting of the two films suggests contrast rather than similarity, it does share an acute suspicion of the capacity of technologically rearranged 'ideal' dispositions of space that are shown to lead to a degenerated civilization. It is worth recalling again at this point that both the underground railway and the London sewer systems were *the* great progressive urban developments of their day. It is no accident that another of Ballard's novels, *The Drowned World* (1962), projects a future London submerged with much of Western Europe following an ecological catastrophe as the city is reclaimed by nature as an extensive tropical lagoon. With the devolution of the physical landscape, the central character is seen to fight against the atavistic urges unleashed by the new environment. The great signifier of technological progress – the city – has turned upon humanity.

Both *Death Line* and *Creep* share what seem to be contradictory conceptual frames; an urban Gothic actuated by atavistic projections into the modern city versus a technological progressiveness that brought the underground railway into being in the first place. Despite Ballard's work demonstrating that technological progressiveness and the vertical city can be just as debilitating of the human condition, the temptation is to allow the former to overwhelm the latter as an instinctual suspicion of anything subterranean much like the Victorian hysteria over the idea of an inhabitable underground. But each film challenges such a simplistic response in the relative complexity of their monsters. They both elicit the form of sympathy to be found in some Gothic monsters pioneered by Mary Shelley in her novel *Frankenstein*, a text which of course actuates a Gothic landscape while questioning the morality and consequences of technological progress. 'The Man' of *Death Line* cannot but provoke strong disgust. He is physically repellent suffering from septicemic plague caught from a sewer rat, constantly dribbling (a possible symptom of the disease like his scaly skin rather than his diet), cannibalism, and his language comprising of inarticulate animalistic grunts and whines. Likewise, Craig from *Creep* is physically deformed, has an inhuman grey pallor, is sadistic, just as inarticulate generating an uncanny high-pitched screech, and is most likely a cannibal as well. And yet the actions of 'The Man' demand sympathy alongside horror. We first see him bowed over his bedridden and feverish mate in clear distress that becomes despair as she dies. He is clearly in agony due to the plague sores on his skin, and in terrorizing Patricia one of the hapless students whom he has snatched from Holborn underground station in what ultimately appears to be attempted rape, suggests that he is driven at some level by the need to perpetuate his 'family line', much like Frankenstein's Monster who forces his maker to assemble a mate. Moreover, in a further resemblance to Shelley's monster he is a victim of the society he terrorizes demonstrating more compelling human traits than we find among the other characters who all seem to be emotionally and morally detached to a lesser or greater degree.

Equally, in *Creep* Craig's origins are revealed when Kate reaches the laboratory in which he was created; the bottles of deformed embryos preserved in alcohol and gruesome surgical instruments are juxtaposed with the ephemera of childhood and a photograph of Craig and the scientist who created him and experimented on him in a chilling father and son pose. The scene most designed to provoke disgust and horror towards him is also the most revealing of his victimization. With Mandy earlier snatched from her partner Jimmy and trussed up in a gynaecological examination seat, Craig has an aural flashback to a laboratory full of screaming children the moment before he conducts a ritualized travesty of surgical preparation which he obviously witnessed many times. The repellent quasi-sexual nature of what he does to Mandy with a long saw-like instrument (carried out, thankfully, out of shot) reveals less about Craig, perhaps, than the perverted science and scientists who created him. While it is easy to focalize horror onto Craig as Kate clearly does in fear for her life, for the viewer this late establishment of Craig as victim merely repeating the acts performed by the scientists and made commonplace growing up in such a perverse environment, is an arresting plot development that forces a narrative revaluation.

In each film, the real monsters are the bankrupt capitalists who abandon 'The Man's' ancestors to a lonely death in a collapsed tunnel, and the scientists who performed their gruesome experiments on Craig and his dead fellows. Late in both films the very thing that marks them out as degenerated atavistic throwbacks, their lack of speech, is also partially reversed but not in a way to completely recover their humanity. 'The Man' eerily splutters out 'mind the doors' which increases in confidence and pitch as he tries and fails to quell Patricia's panic and revulsion, while Craig repeats the last words of Mandy as she begged for her life almost goading Kate to kill him. If anything, Craig seems to understand the meaning of the words he is repeating and while this is not the case with 'The Man', he seems to understand the purpose of language even if the one from above ground is not his – the intonation of whines and grunts exhibited earlier in the film signal a sort of degenerated language. This direct reminder to the viewer of their humanity at the violent climax of each film qualifies any ostensible narrative relief that their deaths bring. They are monsters, yes, but killing them is no clear-cut solution to the issues their existence represents. Equally, the lives of the women whom they have perse-cuted are likely to have been marked permanently. While this is left to the viewer to imagine at the conclusion of *Death Line*, Kate's position on the plat-form of Charing Cross underground station mistaken for a homeless beggar actualizes the point.

At its most pessimistic, the Underground in both these films appears to bring together the contradictory negative perceptions of the subterranean metro-polis from the nineteenth and twentieth centuries. From the nineteenth, the underground is both signifier of progress and the threat implicit in uncovering a historical cesspit of the preceding eras of the city. In the twentieth century, the authoritarian urban utopias of the modernist pioneers seems embedded in the initial order and simplicity of the underground railway perhaps reaching its apogee in Harry Beck's Underground map, but it also seems to be the har-binger of the apocalypse among the material contradictions of an aging techno-logical marvel. As Walter Benjamin observes:

> Each Epoch not only dreams the next, but also, in dreaming, strives toward the moment of waking. It bears its end in itself and unfolds it – as Hegel already saw – with cunning. In the convulsions of the commodity economy we begin to recognize the monuments of the bourgeoisie as ruins even before they have crumbled. (Benjamin 270)

So, is the underground railway and more broadly underground London 'ruins even before they have crumbled'? It is certainly tempting to see in the brief moment of unity and coherence of the new underground railway or the laying out of the sewer, its almost immediate ruin in response to the mutations of urban expansion, decay, and redevelopment of the city above which an abstraction like Beck's Underground map represents only the desire for order, a trope of coherence, not its realization. But one might equally argue that the appropriation of the Underground in these two films is a potent metaphor used to point to the continued failings of the world above. As a dark mirror held up to the only apparent brightness of the surface, it is a stark reminder of the human cost of the prosperity notionally located above. The underground railway might continue to rationalize transport for the city and the hidden world of forgotten lines, tunnels, stations and peoples thrust aside as the underground is refocused to the needs of the world above, but what is discarded into the darkness is the very material history of the metropolis. In both films, 'what lies beneath' refuses to be forgotten.

Notes

[1] *The Times*, 30 November 1862
[2] Fred T. Jane, 'Round the Underground on an Engine', *English Illustrated Magazine*, August 1893

Works Cited

Ballard, J. G. (1998), *High Rise*, London: Flamingo
Ballard, J. G. (2006), *The Drowned World*, London: HaperPerennial
Benjamin, W. (1935), 'Paris, Capital of the Nineteenth Century', cited in Pike, *Subterranean Cities*, 270
Byron, Lord George Gordon (2009), *Manfred: A Dramatic Poem*, London: BiblioBazaar
Gaiman, N. (1996), *Neverwhere*, London: Headline
Hill, T. (1999), *Underground*, London: Faber and Faber
Jane, F. T. (1893), 'Round the Underground on an Engine', *English Illustrated Magazine*, August
Jerrold, B. and Gustave Dorré (1872), *London: A Pilgrimage*, London
Le Corbusier (1987), *City of Tomorrow*, (1929), New York: Dover
Maxwell, R. Jr (1992), *The Mysteries of Paris and London*, Charlottesville, VA: University of Virginia Press
Mayhew, H. (1865), *The Shops and Companies of London and the Trades and Manufactories of Great Britain*, London
Mighall, R. (1999), *A Geography of Victorian Gothic Fiction: Mapping History's Nightmares*, Oxford: Oxford University Press
Pike, D. L. (2005), *Subterranean Cities: The World beneath Paris and London, 1800–1945*, Ithaca and London: Cornell University Press
Pinks, W. J. (1865), *History of Clerkenwell*, London
Wells, H. G. (2005), *The Time Machine*, London: Penguin
Williams, C. (2004), *London Revenant*, London: The Do-Not Press
Wolmar, C. (2005), *The Subterranean Railway*, London: Atlantic Books

Index

Lightning Source UK Ltd.
Milton Keynes UK
19 January 2011

166012UK00001B/58/P